ESSEX AIRMEN
1910–1918

Nº 4. "THE FINEST JOB OF ALL."

Words by
EDWARD LOCKTON.

Music by
ERIC COATES.

God made the land for sol-dier men, He made the sea for

ESSEX AIRMEN
1910–1918

JOHN BARFOOT

TEMPUS

First published 2006

Tempus Publishing Limited
The Mill, Brimscombe Port,
Stroud, Gloucestershire, GL5 2QG
www.tempus-publishing.com

British Library Cataloguing in Publication Data.
A catalogue record for this book is available from the British Library.

ISBN 0 7524 4133 7
 978 0 7524 4133 7

Typesetting and origination by Tempus Publishing Limited
Printed in Great Britain

CONTENTS

THE FINEST JOB OF ALL

God made the land for soldier men,
He made the sea for sailors,
and Regent Street for pretty girls
and Jermyn Street for tailors,
He made the air for other folk,
(Ho! dont you hear the call?)
He made the air for you and me,
'The finest job of all'
God made some men for Parliament,
and some for pious Rectors,
He made some men for writing jobs,
and even made 'objectors'
but you and me he blessed the most,
(Ho! Dont you hear the call?)
He gave us wings to scour the heavens,
'The finest job of all'
He gave us wings to scour the heavens,
'THE FINEST JOB OF ALL'.

Opposite are the lyrics of a patriotic song by Edward Locton, set to the music of Eric Coates, published as '*THE FINEST JOB OF ALL*' by West & Co. in 1918. They were dedicated to the airmen fighting the first war in the air.

This almost forgotten song of the First World War struck a chord with the author, who had researched these early airmen, many of whom had also been forgotten. Essex pioneer aviator B.C. Benny Hucks is remembered today, also the three wartime airmen Lieutenant William Leefe-Robinson, Lieutenant Frederick Sowery and Second Lieutenant Wulstan Tempest who were stationed on Essex aerodromes when they destroyed German airships, but how many of us know the name of an Essex-born airman who also shot a Zeppelin down in flames?

Essex Airmen 1910-1918 remembers the young men of my county, born in the reign of Queen Victoria, who heard the call and fought the first war in the air, and to whom this book, along with '*THE FINEST JOB OF ALL*' is dedicated.

John Barfoot
Romford
Essex
2006

ACKNOWLEDGEMENTS

My sincere thank you to each of the following, as without your help this tribute to the early aviators of my county would not have been possible: Christine Adam, Faulkbourne Historian; Derek Barber, Benfleet Historical Society; John E. Barfoot, twenty-first-century technical adviser; Peter Chapman, The Australian Society of WWI Aero Historians; Peter Chapman, Essex Chapter C&C; E. Frank Cheesman, C&C international; Peter Devitt, Assistant Curator RAF Museum; Ian Dowling, Redbridge Library Archive Service; David Empson, C&C International; Ken Feline, C&C International; Nick Forder, Museum of Science & Technology, Manchester; Desmond Furze, C&C International, son of Lieutenant Stanley Jack Furze RAF; Jeff Harvey, C&C International; Tan Hook, Essex Regiment Museum; Colin and Barbara Huston, C&C International; Kevin Kelly, C&C International; Jan Keohane, FAA Museum; Paul Leaman, C&C International; Phillip Ledger and family of Lieutenant H.M.C. Ledger RFC; Stuart Leslie, C&C International; Simon Moody, National Army Museum; the late Bill Morgan, C&C International; Donald Neate, C&C International; Merle Olmsted, C&C International; C.W.O. Parker, nephew of Lieutenantt W.L.O. Parker RFC; the late Harry Parr, C&C International; Kirsty Petre; Lord Petre of Ingatestone, Essex; Vic Sheppard, C&C International; Leslie Stonell, C&C International; Major Alastair Tower, nephew of Captain Hugh Christopher Tower RFC; Revd Robin Turner, late Rector of Little Baddow, Essex; D.W. 'Joe' Warne, No.60 Squadron RAF Association; the late Douglas Whetton, C&C Great Britain; the late Douglas Wood, C&C International; Amy Rigg and Sophie Atkins, Tempus Publishing.

PART ONE
THE EARLY BIRDS

Although we are about to take wing with the airmen of Essex from the year 1910 onwards, we must first look at the history of aviation in the county that began two years earlier. This was also the year of the first officially recognised aeroplane flight in Britain, which took place at Farnborough in Hampshire, on 16 October 1908. The duration of the flight was 27 seconds and covered a distance of 1,390ft thanks to Samuel F. Cody, who had designed and supervised the construction of the large pusher biplane. Cody was a colourful and fearless ex-showbusiness American, who later applied for British citizenship. The flying machine, because of its size, became known as 'The Cody Cathedral'.

1908 was also the year that an attempt was made to establish the first aerodrome in Essex, situated at Fambridge, east of South Woodham Ferrers on the bank of the river Crouch. The man behind this forward-looking venture, Noel Pemberton Billing, had a career almost as colourful as the brave but unfortunate Samuel Cody, who was destined to be killed in a flying accident within three years. Pemberton Billing already had a reputation as an eccentric MP when he was bitten by the aviation bug and his far-sighted plan was to establish the first flying school in England.

Not to be outdone, in December 1908, the Aeronautical Society of Great Britain formed a committee headed by Major B. Baden-Powell to investigate and select a suitable site on which experiments with flying machines could be carried out. Six basic conditions had to be met, the first of which unfortunately had not been considered important at the time by Pemberton Billing. These were:

1. Accessibility from London.
2. Surrounding open countryside for several miles.
3. Exposed ground for kite flying as well as sheltered ground for aeroplanes.
4. Sloping ground for gliding and models.
5. A large expanse of water for tests on or over.
6. Possibility of fencing in and keeping private.

A pre-war visitor by air to Essex! Lt Charles H. Collet RMA was forced to land this Short 138 biplane at Hadleigh on Tuesday 3 February 1914. Flt Cdr Collet DSO, like so many of his contemporaries, was killed not by enemy action but a flying accident on Thursday 19 August 1915. (D. Barber)

The site eventually chosen was also in Essex, this time just east of Dagenham Dock, bordered to the south by the river Thames and the stretch of fresh water at Dagenham Breach to the west. Although only 15 miles by road from the City of London, access and conditions were basic to say the least. Officially opened on 5 February 1909, the Dagenham site attracted a number of aspiring aviation pioneers for a few months, the more notable among these were C.A. Moreling with a Voisin biplane and a small airship, Major Baden-Powell with a quadruplane and Deverall Saul with a tandem biplane.

Captain Edward Maitland, known as 'Gee Gee' by his fellow officers in the Essex Regiment, made several attempts to fly the Moreling Voisin biplane at Dagenham. Undeterred, 'Gee Gee' tried again to get the Voisin into the air at Brooklands Aerodrome the following year without success. Capt. Edward Maitland, who had been decorated during the Boer War would eventually, through service in the First World War, become the senior airship officer of the RAF. He was among the first men to fly the Atlantic by airship, when in July 1919 as senior airship officer Brigadier General E.M. Maitland (an early RAF rank). He accompanied HMA R34 and her twenty-two-man crew plus a stowaway on the epic four-day crossing to America and the return flight.

Capt. Edward M. Maitland of the Essex Regiment seated in a Voisin biplane at the short-lived Aeronautical Society of Great Britain Experimental Flying Ground at Dagenham, Essex, opened in February 1909. In spite of having the distinction of being the first organised flying ground in England, the site proved unpopular with the membership and visitors, falling into disuse by the end of the same year. (A.C. Healey)

Air-Commodore Maitland CMG, DSO, AFC lost his life on 24 August 1921, when HMA R38 broke in two, falling into the river Humber, killing forty-five of the forty-nine men on board.

One noteworthy experiment at the Dagenham experimental ground in 1909 involved attempts to steer a large model boat controlled by wireless on Dagenham Breach from the Moreling airship. None of the aeroplanes taken with high hopes to the Dagenham flying ground lived up to expectation and within a year the Aeronautical Society, through lack of support and funds partly due to more suitable aerodrome sites opening at Hendon in Middlesex, Brooklands in Surrey and Eastchurch in Kent, proving to be the more popular, abandoned the Dagenham site at the end of the year.

However, 1909 had been the year of the first aeroplane flight made by an English aviator in a machine of his own design. This event took place on the Lea Marshes at Hackney in Essex, on 13 July. The intrepid aviator was a thirty-year-old ex-Merchant Navy engineering officer by the name of Alliot Verdon Roe, who had been born near Manchester in 1877 and later settled in London employed as an engineering draughtsman.

A keen model aeroplane enthusiast, Roe had already built a number of successful flying model aircraft by the time he entered a *Daily Mail*-sponsored model aeroplane flying competition in 1907, to win a £75 cash prize.

Like so many young men at the beginning of the twentieth century inspired by the Wright brothers, Roe had an ambition to fly, and the generous – for the period – prize money from the *Daily Mail* competition encouraged him to design and build a full-size biplane in a shed at Brooklands. Undaunted by his first creation just managing a few hops, and again short of cash he left Brooklands returning to Putney and began construction of a 20ft span, paper covered Triplane, powered by a 9hp JAP motorcycle engine. When completed he transported the unassembled flying machine by horse and cart to a more spacious lockup under a railway arch of the Great Eastern Railway viaduct at Hackney.

Although the Lea Marshes at Hackney in Essex was not an ideal flying ground, Roe managed a few test hops before achieving a flight of 900ft at a height of 10ft on Friday 23 July 1909. The following year the infant Avro Co. was established in Manchester. Two days after Roe became the first Englishman to fly an aeroplane of his own design, the daring Frenchman Louis Blériot flew the English Channel in a monoplane of his own design and England was no longer an island.

The goings on at Dagenham in 1909 attracted an aspiring engineer with an interest in aviation and an eye for business by the name of Frederick Handley Page, who set up the first Aero Engineering Co. in Britain at nearby Barking Creek; this eventually led to the first aeroplane flight across London. See the chapter on the Petre Brothers for details.

Following the formation of the Royal Flying Corps in April 1912, Handley Page secured a contract from the War Office and to deal with this extra influx of orders, the Handley Page works moved to a more suitable site at Cricklewood Lane, between Kilburn and Hendon, in September the same year.

Barking Creek did not sever its connection with the infant aviation industry, and three years later with Britain under aerial bombardment by German Zeppelins, a large wooden shed 266ft long, 50ft wide and 40ft high, was erected with great haste on a site at 277 Creekmouth Road, adjacent to the ex-Handley Page workshops. This large structure was for the proposed construction of a rigid airship, to combat the Zeppelin menace.

Thomas R. MacMechan and Walter K. Kamp, American citizens, were behind the proposed 'Zepp killer', just one of the many counter measures proposed before .303 incendiary ammunition issued to Home Defence pilots in 1916 put an end to the Zeppelin menace. Construction of the wooden-framed, twin-engine (driving four propellers) airship began at the Barking site in May 1915.

When the Admiralty took over the site and construction of the airship the following year, the project became known as the Marshall Fox Airship – after its designer. Like so many wartime projects the airship was not completed and eventually broken up for salvage and Barking Creek and the 'Zepp killer' faded out of Essex aviation history.

Pemberton Billing's early aerodrome-cum-flying school had attracted some custom during 1908–09. Encouraged by the long hops attained by an under-powered Howard-Wright biplane at Fambridge, Jose Weiss attempted flights in a monoplane of his own design and a powered glider with little success.

The most successful aviator at Fambridge appears to have been Robert McFee, an American, who arrived on site in August 1909 and built in just six weeks a small monoplane of his own design powered by a 35hp JAP engine. Undeterred by the first four attempts that each ended in a crash, McFee flew his single-seat monoplane for the first time in October that year. However, dissatisfied with the marshes surrounding the site – and no doubt the weather! – McFee pulled out of the Essex aerodrome in November, eventually taking his machine to France.

The AV Roe Mk 1 Triplane in flight from the nearby railway arches which were serving as a workshop on the Lea Marshes Hackney, Essex, around July 1909. Two famous British aircraft manufacturing companies, Avro and Handley Page, evolved from humble beginnings in Essex. (*Flight*)

The unsuccessful Molesworth 'Britannia' triplane of 1911, modified from the equally unsuccessful Mackensie-Hughes 'Britannia' triplane built by A.W. Smith at Barking, Essex the previous year. (The Aeronautical Society)

A Zeppelin hunter airship under construction in its large shed at Barking, *c.*1915. Originally a private American-backed venture, the MacMechan airship project was taken over by the Admiralty to be renamed the Marshall Fox airship. Although, as can be seen, the construction was well advanced, the hunter airship was never completed; the aeroplane and incendiary bullet had ended the Zeppelin threat. (JMB/GSL Collection)

Fambridge 'Aerodrome' again had a brief lease of life early in 1914, when unsuccessful attempts were made to fly a Talbot hydroplane from the river Crouch, after which Fambridge, like her sister pre-war Essex aerodromes at Dagenham and Barking, was abandoned.

The outbreak of war put an end to the popular 'Aerial Derby' sponsored by the *Daily Mail*. The first of these round London air races had taken place on 8 June 1912, the circuit starting and finishing at Hendon Aerodrome, with turning points at Kempton Park, Esher, Purley, Purfleet, Epping and High Barnet and covering 81 miles. In spite of the poor weather it was estimated that 3 million people turned out to watch, 45,000 actually paying for admission to Hendon on the day.

Essex people turned out again in large numbers to watch the 2nd Aerial Derby on 20 September 1913, the Epping turning point attracting many of the spectators.

Spectators at the West Thurrock turning point during the third and last Aerial Derby on 6 June 1914 saw little of the race due to fog! Flying conditions were so bad that only eleven of the twenty-one entrants took to the air. Free balloons drifting across the county became a common sight during the war, carrying naval personnel under training as airship pilots from the Wormwood Scrubs Depot on the prevailing wind. They had been preceded in the peaceful days of 1913 by balloons of the Welsh airship pioneer Ernest T. Willows, who had opened a school for would-be balloonists at Hendon that year. Two of the more notable flights over Essex by the 50,000 cubic feet spherical balloon ended with Willows and his passengers descending at Nazeing and Little Waltham. Ernest Willows has quite rightly been called 'The Father of British Airships'; in 1910 he had been the first British airman in an airship of his own design to fly the Channel. It would be his pre-war pioneering experience with non-rigid airships, that later stood the RNAS in good stead in the development of the successful U-boat hunting non-rigid airships, known in service as 'Blimps'.

In 1916 Ernest Willows was invited to join the RFC as an acting temporary lieutenant and became involved with the development of observation balloons and in 1917, the London Balloon Apron. The county of Essex played a very active role in the air defence of London during the First World War. Aerodromes such as Suttons Farm at Hornchurch literally sprang up overnight when the threat of the aerial bombardment of the city became a reality.

Now let us take a look at those 'Early Birds' of Essex: the remainder of Part One is devoted to the aviators born in the county that had already spread their wings before the start of the First World War.

Bentfield Charles Hucks

The tiny hamlet of Bentfield End near Stansted Airport in Essex, mentioned in Domesday Book of 1086, was the birthplace of British aviation pioneer Bentfield Charles Hucks.

B.C. Hucks, known as 'Benny' to family and friends, was born on 25 October 1884. His father, a respected consulting engineer, intended his son to follow in his profession; however, by the turn of the century teenager Benny, already obsessed with the internal combustion engine and automobiles, had his own ambitions.

Bentfield Charles Hucks, a famous pre-war Essex aviator, seated at the controls of his Blériot Monoplane around 1913. Although his grave is close by the well-tended memorial to Karl Marx in Highgate Cemetery, London, it was impossible to find on a visit in 1999, as, due to lack of maintenance, the plot was very badly overgrown. (RAF Museum)

In 1904 he convinced his parents that his future lay in the growing motor car industry and subsidised by his father, commenced a three-year apprenticeship at 8s per week. Benny worked hard and thanks to his father's allowance soon became the proud owner of a second-hand motor car. He also acquired a passion for driving the public highways at breakneck speed, for which he on several occasions was fined, until the inevitable day arrived in 1907 when he received a three-year driving ban.

The attraction of flying as free as a bird to a person of Benny Hucks's temperament is obvious, although aviation was still very much a wealthy man's pastime, well beyond his modest means. His fate was sealed, however, when wealthy businessman-cum-aviator, bound for fame and more fortune, Claude Grahame-White, employed Hucks as a mechanic for his second attempt to win the coveted £10,000 prize offered to the first airman to fly from London to Manchester in under 24 hours.

The 1910 *Daily Mail*-sponsored air race developed into a duel between Grahame-White and the French aviator Louis Paulhan, both men flying 50hp Gnome rotary engine powered biplanes designed by Henri Farman who favoured the pusher layout for his machines. Louis Paulhan won the 185-mile race by completing the epic journey in just under 14¼ hours on 28 April, but Grahame-White, on landing with engine failure and being informed the news, won the respect of press and excited public who had followed the ups and downs of the two aviators by sportingly calling 'three cheers for Paulhan the winner'.

When the White Star liner *Cymric* docked at Boston Massachusetts on 1 September 1910, Benny Hucks was one of three mechanics who accompanied Grahame-White on his tour of America, where Grahame-White became the first British aviator to win an international air race. Tall, dark and handsome, Grahame-White became much sought after during the tour by his exploits in the air, that included a flying visit to Washington DC and circling the Capitol Dome before landing his Farman biplane in Executive Avenue close to the White House, with less than a metre clearance on either wing tip.

Even more amazing was the fact that Grahame-White found time from his round of social and business engagements to instruct Benny Hucks in the basic skills of an aviator and allowed his mechanic to make several short flights, before they returned to England on the SS *Mauretania* at the end of November.

Early in the new year Robert Blackburn, an aspiring aeroplane designer, offered Hucks a job as test pilot for his latest monoplane design fitted with a temperamental Isaacson radial engine. As an unqualified aviator turned test pilot, Benny Hucks first earned his £3 per week by putting his mechanical skills to good use and soon had the Isaacson engine running to his satisfaction.

Benny Hucks eventually made his debut as test pilot for Robert Blackburn at Filey Sands on the Yorkshire coast on 8 March 1911. Unfortunately, during a turn Benny lost flying speed, stalled and side-slipped on to the beach. Dame fortune smiled upon the antics of the would-be aviator and Benny walked away from the crumpled but repairable wreckage of wood and fabric.

Undeterred by this mishap, Robert Blackburn established his Flying School at Filey, adding a larger two-seat version of his monoplane design and promoting test pilot B.C. Hucks to Chief Instructor. Existing records indicate that B.C. Hucks qualified for RAeC certificate No.91 at Filey Sands on 30 May 1911 in a Blackburn Monoplane.

Although Francis Conway Jenkins, a contemporary of B.C. Hucks, had been born in London on 25 January 1888, his parents were residents of Westcliff-on-Sea. Awarded his RAeC on 2 May 1911, Conway Jenkins survived a number of crashes early in his career to serve in the war. By 1918 he was director of Aircraft Parks & Depots. Brig. Gen. F. Conway Jenkins died 23 February 1933. (RAF Museum)

Benny Hucks had actually taken his test before official observers from the Royal Aero Club on 18 May, the day after he had established a height record of 1,200ft for the north of England.

Because of a technicality Hucks had to make a second flight for his 'ticket', during which the 40hp Isaacson radial engine seized and sheared the propeller shaft. Although Hucks was injured in the resulting crash, he had satisfied the Royal Aero Club officials enough to qualify.

Whilst recovering from the accident, he accompanied his employer Robert Blackburn to France to observe the start of the Paris–Madrid Aero race starting at Issy on 21 May. Unfortunately the start of the race had to be delayed when the French war minister M. Berteaux was killed in an aircraft accident. He was one of twenty-two Frenchmen who died in aviation-related accidents during 1911.

The *Daily Mail's* £10,000-sponsored Circuit of Britain air race tempted nineteen competitors to the start line at Brooklands Aerodrome on Saturday 22 July 1911. Among the hopeful entries were two Blackburn Mercury Monoplanes, fitted with tried and tested air-cooled 50hp Gnome rotary engines.

All of the test-flying for the two machines had been carried out by Hucks and although he was forced to retire during the second lap with engine trouble and F. Conway Jenkins, the other pilot, overturned his Blackburn monoplane on take-off, the British-designed machine had attracted a number of enquiries, prompting Blackburn to send Hucks on a promotional tour of the West Country.

Beginning at Taunton on 7 August 1911, the tour lasted three months during which Benny Hucks made no less than ninety flights and covered 1,000 miles, establishing his reputation as a skilled aviator and the Blackburn Mercury II as a reliable machine. It was during this period that Benny Hucks undertook one of the earliest experiments attempted in Britain of ground-to-air communication by wireless transmission.

All good things must come to an end as did the tour, and Benny Hucks, putting public acclaim behind him, returned to the Blackburn Flying School as an instructor. However, the successful three-month promotional tour by the Blackburn Co. pilot had not gone unnoticed by rivals, including Claude Grahame-White, who had established an aerodrome at Hendon to hold regular aviation meetings. At the offer of a six-month contract from his former employer to fly a 50hp Blériot XI monoplane for exhibition and racing on a regular basis, Benny Hucks wasted no time in saying farewell to Robert Blackburn and headed south to join the Grahame-White Co. at the London-based aerodrome.

He arrived just in time for the wedding of Claude Grahame-White to Miss Dorothy Caldwell Taylor on Thursday 27 June 1912. The ceremony took place in the parish church of Widford near Chelmsford in Essex.

Among the 200 invited guests were well-known aviators of the period, including Tommy Sopwith, Gustav Hamel, Robert Loraine and Benny Hucks who all arrived by air, landing in the spacious grounds of 'Hylands', the country residence of Sir Daniel and Lady Gooch where the reception was due to take place.

With church bells pealing, the new bride and groom walked under the crossed staves of Chelmsford Boy Scouts forming a guard of honour as Benny Hucks, who had been circling overhead in his Blériot during the service, swooped in low showering the happy couple and guests with confetti.

During July and August, Benny Hucks became one of the pilots taking part in a Grahame-White Flying Circus backed by Lord Northcliffe and the *Daily Mail*, who endeavored to warn the government of the growing threat to the Nation posed by the flying machine as a weapon of war. Whilst Grahame-White toured coastal resorts packed with holidaymakers in his sky blue Henri Farman biplane with 'WAKE UP ENGLAND' painted on either side of the nacelle and beneath the lower wings, Benny Hucks gave flying exhibitions with his monoplane at Birmingham, Loughborough and Long Eaton.

Such was the reputation of the Essex aviator at this period that Benny Hucks received yet another tempting offer he could not refuse. It came from wealthy sportsman Harold Barlow who planned to tour Australia and his homeland New Zealand giving exhibition flights. Barlow was prepared to pay the Grahame-White Co. compensation of £1,000 to secure the services of Hucks, who was still under contract.

Benny Hucks once again said farewell to Grahame-White and accompanied Barlow to France in order to collect a new 70hp two-seat Blériot XI-2 that the millionaire had previously ordered. Having tested the new machine first with lead ballast in the rear cockpit and then with a representative of the Blériot works M. Baffier as a passenger, Hucks, now satisfied that all was well, flew his employer back to Hendon in easy stages.

Unfortunately due to ill-health, Barlow was forced to postpone the proposed tour of Australasia. This left Benny Hucks free to take the two-seater Blériot named 'The Firefly' on a tour of England and Scotland, giving flying displays sponsored by the *Daily Mail*.

In January 1913 after the unfortunate death of Harold Barlow, Hucks purchased 'The Firefly' from Barlow's executors, formed his own company with offices at 166 Piccadilly, London and with the aid of a tour manager, began taking bookings for another eventful year.

Throughout that spring and summer Hucks gave numerous flying displays and continued air racing, winning the Shell Trophy for the Aerial Derby Sealed Handicap on 20 September. Not only had Claude Grahame-White taught Benny Hucks the basic skills of an aviator, he had also imparted the art of aerial showmanship that Hucks now put to good use.

When he heard the news that the French aviator Adolph Pegoud was flying inverted and looping the loop intentionally, Hucks travelled to the Louis Blériot Flying School at Buc to see for himself. The sporting Pegoud recognised a kindred spirit in Benny Hucks and explained his theory of inverted flying before climbing into his modified machine to give the English aviator a display of looping the loop and inverted flying.

Benny Hucks had been so impressed by the skill of his French counterpart, he ordered a specially constructed looping Blériot XI as flown by the dashing Pegoud, with the airframe strengthened to withstand the additional pressure on the mainplanes imposed during inverted fight. The new machine had a fixed tailplane with large elevators to increase the aerobatic performance of the former racing design.

On his return to Hendon, Hucks began training for inverted flying by first strapping himself into an inverting chair rig and increasing the duration daily until he could read a newspaper whilst in the inverted position for 15 minutes without ill effects.

Meanwhile, Brooklands Aerodrome in Surrey, a rival to Grahame-White's London Aerodrome secured the services of Adolph Pegoud for the first display of upside-down flying in Britain. A record number of spectators, including Grahame-White, arrived at Brooklands on 27 September to witness the event. Grahame-White wasted no time, and the programmes for Hendon were soon advertising a 'Scientific Demonstration of Upside-Down Flying and Looping-the-Loop'.

When Benny Hucks considered himself ready to emulate the intrepid Pegoud, he sat inverted in his chair rig for 15 minutes, before donning his one-piece flying suit, helmet and goggles. Seated in the cockpit of his machine, he adjusted the special harness designed by the Blériot Co. for inverted flight then, having checked the controls one more time, he called to his mechanic to start the 50hp Gnome rotary.

Airborne at 1,000ft Benny Hucks, satisfied everything was in order, did exactly as Pegoud had advised and became the first British airman to loop-the-loop and fly inverted. Hucks' first public exhibition of upside-down flying took place above Hendon Aerodrome on 1 November 1913 before 50,000 excited spectators. He had established his reputation as a star aerobatic performer.

Due to public demand, Benny Hucks teamed up with Sheffield-born aviator Marcus Dyce Manton to form a two-man Flying Circus. Although nine years younger than

Hucks the two aviators worked very well together on tour during the splendid but fatal summer of 1914. Among the many ironies of the First World War was the fact that on 31 August 1915, Adolph Pegoud, serving with the French Air Service, was killed in action – the irony being that his opponent Corporal Kadulski had been a former pupil of Pegoud in pre-war days.

Benny Hucks began the 1914 season with an exhibition of his brand of aerobatics at Manchester on 1 January, and two weeks later he was guest of honour at an 'Upside Down Dinner' given by the Hendon Aviators at the 'The Royal Automobile Club' where the meal was both served and eaten in reverse order.

During March he returned to Hendon to give a combined demonstration with Gustav Hame, another famous aviator of the period who had also recently succumbed to the upside down bug. Benny Hucks took a busman's holiday from his busy schedule of exhibition flying during April. He escorted the Royal Yacht across the Channel, accompanied by an intrepid cameraman from the Warwick Bioscope Chronicle Film Co. who was busy filming King George and Queen Mary from the air with his hand cranked movie camera at 400ft.

Previously Hucks had captivated Lincolnshire with his 'barnstorming' by flying his monoplane between the towers of Lincoln Cathedral and looping-the-loop. An excited reporter of the *Lincolnshire Leader* told readers, 'If you want to shout with the very joy of living, just take to the air with Hucks'. Unfortunately for Europe, the joys of living in that splendid summer of 1914 were about to become the horrors of war.

Following the invasion of Belgium by the Imperial German Army, Britain had no option but to honour a treaty and declare war on the aggressor. Hucks immediately cancelled his flying display contracts and volunteered his services and the three Blériot machines owned by his company to the Royal Flying Corps.

Headlines on the morning of 26 August in *The Daily Sketch*, reporting a Zeppelin attack on Antwerp with twelve people killed and a hospital damaged, resulted in Zeppelin sightings over England for several weeks. The most persistent and curious of them had been of a Zeppelin hiding among the hills of Cumberland during daylight hours and venturing out after dark. 2nd-Lt B.C. Hucks RFC, stationed at Bournemouth, carried out orders to reconnoitre the Lake District in his ex-'Tornado' Blériot machine with a service number – 619 – painted either side of the rudder. Hucks made a thorough search of the area, enjoying the scenery, but found no sign of a Zeppelin. Convincing the War Office that the 'Cumberland sausage' had been the result of early wartime hysteria proved easier than the excited public, who persisted in reporting the phantom airship for weeks after Hucks had begun to ferry aircraft to France for the BEF.

Not the most robust of men, the gruelling barnstorming schedules of the previous two years had undermined Benny Hucks' health. After a severe bout of pleurisy he was invalided out of the Royal Flying Corps on 21 January 1915.

Both the *Aeroplane* and *Flight* magazines of the period mention that Hucks had actually flown on active service in France early in the war without giving details; however, Hucks is quoted in the weekly journal *Great Deeds of the Great War* Vol.II No.18, published in February 1915, as a British airman on active service at the front saying:

B.C. Hucks with 'The Tornado', his barnstorming Blériot monoplane, at Scarborough in 1914. (JMB/ GSL Collection)

I once came back from a reconnaissance and found a bullet hole through my plane (wing). I did not know when I got that, one of the enemy must have 'spotted' me. One of pilots however had a much more unpleasant experience. He arrived back from a flight with his machine riddled in about 150 places, the tyres of the wheels cut, one of his planes torn with shots, and wounds in his cheek and the back of his head. In addition to that the observer who accompanied him found that a shot had gone clean through his helmet.

Capt. B.C. Hucks talking to HM King George V during his visit to Hendon Aerodrome in 1918. (RAF Museum)

In spite of never fully recovering from pleurisy, Benny Hucks continued flying and in September 1915, he began test-flying and delivering BE2c biplanes for the aircraft manufacturers Ruston and Proctor, until promoted to the rank of captain in the RFC reserve. He returned to Hendon Aerodrome as a test pilot for 'AIRCO', the Aircraft Manufacturing Co., who put his talents to good use.

Hucks flew many of the de Havilland prototypes as well as the production machines whilst with 'AIRCO'. Important war work did not prevent Benny Hucks indulging in aerobatics when he had a suitable machine. Harry Harper, the air correspondent for the *Aeroplane* magazine, recalled Hucks phoning him one morning inviting him out to Hendon to watch a piece of 'acrobatics' he had been practising.

Through his binoculars Harper watched the DH4 biplane flown by Hucks perform the perfect 'falling leaf' manoeuvre to within a few hundred feet of the ground to make a 'dexterous' landing. Harry Harper, who had the highest regard for Hucks as an aviator, was of the opinion that his friend had taxed his strength to the limit carrying out important tests on military aircraft for the war effort when he contracted influenza, then at epidemic proportions in war-torn Europe.

Capt. B.C. Hucks passed away at the age of thirty-four on 7 November 1918 and was buried, according to Highgate Cemetery Ltd, in Grave 39669, to be found in square 118 located in the eastern part of Highgate Cemetery, on Armistice Day 1918. A well-tended monument to Karl Marx is adjacent to square 118, making it easy to find, but as the plot containing Capt. Hucks was so badly overgrown, with many of the headstones laying face down, the author was unable to locate his grave.

Essex airman Benny Hucks is remembered today as one of Britain's foremost aviators of the pre-1914 era, but his contribution to the RFC/RAF during the First World War had been of immense value, not only had he test flown many prototype machines including the FE8 single-seat pusher scout, the 'AIRCO' DH5 with its unique back stagger of the upper plane and among the last of the prototypes, the Rolls Royce Eagle powered DH9a built under licence by the Westland Co. in 1918.

A tangible link with Benny Hucks can still be seen today at Old Warden Aerodrome at Biggleswade in Bedfordshire, home to the famous Shuttleworth Collection of vintage aeroplanes, in the form of an aero-engine starter mounted on a Model T Ford chassis. This device, still in active use today, had been devised by Benny Hucks for 'AIRCO' and became known as the 'Hucks Starter' by the RAF during and after the First World War.

The Petre Brothers

Perhaps not quite as well known as Bentfield Charles Hucks are the pioneer airmen of the Petre family, brothers Henry, Edward and John a Naval airman. Their brothers William and Bernard also served in the First World War.

The Petre family is interwoven into the history of Essex over the centuries. However, for this account of early Essex airmen, we begin with their father Sebastian Henry Petre, the fourth son of the Hon. H.W. Petre, brother of Lord Petre of Ingatestone in Essex.

Henry Aloysius Petre qualified for Royal Aero Club Certificate No.128 at Brooklands Aerodrome, Surrey, on 12 September 1911. (RAF Museum)

Edward Petre qualified for his Royal Aero Club Certificate No.259 at Fairlop, Essex, on 24 July 1912. (RAF Museum)

Sebastian Petre studied law and in 1881 became a partner in the firm of Blount & Lynch, Solicitors in the City of London, which still flourishes today under the name of Blount, Petre and Kramer.

In June 1881 Sebastian married Elise Sibeth, the only daughter of Edmund Sibeth of Cleveland Square, London. After the wedding, Harry (Sebastian's family name) and Elise lived in Yorkshire, until 'Tor Bryan' their family home had been completed at Ingatestone.

Sebastian and Elise were blessed with five sons, Henry, Edward, John (known in the family as Jack), William and Bernard. Two daughters, Mary and Sybil (known as Bill), completed the family.

It was Henry Aloysius Petre, born 12 June 1884, the eldest of the aviator brothers and Edward, two years his junior, born 27 April 1886, who were to be caught up in the heady excitement of aviation then sweeping Edwardian England. They were inseparable in their quest for knowledge of powered flight and at Brooklands Aerodrome in Surrey they designed and built their own monoplane that was exhibited by Leo Ripault & Co, during the 1910 Olympia Aero and Motor Boat Show.

The following year Henry Petre became known in the aviation fraternity as 'Peter the Monk' and Edward Petre rejoiced in the name of 'Peter the Painter' after the notorious criminal involved in the famous Sidney Street Siege of 1911 that took place in East London.

During the summer of 1911, the Petre brothers, having had little success with their flying machine, decided to visit Barking Creek, the birthplace of the Handley Page Aircraft Co.. Henry and Edward had intended to seek advice from Frederick Handley Page, a competent twenty-six-year-old engineer, who had not only set up the first Aero Engineering Co. in Britain at Barking two years earlier, but had also designed a successful monoplane.

As luck would have it, Handley Page had recently fallen out with and sacked Robert Fenwick, his test pilot, and offered the vacancy to Edward Petre even though he was an unqualified aviator at the time! 'Peter the Painter' and his elder brother Henry had obviously impressed the shrewd businessman Frederick Handley Page. Edward remained at the Barking Aero Works assisting with the design and test-flying of the Handley Page Type D monoplane. During this time Henry returned to Brooklands and qualified for his RAeC Certificate (No.128) on 12 September 1911, flying a Hanriot monoplane, ten months before his test pilot brother qualified as an aviator. Edward was still teaching himself to fly in April 1912; much of his time, energy and enthusiasm had been absorbed in the design and construction of the latest Handley Page machine, a two-seat monoplane designated Type E, fitted with a reliable 50hp Gnome rotary engine in readiness for the Army Aeroplane Competition for the proposed formation of the Royal Flying Corps in May.

The Barking Creek site housing the Handley Page workshops proved to be unsuitable for an aerodrome, as had the ill-fated Experimental Ground set up by the Aeronautical Society at nearby Dagenham Dock two years earlier. Undismayed, Handley Page rented a suitable flying field in the form of a well drained and level sports ground at Fairlop on the outskirts of the nearby town of Ilford. Taken by road and assembled at Fairlop, the Type E was test flown by Edward Petre on 26 April. 'Peter the Painter' wisely flew in long straight hops, as he was still learning to fly; the open level obstacle-free fields of Fairlop proved to be an ideal site for an aerodrome.

The unsuccessful Petre monoplane, designed and built at Brooklands Aerodrome in 1910 by the Petre brothers Henry and Edward. (JMB/GSL Collection)

'Yellow Peril', the Handley Page monoplane, at Brooklands Aerodrome just after Edward Petre made the first heavier than air flight across London from a sports ground at Fairlop on the outskirts of Ilford. (JMB/GSL Collection)

Edward began flying circuits and soon felt confident enough to fly the monoplane from Fairlop back to the small Handley Page ground at Barking a little over 7 miles away by air. Gusting wind conditions were responsible for the crash that occurred as he attempted to land. Fortunately Edward had not been injured and with his enthusiasm and energy the machine was rebuilt and flying again within two weeks.

The wings of the repaired monoplane were re-covered with fabric and doped yellow before it was again transported to Fairlop by road. At first the yellow-winged machine was called *The Antiseptic*, until Edward Petre dubbed it *The Yellow Peril*. It was in this machine that Edward qualified for his RAeC Certificate (No.259) at Fairlop on 24 July 1912.

Three days later 'Peter the Painter' gave the expanding Handley Page Co., in the throes of moving to larger premises near Hendon, a boost by making the first heavier than air flight across London, by flying from Fairlop to Brooklands Aerodrome in Surrey. In 1912 flying over built up areas was prohibited, so Edward, after taking off from the playing fields of Fairlop, flew across country to Rainham and followed the course of the Thames to Kew before heading for Brooklands.

The 50-minute flight covering 55 miles had been made in gusting conditions. 'Peter the Painter' had returned to Brooklands in triumph, a fully fledged birdman. The Handley Page monoplane with its crescent-shaped mustard yellow wings and blue doped fuselage was the centre of attraction.

At the Handley Page Barking works, the proposed military version of *The Yellow Peril* neared completion. It would be the last Handley Page machine built on that site. This machine was fitted with a more powerful 70hp rotary and a single cockpit that housed the pilot and passenger sitting side by side. Henry Petre, who was assisting his brother in the construction of the new machine, unknown to Handley Page who was immersed in business affairs and the imminent move of the company, had designed and constructed a pair of swept back wings with straight leading edges, to replace the curved wings of the original Handley Page specification.

On his return to Barking, younger brother Edward, in the parlance of the day, 'blew a gasket' as no doubt Handley Page would also have done if he had known what 'Peter the Monk' had been up to in his absence. With little time to spare before Handley Page arrived to inspect the Type F, the offending set of wings was quickly replaced.

Henry Petre had to decline an offer by Handley Page to fly the Type F at the August 1912 Military Trials, as he had been a successful candidate for the proposed formation of an Australian Flying School and Flying Corps. Officially he began his duties as an aviator mechanic for the Australian Government on 12 months' probation, at a salary of £400 per annum plus travel allowance on 6 August.

Edward Petre entered the Handley Page Type F for the War Office Military Trials held at Larkhill, Wiltshire. Unfortunately on his second flight, the 70hp Gnome rotary proved to be temperamental, forcing Edward to land downwind. Although the machine received only minor damage, it could not be repaired in time to complete the trials. Shortly after this episode, Edward left the Handley Page Co. and returned to Brooklands, where he began flying as test pilot for the Martin Handasyde Co.

A Martin Handasyde monoplane delivered to the Royal Flying Corps by Edward Petre during November 1912. (JMB/GSL Collection)

Helmuth Martin and George Handasyde, Edward's new employers, had also entered a monoplane for the Military Trials, a large beast fitted with a 75hp Chenu engine that gave endless trouble and eventually had to be withdrawn. This machine, re-engined with a more reliable 65hp Antoinette, was test flown by Edward, still known as 'Peter the Painter', on 27 September. After several cross-country flights, engine trouble again caused Edward to make a forced landing on 24 October that resulted in serious damage when the large machine overturned before coming to a stop. Fortunately once again 'Peter the Painter' had escaped injury.

Luck was still Edward's passenger when he was testing another Martin Handasyde machine at Brooklands on Saturday 9 November and he again escaped injury. An eye witness claimed 'He, whilst finishing a magnificent spiral *vol plane*, made a miscalculation and had a fall, but was luckily unhurt, the only damage done being to the machine' Unperturbed as ever 'Peter the Painter' took to the air again on 17 November in the same machine. Two days later he delivered another Martin Handasyde machine ordered for the Royal Flying Corps to Farnborough. Edward returned to Farnborough during early December, testing the aircraft prior to their acceptance by the Royal Flying Corps.

On Sunday 15 December, Edward, who had returned to Brooklands, began test-flying the latest Martin Handasyde product. Although just nine years old, powered flight had already claimed over 120 lives, so 'Peter the Painter' was well aware of the risk he was undertaking when he planned to fly from Brooklands to Edinburgh on Christmas Eve 1912. Taking off from Brooklands Aerodrome at 0910hrs in the reliable 65hp Antoinette powered Martin Handasyde monoplane, as Edinburgh was 4½ hours away by air, his intention was to fly all the way non-stop. The weather, however, became increasingly turbulent and 3 hours into the flight Edward is thought to have attempted an emergency landing at Marske on the coast, where he crashed and died of his injuries. Following an investigation by the Accidents Committee of the Royal Aero Club, the verdict was given that the aircraft wings had collapsed in flight.

Before setting out for Australia, Henry Petre examined the wreckage of the monoplane his brother had been killed in and agreed with the findings of Martin, the designer, that there was no evidence of wing failure in flight. Martin's theory was that Edward, weary of battling the elements for 3 hours, attempted to land and lost control due to the violent turbulence near the cliffs.

Fearless to the last, 'Peter the Painter' did not live to serve his country in the forthcoming First World War, during which, in the spring of 1915, Martin Handasyde became Martinsyde Ltd and played an important role in supplying the RFC with both Martinsyde-designed and -built subcontracted machines throughout the remainder of the conflict.

Henry Petre arrived in Melbourne at the end of January 1913. He had been one of the many applicants to reply to an advertisement for the 'Appointment of two competent Mechanists and Aviators' first published in the *Commonwealth Gazette* of 30 December 1911. This advertisement had also appeared in the British daily press, and it was to be the modest start of an Australian Flying Corps and a home-based Military Flying School.

There had been no shortage of volunteers for the two positions, the inducement of £400 per annum plus travel allowance had seen to that. Henry Petre had been short-listed to a group of seven that included the colourful Samuel Cody, the showman aviator – credited as being the first man to fly an aeroplane in Britain. In the event Henry Petre and Harry Busteed were chosen as the aviator mechanics, with the flamboyant Cody as organising engineer.

Both Cody and Busteed were eventually to pull out of the proposed formation of the flying school in Australia. They were replaced by Australian-born Eric Harrison, who had been taught to fly at the Bristol School, Wiltshire in 1911. Henry, who had taken up his duties for the Australian Government on 6 August 1912, set about his first task by visiting the British Deperdussin Co. to check upon the progress of machines that had been ordered for the Australian Flying School. Facilities were also made available for him to visit the Central Flying School and Royal Aircraft Factory at Farnborough, to confer with those of the establishment who could advise him of the tasks he would encounter in Australia.

The proposed site of the Australian Central Flying School was to have been at Canberra in the Federal Territory. When Henry inspected the area, he reported it as being unsuitable for a flying school due to the nearby mountains and the altitude. Off the record, Henry confided that also he had no intentions of being isolated in the Bush.

Eventually a suitable 734-acre site known as Point Cook on Point Phillip Bay was purchased. It was well situated for both land and seaplane operation; also, Point Cook was just a mere 6 miles from the nearest railway station and only 23 miles from the Melbourne post office!

Henry Petre and Eric Harrison seated in a BE2a biplane at Point Cook, Australia, in 1914. (K.Petre)

Among the many other problems that Henry Petre had to overcome was the shortage of trained aero mechanics. He repeatedly wired the authorities that it was 'absolutely necessary' for the safe and efficient operation of the school that they be on hand and ready to start work as soon as the machines arrive from Britain. When at last the aircraft began to arrive, it was found their crates were full of moisture and the aircraft fabric covered with mildew, also the metal fittings were beginning to rust.

Due to the primitive conditions at Point Cook at the time, the aircraft were shipped back to Melbourne for extensive overhauls. It had been the first time that aeroplanes from Britain had been transported over such a vast distance. They had been crated up in the winter and subjected to a lengthy sea voyage. Thanks to Henry Petre, later shipments of aircraft were filled with bags of calcium chloride to absorb and prevent the formation of moisture in the crates. This practice would become standard during the First World War.

It was not until February 1914 that Henry, with fellow instructor Eric Harrison, four mechanics from Britain, one clerk and a caretaker finally occupied the Point Cook site, living in bell tents. Two Australian army hospital tents, the largest available, arrived at Point Cook, but these proved to be too small to house the aircraft and eventually served as a Quartermaster Store and a Mess tent.

Eric Harrison designed a canvas hangar for the aircraft and had it manufactured in Melbourne for the grand sum of £114.1.0. In spite of its fragile appearance the hangar survived the elements for a year. Empty aircraft packing cases provided a solid cook house; this was another practice adopted by the RFC/RNAS overseas during the war, where packing cases provided all year round living accommodation on remote aerodrome sites.

Water for the Flying School had to be carried 4 miles, but thanks to an acetylene gas plant intended for welding, the 'Tilly' type gas lamps were never short of fuel, so at least Point Cook had an efficient lighting system.

Henry Petre made the first aeroplane flight at Point Cook on Sunday 1 March, a contemporary report stating that Lieutenant Petre was at the controls of a Deperdussin monoplane, serial CFS.4. Eight days later Henry escaped injury when the engine of CFS.4 cut out just after taking off. Lacking sufficient height to clear a telephone cable, Henry banked the machine in a sharp turn, lost flying speed and side-slipped into the ground. Henry was not sorry to see the Deperdussin written-off, as it had a lot of vices and was known a 'The Dirty Dustbin'.

By contrast CFS.5, the second Deperdussin, although under-powered, provided an excellent 'roller' in which pupils could acquire the feel of the aircraft controls by 'rolling' along the ground under power, as neither the Bristol Boxkite or the BE2a machines, in use for instruction at this period, had dual control.

Four Australian Army officers arrived at Point Cook for flying instruction and the first course commenced on Monday 17 August 1914. Upon their arrival, they found an office and the first workshop had been completed and two permanent hangers were being erected.

Henry had overcome many difficulties. What no doubt stood him in good stead was having been admitted as a solicitor at the age of twenty-one back in 1905; this helped him with dealing with the official red tape.

With the outbreak of the war in Europe, obtaining replacement aircraft and engines would become even more difficult. So the school workshop began the construction of a machine copied from a Bristol Boxkite that was already in everyday use at Point Cook.

All four officers on the course qualified for their 'wings'. Their certificates were formally presented by their instructors Lt Petre and Lt Harrison by arrangement with the Royal Aero Club of Great Britain, on Saturday 28 November 1914.

Point Cook had also become the assembly point for Australian Flying Corps personnel about to go overseas. Lt Eric Harrison, with Lt George Merz, who had just two days previously completed the first Point Cook flying course, sailed with the Australian National Military Expedition for operations against German New Guinea, on Monday 30 November.

In the event, the services of the two aeroplanes and their pilots were not required and when returned to Point Cook the aircraft had not been unpacked from their crates.

The second course of instruction at Point Cook Flying School began on Monday 1 March 1915, with eight pupils, but Henry Petre would not be there to award the brevets to the successful candidates, as he had handed over command of Point Cook to Lt Harrison.

In February 1915, the Viceroy of India appealed to Australia for trained aviators to serve with the Indian Army Expeditionary Force that had occupied Persian territory in September 1914, to protect the Anglo-Persian oil wells at Abadan from Turkish forces that had entered the war allied to Germany.

Promoted to Captain, Henry Petre was to command the Australian Half Flight, comprised of four officer pilots and forty-one NCOs and men. It had been agreed that the Indian Army would supply the aircraft. When the Australian Half Flight landed at Basra via the Persian Gulf in May 1915, they brought with them mechanical transport that included two well-equipped mobile workshops.

Awaiting their arrival at Basra were two Farman Shorthorns and a Longhorn pusher aircraft with spare engines, along with two Indian Army aviators, an engineering officer and fifteen other ranks. Their aerodrome was sited on high ground at Ma'gil, 3 miles north of Basra, as much of the surrounding area was under water during the flood season.

An Anglo-Indian advance from Basra to Baghdad under the command of Major-General Sir Charles Townshend had already begun, when the first aerial reconnaissance was successfully carried out over enemy positions on Monday 31 May 1915. Major Reilly with Brook-Smith, the two Indian Army airmen attached to the Half Flight, and Capt. Henry Petre, with Lt Burns as observer, confirmed the enemy were retreating from their fortified positions north of Kurna. The next day Major Reilly and his observer Capt. White returned to the advanced landing ground at Busrah to report that the enemy had been driven north of Bahran.

Pushing their Maurice Farman to its limit in the extreme heat, Henry Petre, again with Lt Burn, covered 231 miles flying to Amarah and back on Wednesday 2 June and found that apart from a small number of troops in barges on the river, there were no other sightings of the enemy in the vicinity. Engine trouble on 4 June did not prevent Capt. Petre and Lt Burn from carrying out a 120-mile reconnaissance successfully. Flights over Turkish held territory continued daily throughout June. On the 22nd, Capt. Petre and Lt Burn reported the river Euphrates was in flood, forming a lake about 70 miles in length and 12 to 15 miles wide.

Sunday 4 July 1915 would have been a red letter day for the Australian Half Flight as two Caudron GIII tractor biplanes arrived, but their 80hp Gnome rotary engines would prove to be unsuitable for desert operations, with tragic results.

As the Anglo–Indian advance continued, Capt. Petre, unable to fly having accidentally broken his wrist, led a small detachment by launching up the Euphrates on 19 July, to establish a forward refuelling depot on Abu-Saibiq, a small island 46 miles north of Basra. Henry, in a later report, stated:

> The heat here was intense, never falling below 100 degrees day or night, but owing to one of the aeroplanes having missed the island and gone on to Suk-esh-Sheyukh, we had to remain for three days longer than the period previously determined on.

The Caudron biplanes IFC.3 and IFC.4, piloted by Major Reilly and Lt Merz, played an important role in the Nasiuyah operations and the town was captured on Sunday 25 July.

As anticipated, considerable trouble was being experienced with the rotary engines in the hot climate, while the water-cooled Renault engines of the venerable Farman biplanes proved to be the more reliable.

Henry returned to Abu-Salibiq with his small detachment on Wednesday 28 July to refuel the Caudron machines on their return flight to Basra. Major Reilly with Sergeant Palmer landed at Abu-Salibiq to refuel at 11a.m. on 30 July. The two Caudron biplanes had set from Nasiuyah together for the return journey. IFC.3 Reilly's machine developed engine trouble and he landed near the Arab town of Khamsieh; Merz and Burn, the occupants of the second machine, continued on their way and were never seen again.

A dust storm was rising over the desert and Maj. Reilly decided to remain at Abu-Salibiq over night. He explained to Henry that a weak inlet valve spring had caused engine failure earlier in the day. Fortunately for the crew of IFC.3, the Arabs were friendly in that area. Although Lt Merz, the pilot of the second Caudron, had missed the island for refuelling at the start of the Nasiuyah campaign, Henry did not feel too anxious when the second machine did not arrive. Maj. Reilly had confirmed on take-off that Merz had ample petrol to fly direct to Basra. Maj. Reilly and Sgt Palmer continued their flight to Basra the following morning. On arrival they were welcomed with relief, as IFC.4 and its crew were still missing.

During the evening of Sunday 1 August, Henry's party, encamped on the island, saw a Very light fired from the water east of Abu-Salibiq. After firing a Very in return, Henry set out with his launch in the direction of the flare. Travelling in the dark, the launch's propeller became fouled with weed and they ran aground on a mud bank. Anchored for the night, Henry ordered an acetylene flare to be lit. The beacon burned brightly for over 2 hours. At dawn the rescue party set off again towards the east and soon encountered Lt Wells, Sgt Heath, two Indian sailors and an Arab guide in a large native canoe, loaded with a pack wireless and extra rations for Henry's party.

It was by Lt Wells that Henry was informed that Merz and Burns were missing. For the record, Sgt C.V. Heath would receive the only DCM awarded to a member of the Australian Flying Corps. The citation read 'For conspicuous pluck and determination on 1 August 1915, when he assisted to pole a "Bellum" [a flat bottomed boat] for 28 miles in 12 hours, enduring the most intense heat in order to rescue aviators forced to descend in enemy territory.'

By coincidence, as Henry stepped ashore back at Abu-Salibiq island, Maj. Reilly, flying a Maurice Farman, arrived from Basra. After allowing the 70hp water-cooled Renault engine to cool, Henry decided to accompany Reilly in an airborne search for the missing airmen.

The Farman had covered just 25 miles flying west when the missing Caudron was sighted and Reilly landed and taxied alongside the deserted machine.

On inspecting the derelict they found the aeroplane had made a good landing and as a Gnome rotary spanner and a high tension lead were found on the sand by the machine, it was deduced that yet another bout of engine trouble had forced the airmen down. It was also obvious by the way the fabric on the wings and tailplane had been slashed with swords, the missing airmen had been attacked by a band of Bedouins. The only other clue to their disappearance was two burnt-out smoke bomb canisters.

Maintenance work on a Caudron GIII being carried out in the spacious workshops at Ma'gil Aerodrome near Basra, 1915. (W. Evans)

Taking off again, Reilly flew a low sweep over the area looking for signs of the missing men. On returning to Abu-Salibiq, Henry interviewed the local Sheikh, who had search parties sent out to make enquiries, but as the local Arabs lived in fear for themselves of the marauding Bedouins, Henry was not at all hopeful of finding the missing aviators still alive.

The following day, Henry's detachment was recalled to Basra and the matter of the missing Caudron crew was put in the hands of Political Officers, who eventually discovered that Lt William Burn and Lt George Merz had been killed by the band of Bedouin tribesmen, three of whom were wounded and another shot dead as the officers defended themselves with their revolvers until, heavily outnumbered, they were eventually overpowered.

Although large rewards were offered, the bodies of the missing airmen were never recovered. During August the Mesopotamian Half Flight were reinforced with four single-seat Martinsyde biplane scouts and became A Flight of No.30 Squadron of the Royal Flying Corps, detached from the remainder of the squadron serving in Palestine.

Captain Henry Petre remained at Basra Aerodrome, situated just north of the city at Ma'gil, as a flying instructor when on 23 August, A Flight left for the forward aerodrome at Amarah, in readiness for the next Anglo-Indian advance alongside the river Tigris. Of the four A Flight aeroplanes that flew on to the advance landing ground on Thursday 9 September, a Maurice Farman Shorthorn crashed on the airfield within two days. On 13 September, a Martinsyde Scout also crashed while being test flown.

A Martinsyde Scout for A Flight No.30 Squadron, arriving at Basra by barge on 24 August 1915. Major Reilly of the Indian Army was captured when this machine was brought down by ground fire on 21 November 1915. (W. Evans)

Gnome rotary engine failure again forced a Caudron GIII, this time on a reconnaissance for the advance on Kut-el-Mara, to land in the desert. The crew of IFC.3, Lt W. Treloar and Capt. B. Atkians, were captured by Arab cavalry on 16 September and spent the remainder of the war in Turkish prisons.

A Flight of No.30 Squadron had now been reduced to just two serviceable aircraft, a Farman Shorthorn and a Martinsyde scout, to cover the imminent attack on Kut-el-Amara by the Anglo-Indian Force.

The arrival early in September of RFC Force D, a RNAS contingent with three Short 827 type seaplanes equipped with wireless, to operate from the river Tigris, soon ran into difficulties. Although these large single-engined machines were fitted with 150hp Sunbeams, they required a very long, straight stretch of the river to unstick when loaded with a heavy wireless transmitter and observer. By November two of the RNAS machines had been fitted with land chassis in lieu of floats and operated from the same airfield as A Flight.

Henry's second stint as a flying instructor had been short-lived. As soon as his wrist injury had healed, he rejoined the depleted A Flight at Ali Gharbi and returned to carrying out perilous reconnaissance patrols over the hostile desert.

During his tour of duty in Mesopotamia, Capt. Henry Petre would be mentioned in dispatches no less than three times.

Flying IFC.8, a replacement Martinsyde scout, Henry landed heavily on the rough terrain causing damage, which again reduced the number of serviceable machines in the Flight to one Farman Shorthorn IFC.7 and Martinsyde IFC.6.

Major General Townshend ordered the assault on Kut-el-Mara to begin on Monday 27 September and within two days the Anglo-Indian force had occupied the town. The repaired Martinsyde IFC.8 was flown into Kut by Henry to join the two other serviceable machines on Saturday 2 October, only to be crash landed again by Henry. Four days later, flying Martinsyde scout IFC.6 from an advanced landing ground at Aziziya, Henry carried out the first aerial reconnaissance of Baghdad on Wednesday 6 October; on return he reported that the city was nearly empty of enemy troops.

Reinforcement for A Flight in the form of Maurice Farman IFC.2 flew to Kut from Basra. This brought A Flight strength up to two Farman pusher machines, one single-seat Martinsyde scout and a second Martinsyde under repair. The fragile looking Farman aircraft, in spite of their shortcomings in the desert, had performed very well indeed.

The veteran Shorthorn IFC.1 had been struck off strength after a crash at Ali Gharbi Aerodrome. IFC.2, which had seen service as a training machine in India before the start of the war, was lost in a daring raid carried out by T.W. White and Capt. Yeats-Brown on Saturday 13 November 1915. Their orders were to land behind enemy lines and sabotage telegraph lines to isolate the Turkish forces from their Headquarters in Baghdad.

Their Longhorn came under rifle as they were landing and taxiing up close to the road, and the tips of their 53ft span mainplanes struck a telegraph pole. Still under fire, they set their explosive charges and attempted to escape using the crippled flying bird cage as a propeller driven sand buggy! The plucky pair had carried out a similar escape when they had been grounded in enemy territory a few weeks earlier. This time however, fortune did not favour the brave. Pursued by cavalry, they were captured and became *Guests of the Unspeakable*, as T.W. White entitled his remarkable account of the plight endured by prisoners of war in Turkish hands, published after the war.

Another loss to A Flight was Maj. Reilly who failed to return from a reconnaissance mission flying Martinsyde IFC.6 in preparation for the battle of Ctesiphon on Sunday 21 November. Shot down by small arms fire, Maj. Reilly attempted to escape on foot before he was captured.

The bane of Henry's life at this period, Martinsyde scout IFC.8, was finally written off on the day after the start of the battle of Ctesiphon. Turkish small arms fire damaged the engine of the little biplane, forcing Capt. E.J. Fulton to land and be led away into captivity. The loss of the two pilots and their aeroplanes from the meager resources of A Flight at a critical period in the campaign had serious consequences. In spite of the valiant efforts of Capt. Petre, flying reconnaissance sorties in the remaining operational Shorthorn IFC.7, the Anglo-Indian force, in fierce fighting at Ctesiphon and the retreat back to Kut, lost one third of its force – killed or wounded. At Kut the exhausted survivors came under siege from the Turkish Army quickly encircling the town.

Suitable aircraft (at that period) for the desert campaign arrived at Ma'gil (Basra) for No.30 Squadron in the form of four BE2c biplanes, better late than never they had been dispatched to Kut by barge. The BE biplanes were assigned to B Flight as by the end of November the remnants of both A and B Flights at Kut had just three serviceable machines between them. This small force had been whittled down to one Farman

Shorthorn by 7 December, when under orders Capt. Petre flew IFC.7 out of the besieged town as the remaining members of both flights fought as infantry alongside the British and Indian troops, starving in appalling conditions, until General Townshend, with many of his men wounded or suffering from malaria and dysentery, finally surrendered Kut-el-Mara on Wednesday 29 April 1916, after two relief columns and attempts to supply the defenders by running the Turkish blockade of the Tigris with sandbagged river steamers had failed.

During the 143 days of the siege, the pilots of No.30 Squadron and the RNAS unit had carried out the first airlifts of the war, by dropping as many sacks of food to the starving garrison as their primitive aeroplanes would allow them to carry into the air during the hours of daylight. Among the airmen involved in this dangerous work was Capt. Petre, who had been the last man to fly out of Kut.

Of the four Australian Flying Corps and two Indian Flying Corps pilots of the original Mesopotamian Half Flight, only Capt. Henry Petre had survived the ill-fated campaign. By May 1916, when No.30 Squadron moved back to the aerodrome at Sheikh Said, such had been the strain imposed on their physical health by the rigors of the campaign that six of the eight pilots were hospitalised.

The RNAS detachment returned with its seaplanes to Egypt at the end of June 1916 and October saw the Mesopotamian Half Flight attached to the RFC finally disbanded. All surviving Australian personnel were also sent to Egypt to join two Australian Flying Corps squadrons. Major Henry Petre DSO, MC, returned home to England, where, after convalescent leave, he became the first Commanding Officer of No.75 Home Defence Squadron, formed at Goldington, Bedfordshire on 1 October 1916.

Transferred from the Australian Flying Corps to the Royal Air Force in April 1918, Maj. Henry Petre retired from the RAF in 1919. Between the two world wars, Henry married a lady who, as Kay Petre, became well known during the 1930s for her skills as a racing car driver at Brooklands.

The start of the Second World War saw Henry back in uniform, at one period serving as a gliding instructor. 'Peter the Monk', alias Henry Aloysius Petre, pioneer aviator of Ingatestone, Essex, passed away on 24 April, 1962, aged seventy-eight years.

Henry and Edward had been the eldest of the Petre brothers. William, born two years after Edward in 1888, served with the Army Service Corps overseas until posted to Home Establishment on 13 August 1917. Captain William Petre, who had been mentioned in dispatches, transferred to the Royal Flying Corps on 23 March 1918. After the war William became an estate agent and married Margaret in 1925. Should any of their three daughters or grandchildren read this, the author would be pleased to hear from them, to enable him to fill the missing details of Capt. William Petre's service with the Royal Air Force.

Bernard, the fourth Petre brother, born in 1891, was an engineer and served as a captain in the Army Service Corps, prefixed Royal in November 1918. Bernard was also mentioned in dispatches during the First World War.

Squadron Commander John Joseph Petre DSC, CG, born 11 April 1894, was the youngest of the five Ingatestone brothers. A draughtsman at the start of the First World War, he volunteered for the Royal Naval Air Service.

Flt Lt John (Jack) Petre, fourth from left, at Dover Naval Air Station 1915. (RAF Museum)

Flt Lt John Petre at the controls of a Nieuport 11 at Dunkirk. (RAF Museum)

Twenty-seven days after his entry into the RNAS, Flight Sub-Lieutenant John Petre qualified for his RAeC flying an EAC biplane at the Naval Flying School, Eastbourne on Wednesday 14 October 1914. Posted to Eastchurch Naval Air Station on 27 October, John Petre continued his training until the end of the year. On 12 January 1915 he commenced a four-week course at Grain Naval Air Station prior to his posting to 1 Wing Seaplane Base at Dunkirk.

Having flown many of the varied land and seaplanes in service without serious mishap for six months, John Petre had been promoted to the rank of Flight Lieutenant on 7 April 1916. During the same month, two single-engined 100hp pusher flying boats were delivered to the Seaplane Base.

Flight Lieutenant Petre escaped serious injury on Monday 24 May, when the Gnome rotary engine of the Franco-British Aviation flying boat cut out just after taking off. FBA 3134 was repaired and flown again only to be written off by a fellow officer on 5 December the same year. The two FBA machines flown by John Petre at Dunkirk were of French design and construction. He also suffered a minor mishap in FBA 3113, when he damaged an elevator in a collision while taxiing back into the busy harbour on 18 June at the end of an anti-submarine patrol.

As the war in the air intensified the demands on the RNAS led to a rapid expansion of the service. Flt Lt Petre was posted to 'B' Group, 1 Wing, when formed at St Pol near Dunkirk on 22 November 1915. 'B' Group were equipped with French-built single and two-seat Nieuport sesquiplane.

A mention in dispatches for meritorious work in connection with a bombing raid on sheds at Ostend docks on 30 December 1915, gives scant detail of this particular action and the many and various raids carried out by Flt Lt Petre and 1 Wing in the Dunkirk area during the closing weeks of 1915.

Foul flying weather in the form of gales, sleet and rain for the first ten days of 1916 restricted the actions of 1 Wing at St Pol. A heavy leather knee-length coat and sheepskin lined boots afforded John Petre some protection from the icy slipstream in the open cockpit of the Nieuport and bear grease covering the parts of his face exposed by his leather flying helmet and goggles lessened the ever present risk from frostbite. In spite of these hardships in the depth of winter, the airmen were well aware they were far better off than the infantry men in the frozen water-logged trenches of the firing line far below. Barring engine failure, 'Archie' – the nickname for German anti-aircraft fire, derived from a ribald pre-war music-hall song entitled *Archibald Certainly Not* – and the increasing number of enemy aeroplanes being encountered daily, the young airmen on both sides of the lines could rely on a hot meal and a warm dry billet awaiting their return.

Flight Lieutenant John Petre was again mentioned in dispatches by the Admiralty on 15 February 1916, 'For continuous meritorious service over the enemy lines'. Another Admiralty communiqué states, 'On May 16th this officer [John Petre] in a Nieuport Scout, fought an action with a German Machine over Dixmunde at 5000ft and after chasing him for 5 miles over the enemy lines, he forced the hostile machine to descend. This was carried out under intense and accurate anti-aircraft fire by enemy batteries'.

Dressed for winter flying, Flt Lt John Petre with a Nieuport scout at Dunkirk
early 1916. (RAF Museum)

John Petre was recommended for promotion to Acting Flight Commander in view of
consistent good services. The following month the *London Gazette*, dated 22 June 1916,
announced that 'Flt Cdr John Petre had been awarded a DSC, in recognition of service
as a pilot at Dunkirk'. On patrol in a Nieuport scout 8751 on Saturday 21 October, John
Petre observed two enemy machines approaching the town of Nieuport at 6,000ft. Diving

from 1,500ft with the element of surprise he opened fire at the nearest machine with forty rounds at 100 yards range, which caused the unfortunate observer, dead or wounded, to fall back inside his cockpit before the stricken machine side slipped and fell vertically, trailing smoke. John Petre wasted no time as the Nieuport scout suddenly came under anti-aircraft fire; zig-zagging, he climbed, regaining height to change the now empty ammunition drum on his Lewis gun. Re-armed, the Nieuport pilot then discovered the crew of the second enemy machine had made its escape. A report received from a local Belgian squadron stated that one of their airmen had witnessed the action and confirmed that the LVG had crashed. Flt Cdr John Petre DSC was decorated with the Croix de Guerre by the French Government on Sunday 12 November.

At the end of 1916, the Royal Flying Corps on the Western Front were short of scout (fighter) squadrons. In an agreement between the Admiralty and the War Office, new Naval fighter squadrons were to be formed from existing RNAS units along the Belgian coast and attached for what should have been temporary service with the RFC in France under the command of General Trenchard. These squadrons were given an 'N' for Naval prefix to avoid confusion with RFC squadrons all ready in action along the Western Front.

These Naval squadrons were still under Trenchard's control when the Royal Naval Air Service and the Royal Flying Corps amalgamated to form the Royal Air Force on 1 April 1918, when 6N became No.206 and 8N became No.208 Squadron of the RAF. The remaining ex-Naval squadrons also had 200 added to their original number to fit in with the new service.

John Petre became acting Squadron Commander when 6N Squadron was officially formed at Petite Synthe in December 1916. Twenty-four Nieuport 17bis with 130hp were ordered from the French parent company – they were an improved version of the 80hp and 110hp Nieuport machines that John Petre had previously flown in action. 8N Squadron, that had been formed a few weeks earlier, would be fully equipped with British-designed and built Sopwith Pup and Triplane machines, to become the most successful of the Naval fighter squadrons serving with the RFC on the Western Front. Experienced pilots of 6N Squadron found the Nieuport 17bis (a variant), with a top speed of 116mph, faster than the standard Nieuport 17 due to the more powerful Clerget and aerodynamically cleaner side-stringered fuselage. Differing little from its predecessors, the 17bis retained the sesquiplane configuration that gave the pilot an excellent downward view compared to most biplanes, due to the narrow chord of the lower wing. However, the 17bis retained the inherent weakness of the previous Nieuport 'V' strutters, a tendency for the lower wings to twist during a prolonged dive or performing aerobatics. The last of the Nieuport 'V' strutters to see service during the war, types 24 and 27, were fitted with a fin and rudder in place of the 'comma'-shaped rudder of their predecessors. The fin made the torque from the more powerful rotary engine easier to control, but the design change came unfortunately too late for some of 6N airmen flying the Nieuport 17bis.

Flight Lieutenant Ernest Norton, flying Nieuport N3184, opened up the scoring for 6N Squadron on 8 February, when he was credited with sending an Albatros two-seat reconnaissance machine down out of control into Houthoulst Forest. N3184 again, this time with Lieutenant John de C. Paynter at the controls, tackled another enemy two-seater that fell in a vertical dive through the clouds before he lost sight of it, on Thursday

1 March. It was a promising start for the new squadron, but unfortunately too good to last. N3186, delivered to 6N Squadron two days previously, crashed taking off on patrol in adverse weather conditions on 11 March. Flight Sub Lieutenant C. Bailey escaped serious injury, but the machine had to be returned to St Pol Aircraft Depot for extensive repairs.

Saturday 17 March 1917 was another bad day for the aluminium doped Nieuports of 6N Squadron: eighteen-year-old Flt Sub Lt Frederick Walker stalled N3201 on take-off and crashed 400ft on to the airfield and died of his injuries. Flt Sub Lt Fletcher had escaped serious injury when he crashed on landing after returning from a patrol just four days earlier. 6N were carrying out long range patrols in spite of the severity of the weather; cold and fatigue were also enemies. The following day, 18 March, N3198 delivered to the squadron nine days earlier, was written off by Flt Sub-Lt R.K. Slater.

As the harsh winter began to relinquish its icy grip, the pilots of 6N Squadron at La Bellevue Aerodrome, attached to 13 Wing, 3 Brigade of the RFC, encountered an increasing number of enemy Albatros and Halberstadt fighters armed with twin forward firing machine guns. The Squadron suffered their first casualty due to enemy action on Thursday 5 April 1917, when Flt Sub-Lt R.K. Slater, in combat with Albatros scouts, lost consciousness after being wounded. N3202 fell in to a spin, crashing behind enemy lines, and Slater became a POW.

The Squadron lost another Nieuport machine the same day when, returning to Bellevue badly shot up after a fight over the lines, N3191 suffered engine failure, crashing onto the airfield from 200ft. Fortunately Flt Sub-Lt M. Kingsford, although injured, lived to fight another day. During the fierce aerial battles that had taken place over the enemy lines during the day Flight Commander Ernest Norton in N3187 had evened the score by crashing a Albatros and sending another down out of control. He would repeat this performance in N3187 on 9 April, but on this occasion was forced to land his badly shot about machine just after recrossing the British lines at Maricourt. Flt Sub-Lt Alfred Thorne was also credited with an Albatros that day, only to lose his life when N3205 was caught in a violent thunderstorm and crashed. The storm was also responsible for the loss of N3190, that crashed as Flt Sub-Lt John de Campbourne Paynter attempted to land; Paynter survived his injuries and was credited with the destruction of at least ten enemy aeroplanes, before being killed during an air raid by German aircraft on No.213 Squadron during the night of Tuesday 18 June 1918.

Squadron Commander John Petre's twenty-third birthday on Wednesday 11 April 1917 coincided with 6N transferring south to an airfield at Morlancourt 12 miles east of Amiens.

Friday 13 April saw yet another flying accident involving a Nieuport machine of 6N Squadron, but this time it involved their commanding officer. Sqn Cdr Petre was still alive when extricated from the wreckage of Nieuport scout N3206, but sadly the gallant twenty-three-year-old Essex airman died shortly afterwards and was buried with honours at Cerisy-Gailly in France.

Squadron Commander C.D. Breese took command of 6N on 14 April 1917 and the squadron continued to hold their own against the enemy, but another Nieuport scout was written off in a landing accident on 23 April and another on the 28th.

During a day of fierce fighting over the enemy lines on Sunday 29 April, Flt Cdr Ernest Norton in N3208 destroyed one and sent another two Albatros V strutters down out of control above Guise. Flt Sub-Lt Winter in N3199 also claimed an Albatros scout driven down out of control and Flt Sub-Lt A.H. Fletcher in N3192 may have accounted for another before he was separated from the remainder of the Flight by a dozen enemy machines and fell wounded into captivity.

The month of May began with the loss of nineteen-year-old Flt Sub-Lt Raymond Berridge, who died of injuries received on the 3rd, following a crash landing at a nearby RFC aerodrome. 6N Squadron was disbanded in August 1917 when pilots, ground crew and aircraft were sent to 9N and 10N Squadrons. Reformed at Dover on 1 January 1918, 6N Squadron became No.206 Squadron with the formation of the Royal Air Force on 1 April 1918.

In May 1917, the aviation magazine *Flight* published the following item:

A Requiem Mass for Squadron Commander John Petre, DSC, the youngest son of Mr Sebastian H. Petre, who lost his life in a flying accident abroad, took place at Ingatestone Hall on April 27th. The congregation included officers of a bombing school and men of the RNAS. By coincidence the service took place on the birthday of an elder brother, Edward Petre, a pioneer of aviation who lost his life in England five years ago. It is hoped to bring Commander Petre's body home after the war.

Hugh Christopher Tower

Weald Hall, for many years the home of the Tower family at South Weald, dating back to Tudor times, was the birthplace of Essex airman Hugh Christopher Tower on 23 July 1886. Hugh's ancestor Thomas Tower (1700–78) purchased Weald Hall in 1745 from Erasmus Smith, an alderman of the city of London. Thomas was at the time of purchase a Controller of Excise. He had previously been a Member of Parliament. On his death, Weald Hall and the estate passed to his brother's son, Christopher Tower (1747–1810).

Christopher married Elizabeth Baker from County Durham and the couple lived principally at Weald Hall, which in turn was inherited by their eldest son Christopher Thomas Tower (1775–1867), who became High Sheriff of Essex.

The family home eventually passed to their eldest son Christopher Tower (1804–83), who transferred Weald Hall to his son, Christopher John Hume Tower (1841–1924). During his eighty-two years Christopher John Hume Tower became Deputy Lieutenant and High Sheriff of Essex. He not only suffered the loss of his first wife and baby daughter during the first year of their marriage in 1865, but during the First World War he had to endure the loss of both sons from his second marriage to Cecilia Hanbury that took place in 1883.

Their eldest son, Christopher Cecil Tower, was born the following year in 1884. He in turn inherited Weald Hall upon his marriage to Cynthia Surtees in 1913. Sadly thirty-two-year-old Lieutenant Christopher Tower, serving with the Essex Yeomanry, was killed in action on the Western Front at Loos on Saturday 2 October 1915.

A youthful Hugh Christopher Tower as a sub-agent in Wiltshire before the start of the First World War. (A. Tower via H. Parr)

Studio portrait of Lt H.C. Tower in Royal Flying Corps uniform around 1914. (A. Tower via H. Parr)

Fate decreed that his younger brother Hugh Christopher Tower would survive him by only eleven months. Hugh attended Sir Anthony Browne's School at Brentwood as a day boy from 1898 to 1902. He successfully passed an examination in estate management at the Surveyors Institute and was, at the outbreak of the war, a sub-agent on the estates of Lady Heytesbury and Sir Edward Antrobus in the county of Wiltshire.

Hugh Tower qualified for Royal Aero Club Certificate No.466, in this Bristol Box kite at Larkhill, Salisbury Plain on 23 April 1913. (A. Tower via H. Parr)

During his leisure time in Wiltshire the young land agent became a skilled aviator at the age of twenty-six, having obtained his Royal Aero Club Certificate in a Bristol Box kite at the Bristol Flying School, Larkhill, Salisbury Plain on 23 April 1913. Hugh volunteered for the RFC Special Reserve as the war clouds gathered and, as Second Lieutenant Hugh C. Tower, reported for duty with the Royal Flying Corps at Farnborough on Saturday 15 August 1914. He flew to France in April 1915 and by the time of his return to England six months later he had been promoted to Captain.

He then served as a flying instructor with 1 Reserve Aeroplane Squadron until his posting to the newly formed No.60 Squadron as a Flight Commander at Gosport Aerodrome in April 1916. No.60 Squadron was then in the process of working up to a Front Line squadron, under the command of Major F.F. 'Ferdie' Waldron. The new Squadron moved to France via St Omer on 28 May, where it became equipped with aircraft of French manufacture owing to an acute shortage of British-built aeroplanes. No.60 Squadron was intended as reinforcement for the BEF and attached to the 13th Army Wing in readiness for the start of a massive offensive on the Somme, occupying an aerodrome at Bois d'Inghem, 15 miles west of St Omer.

The experienced flight commanders began preparing the young pilots, some just out of flying school with a minimum amount of flying hours in their Log Books, for the idiosyncrasies of the Morane-Saulnier aeroplanes they would shortly fly in action.

C Flight, under the command of Capt. Hugh (Jimmy) Tower – how he came by the name of Jimmy in the squadron is a mystery as yet unsolved by the author – were equipped with the MS type two-seat BB biplanes which by this stage of the war were fitted with ailerons in place of wing warping and the 100hp Le Rhone rotary engines made them the fastest machines in the squadron.

A Flight received Morane-Saulnier type N single-seat 'Bullet' monoplanes fitted with a Lewis gun firing through the propeller arc with the aid of hardened steel deflector plates bolted on to the back of the propeller blades. Fitted with a 110hp Le Rhone rotary engine, the single-seat scout came with a reputation of being very difficult to fly, having no fixed tailplane or ailerons. The speedy Bullet still had wing warping and, like the Morane biplane and Parasol, balanced elevators pivoted about a third of the way back from the leading edge that made the fore and aft control very sensitive for the inexperienced.

B Flight were in turn issued with Morane-Saulnier LA high wing two-seat monoplanes. Known in the RFC as the 'Parasol', these machines, fitted with an 80hp rotary, were the safest of the three types of Morane aircraft to fly and were flown initially by the least experienced pilots before they graduated to the faster biplane or Bullet.

Amongst the problems that beset the new squadron about to go to war would be not having a practical interrupter gear, enabling the machine gun to fire through the propeller arc. The metal deflector plates fitted to the back of the propellor blades of the Bullet to allow the gun to fire most of the rounds through the propellor arc. was, in practice, far from perfect. During the sixteen-day training period with their new warplanes, No.60 Squadron had at least two propellers shattered during target practice. The odd ricochet bullets off the steel deflector plates were lethal; even if the aeroplanes had been more stable in flight, close formation flying was not possible due to the deflected bullets whining in all directions when the guns were fired. Among the mishaps of this training period in June were a Bullet crashed by Lt J.N. Simpson on 3 June and a Parasol written off by Lt G.D. Keddie on the 8th.

Before No.60 Squadron moved to Vert Galand Aerodrome 5 miles south of Doullens on Friday 16 June 1916, all the Parasol machines were returned to No.1 Aircraft Depot and exchanged for Bullets. C Flight, under Capt. Tower, handed their two-seat biplanes and observers over to B Flight and were equipped with Bullets. Six months earlier these French machines had held their own in the battles above the lines, but by the summer of 1916 they were obsolete and within weeks would be well outclassed by the new breed of Albatros fighter aircraft making their debut at the front.

The Squadron's first offensive patrols over the lines were carried out on Saturday 17 June, and flying in pairs, alternating two Bullet monoplanes with two biplanes, but as the aerial opposition increased with the build-up for the Somme offensive, the patrols were soon made at Flight strength. Another hazard facing the Bullet in action was the fact the French scout was frequently mistaken for the Fokker monoplane and fired on by friend and foe alike, including British anti-aircraft guns.

On one occasion Capt. Tower's Bullet was attacked from the rear by a French pilot in a superior Nieuport. As the Bullet dived out of the line of fire, the large under-wing RFC cockades became visible to the French aviator who made amends by escorting the Bullet back to No.60 Squadron aerodrome and landing to apologise in person.

Capt. H.C. 'Jimmy' Tower at the controls of a No.60 Squadron Morane-Saulnier BB Biplane. (D.W. Warne)

Experiments were then carried out with recognition aids, resulting in the large spinner, cowl, fuselage to just aft of the cockpit and wheel covers receiving a coat of bright red roundel paint; that if nothing else, made the little monoplane look more aggressive.

A spate of engine trouble on 23 June forced Lt D.B. Gray to land his BB Biplane and Capt. H.A. Browning-Patterson crashed a BB Biplane on take-off. Three days later 2nd-Lt A.D. Bell-Irving and Lt H.H. Balfour also escaped serious injury when their Bullets were crashed on landing after offensive patrols.

By dusk on the first day of the Battle of the Somme, Saturday 1 July 1916, the BEF had suffered 60,000 casualties dead and wounded. The heroics and the horrors of that summer day have been recorded for future generations and are beyond the scope of this modest tribute to the airmen of Essex, but it was also the day on which the airmen of No.60 Squadron forced down their first enemy aeroplane.

The CO of No.60 Squadron, Major Waldron, set an example by leading a flight of Bullets into action that resulted in an LVG two-seater being forced to land behind enemy lines near Bapaume, the first of the 460 enemy aircraft claimed by the pilots of No.60 Squadron before the end of the war. The second day of the Somme offensive again found No.60 Squadron carrying out offensive patrols and escorting six RE7s of No.21 Squadron carrying a 360lb bomb apiece to raid the German Headquarters and the railway station at Bapaume. Another LVG was driven down, this time by B Flight Morane Biplanes and a Fokker monoplane sent down out of control. The same patrol forced another unidentified machine to land behind enemy lines. It had been a promising start for the new squadron.

With tails up, Maj. Waldron led four Bullets of A Flight on a morning offensive patrol looking for trouble and found it in the form of twelve enemy machines, a mixed bag of two-seater and Fokker monoplanes that dived out of the sun. In the ensuing dogfight 'Ferdie' Waldron received a fatal wound and died within minutes of crash landing in enemy lines. Such are the ironies of war that the Commanding Officer of No.60 Squadron, who had been credited with the squadron's first enemy aircraft, also became the squadron's first fatal casualty. Capt. R. Smith Barry took over the command of No.60 Squadron at this difficult period, but the loss of the aggressive 'Ferdie' Waldron was a blow to the morale of the younger pilots.

A combined bombing raid by a mixed bag of BE2c, RE7, and Martinsyde machines came under attack from enemy aircraft on 11 July. C Flight of No.60 Squadron led by Capt. Tower drove off the enemy scouts that had wounded both Lt-Col Hugh Dowding (of Second World War fame), leading the raid in a BE2c, and his observer. One of the enemy aeroplanes fired at by Jimmy Tower was observed to go down under control.

The day following saw the incident involving a French machine firing at Jimmy Tower's Bullet in mistake for a Fokker monoplane. The new CO of No.60 Squadron, recently promoted to Major, escaped serious injury when he crash landed his Bullet returning from a patrol. This accident was no reflection upon the flying abilities of Smith Barry, who was a first-class pilot and later during the war created the Gosport School of Special Flying; it was just another example of the many mishaps suffered by the unfortunate pilots equipped with this outdated monoplane.

On the morning of Friday 21 July, enemy observation balloons were the target for two No.60 Squadron BB biplanes armed with electrically fired Le Prier rockets fitted to guide tubes attached to the interplant struts. One balloon was attacked without result, the other pilot looked for his target in vain; it had been lowered in double quick time by a motorised winch as the ground crew had been warned of an attempt on the other balloon. Not to be outdone, the pilot fired his rockets at enemy troops on parade in the village of Combles. Returning from a patrol of Achiet-Combles-Marcoing to cover B Flight's attempted balloon bust, Capt. Jimmy Tower overturned his Bullet on landing.

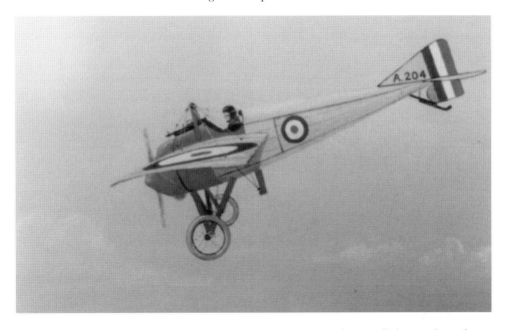

A painting of Capt. H.C. 'Jimmy' Tower on the wing in a Morane-Saulnier 'Bullet' monoplane of No.60 Squadron RFC. (M.C. Olmsted)

Capt. Jimmy Tower with the wireless equipped LVG observation biplane he forced down behind British lines on 28 July 1916. (A. Tower via H. Parr)

On the evening offensive patrol, A Flight lost their commander, Capt. Norman Browning-Paterson, who fell to his death in a burning Bullet as the tenth victory to the guns of the bespectacled 'Ace' Second Lieutenant Kurt Wintgens, who had caught the experienced twenty-two-year-old pilot off his guard.

No.60 Squadron recorded another casualty on 26 July; Lt L.E.Whitehouse of B Flight crashed a BB biplane whilst making an emergency landing near a casualty clearing station at Verquin for his observer who had been shot through the foot.

Three enemy aeroplanes were shot down by No.60 Squadron Bullets on 27 July and Capt. Jimmy Tower forced a wireless equipped LVG observation machine down behind British lines the following day. This machine brought the total of enemy aircraft claimed for the month of July 1916 to twelve, four of which had been forced to land; and this in spite of the various mishaps by the airmen of No.60 Squadron.

Two out of a patrol of four 60 Squadron BB biplanes were shot down on Sunday 30 July. Capt. L.S. Charles, although badly wounded, managed to land his Morane; unknown to him his observer Lt C.Wiliams had been killed in the air battle. The gallant twenty-one-year-old Leslie Charles later died of his wounds as a prisoner of war.

Although both the pilot Lt Lewis Whitehead and his observer 2nd-Lt W.E. Bryant were also wounded in the fight, they managed to land their damaged BB biplane at Baizieux Aerodrome. German anti-aircraft guns accounted for another two of B Flight's Morane Biplanes on Wednesday 2 August. Lt John Ormsby and his observer, nineteen-year-old 2nd-Lt Henry Newton, both died of their wounds as prisoners of war. Sgt Pilot Alexander Walker and his observer, eighteen-year-old 2nd-Lt Lyonel Clark, in the second BB biplane were killed after Sgt Walker had been struck by a shell splinter causing him to crash. No.60 Squadron lost yet another pilot and aircraft the following day when 2nd-Lt Claude Ridley failed to return from an attempt to land a spy behind enemy lines. Claude Ridley had volunteered for the special mission that entailed flying a Morane Parasol he had collected from the Aircraft Depot several days previously.

During the past four weeks, No.60 Squadron had lost their commanding officer, two flight commanders, three pilots and two observers due to enemy action. This, plus the numerous mishaps with the accident-prone Bullet, prompted General Hugh Trenchard to send the following letter to Sir Douglas Haig, who would be promoted to field-marshal the following January:

> I have had to withdraw one of the GHQ fighting squadrons from work temporarily and have sent it to St. Andre Aux Bois. This squadron, since the battle began, has lost a squadron commander, two flight commanders and a pilot, killed or missing and yesterday it lost two more machines, with two pilots and two observers, by anti-aircraft gun fire. Besides this, they have had several officers wounded. They have a difficult machine to fly and I think a rest away from work is absolutely necessary.

While at 'rest' behind the lines, the squadron began to replace their Bullet monoplanes for single-seat French-built Nieuport 16 and 17 biplane fighters armed with an over the wing forward firing Lewis gun that dispensed with the steel deflector plates bolted onto the propeller of the Morane. Although still outgunned by enemy fighters, the Nieuport V

Strutters, fitted with ailerons and a fixed tailplane, were an improvement on the pre-war designed Morane aircraft.

Another No.60 Squadron BB biplane was wrecked on Thursday 8 August, when 2nd-Lt Roderick Hill, a replacement pilot who had overturned a Bullet on landing a few days before, crashed taking off with a full war load and an observer for the first time. Had the new pilot got airborne he would have formed part of the defensive cover the 'resting' squadron provided above Montreuil for HM King George V, who was making an inspection of the General Headquarters of the British Expeditionary Force in France.

C Flight, under the command of Capt. Jimmy Tower, received a backhanded compliment when they were informed their 80hp Bullets were to be replaced by the more powerful 110hp Le Rhone version. No.60 Squadron saw the last of their two-seat BB biplanes on 12 August as the squadron was to return to action as a single-seat scout (fighter) squadron, their gallant observers being posted away to other Front Line squadrons.

Wednesday 16 August was a red letter day for No.60 Squadron; the first replacement Nieuport 16s arrived complete with three pilots transferred from No.1 Squadron. These were in turn followed by three more Nieuport 16s and three type 17s, the latter machines proved to be one of the most successful French fighter aircraft of the period.

After a short period of intensive training including formation flying led by Maj. Smith-Barry, the squadron flew back to the war on Wednesday 23 August 1916. The Squadron's rest period had been less than three weeks, but with replacement pilots and the BB biplanes exchanged for Nieuport scouts, the tails of No.60 Squadron were well up.

The arrival of 60 Squadron at Izel-le-Hameau was a spectacular event – four Bullets stood on their nose or turned over completely on landing. Lt Albert Ball, who had flown a Nieuport over from No.11 Squadron as a replacement pilot, witnessed the arrival of his new squadron with a critical eye.

With no less than eleven enemy aircraft to his credit, twenty-year-old Lt Ball, flying Nieuport scouts, would add another twenty during his six-week tour of duty with No.60 Squadron. On Thursday 24 August the pilots of No.60 Squadron were back over the enemy lines. Capt. Jimmy Tower, at the controls of Bullet A204, forced down a two-seat observation machine, possibly an LVG, near Bois d'Adinfer during the morning patrol.

The following morning No.60 Squadron's Bullets sent down two more enemy machines, 2nd-Lt George Smart drove down an enemy scout near Bapaume and 2nd-Lt B.M. Wainright sent a Roland two-seater down out of control south of Arras at 1100hrs. During the same scrap Lt Albert Ball became the first of No.60 Squadron's Nieuport pilots to shoot down an enemy machine that also fell south of Arras.

Bad weather kept the Squadron grounded until the late afternoon on Saturday 26 August when 2nd-Lt A.E. Walters, flying a Nieuport scout, emptied a complete drum of ammunition at an enemy two-seater that fell out of control and out of sight through the clouds below.

Again bad flying weather grounded the Squadron, this time for the whole day on Sunday 27 August, but Lt Ball made up for lost time the following morning; flying and fighting all day, he forced a Roland two-seat fighter to land south of Bapaume at 0700hrs, crashed another Roland east of Ayette and forced an observation machine down to land at Grevillers during an evening offensive patrol. Two more enemy aeroplanes shot down by Ball during the day were not confirmed.

There were enough enemy machines across the German lines to keep the rest of the Squadron occupied; another Nieuport with 2nd-Lt A.M. Walters at the controls tackled an LVG, sending the observation machine down out of control.

The 110hp Bullets of C Flight appeared to be holding their own when Lt Alan Bell-Irving, a Canadian, shot down his first enemy aeroplane, a Roland two-seater that fell in the Bapaume area. Celebrations in the Squadron Mess that evening were, however, overshadowed by the empty chair of 2nd-Lt B.M. Wainright, who had failed to return. The good news eventually reached the squadron that Wainright was alive and well, having chased an enemy machine well in to 'Hun-land' and been shot up hedgehopping on the way back by two fighters and forced to land in enemy occupied territory.

August had begun so disastrously for No.60 Squadron but drew to a triumphant close, with no less than five enemy machines driven down on Thursday 31st, four by Nieuport pilots and one by Capt. Alfred Summers in a Bullet. Lt Albert Ball with his Nieuport and a roving commission had brought his total of enemy machines, that included two observation balloons forced down, to twenty, making him the leading British fighter pilot that autumn and setting a standard that would eventually make No.60 Squadron second to none as a fighter squadron by the Armistice.

Across the enemy lines Captain Oswald Boelcke, the Fatherland's leading fighter pilot, had methodically trained the young airmen he had hand-picked from the best the Imperial Air Service had to offer to form the elite Jasta 2.

Unfortunately for Capt. Jimmy Tower and the RFC, Jasta 2, equipped with the latest two-gun Albatros fighter, entered the battle over the Somme at the beginning of September 1916.

On Sunday 3 September, Lt Philip Joyce, on patrol in a Morane Bullet of No.60 Squadron, fought an unusual adversary, a pusher with twin booms, possibly an AGO CLII, that crashed behind enemy lines after receiving the contents of a drum from his Lewis gun.

Capt. Eustace Grenfell had a narrow escape when his Bullet was badly damaged during combat over the lines on 4 September. Unfavourable weather conditions then prevented the Squadron from getting to grips with the enemy for a few days. During the lull, more Bullets were exchanged for Nieuport machines. On the eve of his posting to Home Establishment, Capt. Frank Goodrich took off to say farewell to No.3, his former Squadron, stalled and died following the resulting crash onto the aerodrome.

Denied the airspace above the British front the Germans were forced to rely more and more on their observation balloons. In readiness for the third phase of the Somme offensive, No.60 Squadron's Nieuports armed with Le Prieur rockets and escorted by Bullets set out to blind the enemy on Friday 15 September, as the BEF sent tanks into action for the first time. Two observation balloons were flamed, their crews jumping to safety by parachute. In fierce fighting, six enemy aircraft were claimed, three by Lt Albert Ball who flew three different Nieuports during the course of the day.

Capt. Alfred Summers accounted for one of the enemy balloons with his electrically fired rockets; unfortunately he failed to return and was later confirmed as killed in action. Fourteen more RFC machines were lost or badly damaged as the latest German fighter aircraft made their debut over the Somme.

On Sunday 17 September a young German flier, selected and trained by Capt. Boelcke, shot down his first *Englander* with his shark-like Albatros biplane; the majority of the eighty allied aircraft he destroyed during the war fell to the twin guns of various Albatros fighters, but Manfred von Richthofen is remembered as 'The Red Baron' flying a red Fokker Triplane, the type in which he was killed in action in April 1918.

Capt. Hugh C. Tower submitted his last combat report to No.60 Squadron on the day von Richthofen made his first kill, but for Jimmy Tower it had been another day of escorting the hard-pressed bombing and reconnaissance squadrons back across the lines. This extract from his combat report is typical of the numerous encounters he experienced daily:

> While leading a formation to meet a returning bombing formation I observed a Roland some two thousand feet below me over Tilloy. I then dived at him, but lost him until I heard his machine-gun firing at me from behind. I then caught sight of him again and dived at him, hunting him down to five thousand feet at Beaulencourt, when I lost him in the clouds and did not find him again. I then proceeded to Beugney.

On the evening of Tuesday 19 September, after another spell of bad weather, Jimmy Tower once again led his now mixed flight of Morane Bullets and Nieuports into action as the formation of FE2b reconnaissance machines they were escorting came under attack from German fighters.

During the frantic, desperate minutes that followed, Jimmy Tower had been seen chasing a Fokker biplane and a long battle ensued during which his Bullet A204 was thought to have collided with the enemy as his monoplane was seen to shed a wing before falling in flames onto Grevillers Wood. Eyewitness accounts of split-second images in an air battle, with death waiting for the unwary, account for No.60 Squadron believing that Jimmy Tower had died colliding with the Fokker with which he had been scrapping.

The experienced Flight Commander at the controls of the Bullet would have been a match for a Fokker, but unfortunately his opponent, also experienced with twenty-seven French and British machines to his credit, flew the latest twin gun Albatros scout. Published under the title of *Knight of Germany* in the 1930s, the translated biography of Capt. Oswald Boelcke contained this account of the death of Capt. Hugh Christopher Tower:

> Six of us rattled into a squadron consisting of eight or ten FEs and several Moranes, the fat lattice tails down below and the Moranes above as cover. I engaged one of the latter and pranced about the air with him. He escaped for a moment, but I got to grips with him again west of Bapaume; one of my guns jammed, but the other shot all the better. I shot up the monoplane from close range until he broke up in flames and fell into the wood near Grevillers in fragments.

Disregarding the superior airframe and engines of the new German fighters, having twice the firepower of allied fighters at this period gave the enemy a tremendous advantage; had Boelcke been an allied pilot, his adversary would have escaped when one machine gun jammed. Jimmy Tower had been shot down by a much respected fighter pilot who, but for an accident, would have become the top scoring ace of the war.

Weald Hall, South Weald, Essex, for many years the home of the Tower family. The older parts were Elizabethan but the east side, shown here, was refaced in Georgian style during the eighteenth century. This fine old building was demolished in 1950. (K. Feline)

Oswald Boelcke lost his life when two Albatros scouts diving for a kill collided on Saturday 28 October 1916. By this time, unfortunately for the Allies, he had organised the single-seat hunting squadrons, giving the advantage once more to the Imperial Air Service and accounted personally for forty allied aircraft. No.60 Squadron fought on with Nieuport machines until they were replaced with SE5s in July 1917, when they were once again able to meet the enemy on equal terms.

As for the Essex airman who gave his life for King and Country, Capt. Hugh Christopher Tower has no known grave, just his name inscribed upon the Arras Memorial for the fallen in France. A staff officer serving as private secretary to the general commanding the RFC – Hugh Trenchard – visited No.60 Squadron on one occasion and had been invited to lunch with Jimmy Tower and C Flight. In his diary Maurice Baring recorded 'On the 19th I heard Tower had been killed, he was gayest and sunniest of pilots'.

A memorial window to Christopher J.H. Tower of Weald Hall and his sons, Christopher and Hugh, both killed in the war, had been placed by Mrs Cecilia Tower in the church of St Peter, and was dedicated on 20 January 1928 by the vicar, Revd F.H. Proctor. The window was unveiled by Christopher, aged thirteen, son of the late Lt Chistopher Cecil Tower, on his birthday.

Weald Hall, for many years the home of Tower family, was demolished in 1950.

A photograph of eighteen-year-old Donald Clappen, awarded Royal Aero Club Certificate No.591, on 15 August 1913. Serving in both world wars, Air Commodore Donald Clappen retired from the Royal Air Force in 1949. (RAF Museum)

Donald W. Clappen

No less than eight Essex airmen serving in the First World War had been born or were living in the Westcliff-on-Sea area. Among this group was a pre-war aviator by the name of Donald Clappen, born on 30 June 1895. Young Donald would first be educated at St Johns College Westcliff, before entering University College, London.

In 1911, influenced by the daily newspapers promoting aviation interest then sweeping the nation, Donald Clappen applied for and was accepted as an apprentice by the expanding Blériot Aviation Co., situated at Hendon Aerodrome. The following year he took to the air for the first time and soon qualified for his Royal Aero Club Certificate flying a Blériot monoplane.

With RAeC no.591 awarded to him on 15 August 1913 and at eighteen years of age, Donald Clappen became the assistant flying instructor for the J.L. Hall Flying School at Hendon. Within a year Donald Clappen had acquired a reputation not only as an aviator, but also as a competent flying instructor.

The following year brought with it a brilliant summer that would have been ideal for the young aviator; unfortunately it also brought the start of a European war destined to change the course of history and cut short the lives of many of his contemporaries.

When the German Army invaded Belgium in August, forcing Great Britain to honour an obligation to a treaty signed with Belgium seventy-five years earlier, thousands of young men were caught up in the great tide of patriotism sweeping the nation, among them the nineteen-year-old airman Donald Clappen, who volunteered his services to the Royal Flying Corps.

A month went by and as rumours abounded that the war would be over by Christmas due to the mighty armies of Britain's allies, France and Russia, crushing the Central Powers, Donald Clappen, keen to do his bit for King and Country, growing impatient with the powers in charge of the RFC, volunteered for the infantry and became a private in the 1st Battalion, the London Scottish Territorials.

On the Western Front in 1915, he fought in the trenches, taking part in the battles of Neuve Chappele in March, Aubers Ridge in May and Loos in September. The mud and squalor of trench warfare prompted many men on both sides of the lines to volunteer for a transfer to the air service. There can be little doubt that Clappen was pleased to finally receive a transfer to the Royal Flying Corps in the autumn of 1915 – with the prospect of another winter in the trenches looming – 2nd-Lt D.W. Clappen returned to Hendon Aerodrome where he had been taught to fly in 1913. After a stint as a flying instructor at Gosport Aerodrome in Hampshire, he returned to Hendon and reported to No.2 Aircraft Acceptance Park as a test and ferry pilot. Although not a member of a Home Defence squadron, Donald Clappen was one of the miscellaneous group of flying instructors, test and ferry pilots who were to play an active role in the Air Defence of Britain during the First World War.

German Army and Naval airships, mainly of the Zeppelin-type, had bombed Britain under cover of darkness since January 1915. Their main target, London, easily recognisable, in spite of a blackout, by the teltale river Thames. The propaganda value of the 'Zepp' raids alone, apart from the disruption of the production of munitions, was like the size of the airships – enormous. The defeat of these hydrogen-filled monsters of the night was due to the introduction of .303 incendiary ammunition and the courage of the Home Defence pilots in the autumn of 1916.

As the death knell sounded for the Fatherland's war-winning terror weapon, a warning bell rang in Whitehall when a single engine German biplane bombed London at midday on Wednesday 28 November 1916. The bombs fell close to the Admiralty building. The Imperial German Army, having been made to realise the vulnerability of the Zeppelin when flown long distances over land, disbanded their Airship Service and concentrated on large bombing aeroplanes.

Overnight in the autumn of 1916 the dreaded 'Zepp' had become the comic 'Gasbag' to the civilian population of Britain. The new year, however, brought a deadlier menace: twin-engine Gotha bombers that followed the example set by two intrepid Imperial Navy aviators in their single engined LVG biplane that bombed London in daylight.

The Belgium-based Gotha bombers made their debut over Essex on the evening of Friday 25 May 1917 heading towards London via the river Crouch. Either probing the defences or thwarted by thick clouds, the twenty-one-strong enemy formation flew over Kent scattering bombs in their wake before bombing Folkestone, leaving behind ninety-five dead and 195 injured.

It was soon realised that the venerable BE2 biplanes that had served so well as 'Zepp busters' were no match for the well-armed Gotha, and various RFC establishments testing and delivering new machines to France were put on standby to assist the ill-equipped Home Defence squadrons to meet the new aerial menace.

'Presents from the Kaiser', an Essex artist's painting depicting the daylight bombing raid of London on Wednesday 13 June 1917. (L. Stonell)

Lieutenant Donald Clappen piloted one of the sixty-two machines that flew defence sorties on the evening of Tuesday 5 June when twenty-two Gothas again crossed the coast heading for London. Airborne from Hendon in a 275hp RR Eagle engined DH4, Clappen certainly had the speed to overtake and harass the raiders, but having patrolled his designated area in A7471 for 2 hours as ordered he returned to No.2 AAP without a sighting of the raiders.

The astute enemy squadron commander leading the bombers had noted an increase in the easterly wind that would endanger the return trip across the North Sea if low on fuel, so the secondary targets of Sheerness and Shoeburyness were bombed instead with thirteen civilians killed and another thirty-four injured; but London did not have long to wait before it was back in the firing line.

Eighteen Gothas, led by their able commanding officer Capt. Ernst Brandenburg, flew across London on the morning of Wednesday 13 June delivering 'Presents from the Kaiser'. What would have been a fine feat of arms by the German airmen was flawed by the one bomb aimed at the East London Docks, falling instead on an infant school killing sixteen little children of six years of age and under.

Once again Lt Clappen patrolled as one of a mixed bag of ninety-four RFC and RNAS aeroplanes sent aloft to intercept the raiders. No.2 AAP had no less than two DH4 and a DH5 machine scrambled. Clappen in DH4 A7477 was ordered up at 1215hrs after the raiders had left the London area, as a second wave had been anticipated. Apart from the sixteen infants, a further 146 civilians were also killed and 432 injured. Chased back across Essex heading for the coast, the Gothas were attacked by a variety of aircraft. One unfortunate observer from No.35 Training Squadron caught in the crossfire from the Gothas in an exchange of fire above Ilford, died from a bullet wound in the neck.

Lieutenant Clappen flew another uneventful defence sortie on Wednesday 4 July, but it would be Saturday 7 July he would have cause to remember. Airborne from No.2 AAP at 0930hrs on patrol above Essex, he encountered the Gotha squadron returning for their second daylight raid on London. Positioning DH4 A7483 for an attack on the rear machine of the formation he opened fire with the synchronised Vickers gun that immediately suffered a stoppage that he could not clear in the air. Home Defence pilots at this period were plagued with machine gun problems, as the more experienced armourers were with front line squadrons. Ignoring the Gotha's rear 'belly' gun, fired through a large aperture to eliminate the blind spot under the tailplane, Clappen manoeuvred the DH4, still flying behind but now beneath the bomber giving his gunner Air Mechanic Wills in the rear cockpit the opportunity to bring his ring mounted Lewis gun to bear and open fire. Several times as the formation droned on towards London Clappen was forced to take evasive action as several of the formation dropped back on either side of their harassed comrade to give covering crossfire.

Above Hornchurch, AM Wills signalled to his pilot he was down to the last drum of ammunition. Throwing caution to the wind, Clappen then closed with the enemy machine, giving the young mechanic a point-blank target. Wills emptied the last drum into the fuselage as the Gotha droned on apparently unscathed. Out of ammunition Clappen quickly turned the DH4 away and dived out of range of return fire.

Without warning the RR Eagle engine that had performed so well seized as Clappen flattened the DH4 out. Clappen knew he had ample height to glide to Hendon where he made a text book landing. In spite of the withering cross fire from the German gunners, A7483 had bullet holes in just the centre section of the upper plane and tailplane. To be fair to AM Wills, one of the four Gothas that crashed on landing returning to Belgium may have been seriously damaged by his machine gun fire.

Such was the hue and cry following the second daylight raid by German heavy bombers that front line squadrons were rushed back from France to fill the gap in Home Defences until modern fighters could be found to fill it. With the hurried formation of No.44 Squadron with Sopwith Camels based at Ilford on the outskirts of East London in July 1917, the daylight raids on the city ceased, but the night raids by the 'Wong Wongs' as the Gothas were called due to the continuous 'wong-wong' sound of their twin engines.

Promoted captain, Donald Clappen served at Farnborough before becoming the officer in charge of flying at Brooklands Aerodrome in 1918. Major Donald Clappen remained with the RAF after the Armistice and served two tours of duty in Iraq. During the Second World War he served in the Middle East from 1939 to 1943. Returning to the UK he was station commander at RAF Cosford.

Air Commodore Donald Clappen finished his lengthy service with the Royal Air Force as senior technical officer with HQ Bomber Command in 1949.

In retirement the early Essex aviator lived at Great Missenden, Buckinghamshire, where he died on 30 November 1978.

PART TWO
THE WAR BIRDS RFC/RAF

In Part Two we remember Essex men who volunteered for the Royal Flying Corps and later served with the Royal Air Force when formed in April 1918. They came from all walks of life, but had one thing in common; they had volunteered to fight in the air for King and Country.

Essex Men with No.48 Squadron

When No.48 Squadron of the Royal Flying Corps arrived in France in the spring of 1917 equipped with the latest British fighting aeroplane, the morale of the squadron was high. The new two-seat biplane was the equal to the enemy in speed and armament and despite a disastrous debut over the lines on Thursday 5 April 1917 when four out of a flight of six Bristol F2A Fighters, including the Flight Commander Captain William Leefe-Robinson, the 'Zepp VC', were shot down.

This episode formed part of the period remembered by First World War aviation historians as 'Bloody April', the month in 1917 when the Royal Flying Corps suffered the loss of 316 airmen and over 150 aircraft due to the superior fighting machines and tactics of the enemy airmen on the Western Front.

Undaunted by the initial teething problems with their new machines, the men of No.48 Squadron quickly evolved their own tactics and the Bristol Fighter acquired a reputation that was second to none, rating along with the SE5a and Sopwith Camel as the best British fighting planes of the war.

Seven Essex airmen are known to have flown Bristol Fighters with No.48 Squadron, and two who flew together as pilot and observer (gunner) were credited with fifteen enemy aeroplanes between them.

Ralph Luxmore Curtis, born 1898, was the son of gentleman farmer William Curtis and his wife Amy of Berwick Manor, Rainham, Essex. Ralph, who was just sixteen years of age when Britain went to war, served with the Royal Fusiliers before a transfer as second lieutenant to the Royal Flying Corps in September 1916. Awarded his RAeC certificate and his 'wings' on 17 February 1917, he completed his flight training in the UK before his posting to No.48 Squadron in France.

Desmond Percival Fitzgerald-Uniacke, born in 1895, lived in Upminster, Essex at the start of the war. He saw service with the Royal Inniskillen Fusiliers and 1 Irish Rifles, seeing action in the ill-fated Gallipoli campaign and, after the evacuation, he served in Salonika.

Uniacke transferred to the Royal Flying Corps in May 1917. Second Lieutenant Uniacke (listed as Fitzgerald-Uniacke in some RFC records) joined No.48 Squadron the following month and was officially confirmed as an observer in August that year, by which time he had already claimed six enemy aircraft while flying with Lt Ralph Curtis as his pilot.

Second Lieutenant Uniacke replaced Second Lieutenant Alan D. Light as Lt Curtis's observer when Light suffered head injuries in a crash landing among trees, following engine failure just after take-off from La Bellevue Aerodrome in A3334 on Monday 4 June 1917. Curtis was uninjured, but Alan Light's injuries put him out of action for three weeks. It was during this period that Curtis flew a morning patrol in A7107 with 2nd-Lt Laurence William Allan, an experienced observer from Coventry. In an encounter with enemy scouts above Fresnes-les-Montauban, they shot down an Albatros DIII that crashed behind enemy lines at 0730hrs on Saturday 16 June.

Tuesday 3 July 1917 saw the first success of the formidable combination of Curtis and Uniacke who were flying A7149 as part of the patrol of No.48 Squadron Bristol Fighters that ambushed four Albatros scouts escorting an observation machine.

The crew of A7149 sent the two-seater down out of control, as the remaining Bristols fought with the defending enemy fighters, sending two of them down in the Queant area.

Two days later Curtis and Uniacke, carrying out an evening patrol in A7153, encountered a flight of Albatros scouts. During the ensuing battle two were shot down; the one claimed by the Essex men was last seen falling out of control over Bapaume.

At 0550hrs on Saturday 7 July, another Albatros scout fell to the guns of the Essex airmen flying Bristol Fighter A7107. It happened during a dawn patrol that ended in another fight to the death over the lines, when the unfortunate pilot of a green and yellow Albatros DV crashed to his death near Vitry.

No.48 Squadron moved from Bellevue Aerodrome under the 13th Wing, 3 Brigade, to Bray Dunes Aerodrome and was attached to the 14th Wing of the 4th Brigade on Tuesday 10 July 1917. The move to the coastal aerodrome would be no respite from daily air battles over enemy lines and by Wednesday evening No.48 Squadron were again on patrol looking for trouble. Three enemy aircraft were claimed the following day by the Bristol crews of No.48 Squadron, making up for lost time.

Curtis and Uniacke in A7121 were part of an escort of Bristol Fighters for a formation of DH4 bombers on Saturday 28 July. The bombers came under attack from ten Albatros scouts and during the melee, Uniacke emptied half a drum of ammunition from his Lewis gun at a blue green Albatros DIll that stalled and fell out of the fight in a falling leaf for 2,000ft, before entering a vertical dive into the ground mist covering Ghistelles.

The confidence placed in the new Bristol Fighter by the men of No.48 Squadron was being repaid; crews such as Curtis and Uniacke, fighting back to back, had found their machine could be handled like a single-seat fighter in combat, with the added protection of the observer's Lewis gun guarding the rear during the deadly aerial battles daily over the Western Front.

On Tuesday 31 July 1917, the third battle of Ypres began. Unfortunately for the BEF, the weather hampered the planned air operations during the first eight days, but Curtis and Uniacke again made up for lost time on Thursday 16 August when on patrol in A7151 they gave chase to an Albatros two-seater up to no good along the lines, escorted by three single-seat Albatros DV fighters with red fuselages. Curtis singled out one of the escorting Albatros fighters, firing 200 rounds before the belt-fed Vickers suffered a stoppage in the breach. By then, less than 100yds separated the Bristol Fighter from its prey and Uniacke now with the V-strutter in the sights of his Lewis gun emptied a drum of ammunition. As he replaced the empty drum, he watched the out-of-control Albatros followed by a funeral plume of black smoke end as a bonfire in a field near St Pierre-Capelle.

Split up from the remainder of the flight, the lone Bristol Fighter was pursued towards the British lines by three enemy aircraft. As the first of the Albatros scouts came within range, Uniacke opened fire in short bursts; at this point two of the enemy pilots gave up the chase and turned back. Undaunted, the third Albatros closed to within 200 yards to be greeted with a well-aimed burst that emptied the drum of Uniacke's Lewis gun. Curtis by this time had rectified the stoppage in the forward firing Vickers gun and flinging the Bristol Fighter into a tight turn, he opened fire at the persistent foe that suddenly fell out of control spinning towards the St Pierre Canal.

By the end of August 1917, Curtis and Uniacke had sent down three more of the Albatros scouts of the type that had wreaked havoc among the obsolete British aeroplanes in the spring of that year.

German airmen found they were now encountering British warplanes fitted with Constantinesco oil impulse synchronising gear that allowed the Vickers guns fitted to the Bristol, SE5 and Camels a rate of fire of up to 800 rounds per minute through the propeller arc. RFC pilots were once again on equal terms with their opposite numbers.

No.48 Squadron lost three aircraft, plus an observer killed in action and another wounded during August 1917. Thirty-seven enemy aircraft were claimed during this period by the men of No.48 Squadron, falling as usual behind enemy lines. The German Air Service continued to counter the on-going offensive strategy of the RFC in the air from behind their own lines; this wise policy was proved correct in July when the leading German ace with fifty-seven allied aircraft to his credit was wounded in action and forced to land. Had Manfred von Richthofen been a British pilot, he would have remained a prisoner for the rest of the war. Returning to the fray in a matter of weeks, the Red Baron shot down another twenty-three British aeroplanes before he crossed the allied lines in error on 21 April 1918, to be given a hero's funeral by the Royal Flying Corps.

Time was also running out for Curtis and Uniacke who had been in action daily over the enemy lines since June. Squadron records unfortunately give no indication of how the two men used their off-duty hours; united daily in shared tension and great danger no doubt forged a very special bond of friendship.

A grey-green Albatros attacked a Bristol Fighter of No.48 Squadron on patrol over Dixmuide behind the enemy lines on Sunday 2 September 1917. Uniacke, in A7224, swung his Scarf ring mounted Lewis gun to counter the attacker at the same moment the German pilot came under fire from a second Bristol Fighter. The pilot, Lt Keith Park, at the controls of A7170 fired a long burst forcing the Albatros to dive under A7224 and Uniacke opened fire at the luckless foe. Park, pursuing the grey-green machine, fired a second burst; it stalled and dived through the clouds apparently out of control. Keith Park the pilot of the Bristol Fighter that came to the aid of the Essex airmen, was himself shot down twice. He survived the war as the commanding officer of No.48 Squadron, with twenty enemy aircraft to his credit. This gallant New Zealand airman had an important role in the Second World War and retired as Air Chief Marshal Sir Keith Park GCB, KBE, MC, DFC, DCL.

Wednesday 5 September was another action-filled day in the lives of Curtis and Uniacke. On early morning patrol, a flight of Bristol Fighters dived on five enemy two-seaters; Curtis and Uniacke, manning A7170, fired at one DFW, Uniacke emptying a drum of ammunition from 60 yards. The two-seater dived away with another Bristol on its tail, the crew of which lost sight of the enemy machine over Middelerke.

The same morning, Curtis flew A7155 with 2nd-Lt H. Munro in place of Uniacke, escorting RE8 machines attempting to range heavy artillery on to hostile batteries. Circling high above the Harry Tates busy correcting the fall of shells with Morse code, the Bristol Fighters waited for the arrival of enemy aircraft alerted by the black smoke of exploding anti-aircraft shells around the unperturbed artillery fliers.

The escorting Bristol Fighter crew had seen the Huns even before the anti-aircraft fire aimed at the Harry Tates ceased, warning their crews of the approaching enemy machines. Curtis stood the Bristol on its nose and dived on to an Albatros about to attack an artillery machine. As the gap between the Bristol and the Albatros closed, Curtis opened fire with a 100-round burst and at 200 yards, in a desperate attempt to shake the Bristol off his tail, the enemy pilot turned head on to be met with a further 200 rounds from the combined guns of Curtis and Munro. As a last resort to escape, the Albatros pilot dived towards the coast with the crew of the Bristol Fighter in pursuit and both crew members firing, until, bursting into flames, the Albatros fell into the sea.

Curtis and Uniacke were again over the enemy lines, carrying out a photographic mission in A7224 on Friday 14 September. GHQ was planning a bombing raid upon Ghistelles Aerodrome. The Bristol attracted the attention of three green and yellow Albatros scouts and during the ensuing fight, Uniacke hit one V strutter with a burst at 100 yards' range, the enemy machine dived away spinning apparently out of control.

The following day, Saturday 15 September, No.48 Squadron moved from Bray Dunes to Leffringoucke Aerodrome near Dunkirk. The move did not interrupt the daily offensive patrols and several enemy aircraft were claimed. Squadron records indicate the last enemy machine claimed by Curtis and Uniacke, again flying A7224, fell on Monday 17 September, when they sent an enemy two-seater down out of control, having fired 250 rounds at it from 100 yards' range.

Nineteen-year-old Second Lieutenant Ralph Luxmore Curtis, No.48 Squadron RFC, killed in action over the enemy lines on 21 September 1917. (RAF Museum)

On Friday 21 September 1917, Curtis and Uniacke took off in A7224 to carry out an offensive patrol over Ostende. When the remainder of the patrol returned, the crews reported combats with enemy fighters in which Curtis and Uniacke were last seen falling behind enemy lines to the north of Roulers. There is little doubt that a Bristol Fighter, claimed by the commander of Jagdstaffel 27 as his fourteenth victory, was A7224. The pilot of the enemy machine, twenty-four-year-old Lieutenant Herman Wilhelm Goring, a pre-war infantry officer, had seen action in the army on the Western Front before volunteering for the Imperial Army Air Service. After a stint as an observer during which he claimed two French machines, he commenced pilot training in June 1915. The experienced German fighter pilot reported attacking the British machine from underneath, hidden by the tail plane. As Curtis put the Bristol Fighter into a spin to escape both he and Uniacke were wounded, forcing them to crash land behind enemy lines. Although suffering a head wound, twenty-two-year-old Uniacke attempted to help his comrade, but nineteen-year-old Ralph Curtis died in his arms.

Desmond Fitzgerald-Uniacke survived his wounds and the hardships of being a prisoner of war, but unfortunately due to these war wounds, he passed away in March 1933 at thirty-eight years of age.

The Bristol Fighter was regarded as one of the best aeroplanes of the First World War but in spite of that fact only one of the other five Essex airman known to have flown with No.48 Squadron lived to see the armistice, such was the ferocity of aerial combat over the enemy lines during the final eighteen months of the war.

Lieutenant Arnold Edward Ansell, a twenty-one-year-old married man from Laindon, Essex, had served with the London Regiment before he volunteered for the Royal Flying Corps in November 1917. Posted to No.48 Squadron as an observer, he was credited with five enemy aircraft from May to July 1918, while flying with four different pilots. Lt Ansell returned to the UK for pilot training before being demobilised in March 1919.

Corporal Robert Edwards of Canning Town, Essex, was killed in action on the last day of 'Bloody April' 1917. He did not fall to the guns of an enemy airman but unfortunately whilst flying as observer for Lt Hugh C. Patterson in Bristol Fighter A7105 they collided with a Sopwith Pup of No.66 Squadron returning from patrol. Without parachutes the unfortunate crew of the Bristol Fighter were killed in the resulting crash. Capt. Robert Oxspring, the pilot of the Pup, survived with two broken legs following a partially controlled descent with the Pup falling into a shell crater just behind the front line.

Second Lieutenant Harold Smither from Westcliffe-on-Sea and his observer, Second Lieutenant Harry C. Clark, failed to return from an offensive patrol in Bristol Fighter A7137 on Friday 6 July 1917 during an encounter with six enemy machines, two of which were reported shot down. Two Bristol Fighters were also brought down behind enemy lines, one of them falling in flames. Two days later an enemy machine dropped a message over the lines, confirming all four men had been killed in action. Harold Smither had been credited with three enemy aircraft destroyed during his tour of duty with No.48 Squadron.

The battle of Amiens began at 0420hrs on Thursday 8 August 1918 with the roar of 2,000 British guns followed by a determined infantry assault supported by tanks and aircraft. During the day, No.48 Squadron had four Bristol Fighters brought down by

Bristol F2b Fighter D8061 seen at Filton Aerodrome with presentation markings before service in France with No.48 Squadron. Observer nineteen-year-old 2nd-Lt Bernard McCutcheon from Westcliff-on-Sea and his twenty-year-old pilot Lt Victor Gray manning D8061 were among the four No.48 Squadron aircraft and crews lost in action on Thursday 8 August 1918. (JMB/GSL Collection)

ground fire and enemy fighters. Two badly damaged machines managed to re-cross the British lines before crash landing, the third fell behind enemy lines and the crew, although wounded, survived as POWs. The crew of the fourth Bristol Fighter D8061, carrying out a low patrol in support of the infantry, was observed to suddenly spin into the ground. The pilot, nineteen-year-old 2nd-Lt Bernard John McCutcheon from Westcliff-on-Sea, Essex and observer twenty-year-old Lt Victor Samuel Gray from Suffolk were both killed and, as so many of their contemporaries who fell behind enemy lines, have no known graves. Their names are among the thousand missing airmen listed on the Arras Memorial.

Parachutes again, had they been issued, may have saved the lives of the twenty-four-year-old observer, 2nd-Lt Walter S. Smith of Loughton, Essex and his pilot, thirty-year-old Capt. Archibald W. Field from Leamington. They were on a photographic reconnaissance mission between Cambrai and St Quentin on Wednesday 9 January 1918 when their Bristol Fighter C4816 came under attack from enemy fighters and broke up in mid-air, shedding the left-hand wings before falling out of control near Estrees. 2nd-Lt Walter Smith and his pilot Capt. Archibald Field were buried side by side at Joncourt Cemetery in France.

It is highly probable that more than the seven Essex airmen recorded in this chapter flew with No.48 Squadron during the First World War; these seven, however, highlight the devotion to duty displayed by all the young servicemen of the county serving on land, sea and the air during the war to end all wars.

When Capt. James Child served with No.84 Squadron in 1918, Major Sholto Douglas was the commanding officer. Sholto Douglas had previously served with No.8 Squadron when, on one occasion at the end of December 1915 with James Child as his observer/gunner, they had the memorable encounter with four Fokker monoplanes. (D.Whetton)

The Child Brothers

Jack and James Child were born in Leytonstone – Jack Escott on 5 October 1890 and James Martin, four years his junior, on 20 October 1894. Both served as flying officers with the RFC/RAF during the First World War.

First into the air was younger brother James, a single man who had served with the 13th Durham Light Infantry in France prior to his transfer to the Royal Flying Corps on November 1915. Attached to No.8 Squadron at Marieux as an observer, James – like so many would-be observer gunners straight from the trenches – had no previous flying experience. If he proved to be unsuitable he would soon be back in the trenches where there was no shortage of volunteers with the onset of the second wartime winter.

No.8 Squadron had been formed at Brooklands in January the same year and had arrived in France in May, attached to the VII Army Corps to be engaged in artillery spotting and photographic reconnaissance duties flying BE2c biplanes.

Wednesday 29 December proved to be a memorable day for James, who had survived four weeks of flying over the enemy lines when weather permitted. On this particular morning, two BEs left Marieux Aerodrome at 0925hrs; the pilot at the controls of BE2c 4087 Lt William Sholto Douglas, sat in the rear cockpit, his observer, 2nd-Lt James Child, well wrapped up against the icy blast of the four bladed propeller, sat in front. Their mission this winter's morning, a deep reconnaissance along the enemy lines to Cambrai and St Quentin. Fokker monoplanes were very active on this sector of the front so a second BE2c, 2039, crewed by 2nd-Lt David Glen and Sgt E. Jones, flew along as an escort.

The pair was flying at 6,500ft when suddenly they came under very accurate anti-aircraft fire near Cambrai. The 'hymn' of hate ceased just as suddenly as it began, when six Fokker monoplanes dived out of the wintery sun firing machine guns through their propellers. At this early period of the war, there were two schools of thought among the pilots of No.8 Squadron in how to deal with a single-seater armed with a forward-firing machine gun. 2nd-Lt Glen in 2039 was of the opinion that as the BE was a stable flying machine it made a perfect platform for his observer's Lewis gun, although this had to be fired backwards over the pilot's head and flying straight and level for the observer gunner was the best means of defence. Unfortunately for David Glen, a nineteen-year-old Norfolk man, the Fokker pilots were experienced enough to be able to exploit their forward-firing, belt-fed machine guns to the full. By December 1915 Lt Max Immelmann, flying Fokker monoplanes, had already accounted for seven allied aeroplanes and Lt Oswald Boelcke, another rising star of the Imperial Air Service, had six to his credit.

In spite of the valiant efforts of Sgt Jones to ward off the Fokkers, the stable BE made an easy target and soon, riddled with bullets, fell earthwards into 'Hun-land' with a wounded pilot pursued by two Fokkers to crash near Marquion. Nineteen-year-old David Glen died of his wounds; Sgt Jones, injured in the crash, remained a prisoner in Germany for the duration of the war.

Fortunately for James Child, his pilot Sholto Douglas, unlike the unfortunate Glen, had subscribed to the theory that the best means of defending a stable 'Bus' like the BE2c was to counter the attacker by turning and diving back under the enemy machines, in this case four of them. This he did time and time again in an unequal contest lasting half an hour. So violent were some of the maneouvers carried out by the British pilot that his unfortunate observer on one occasion threw up all over him, temporarily blinding him with vomit, but James Child quickly recovered and immediately had his Lewis gun back in action.

Lieutenant Sholto Douglas wrote a modest account of the one-sided battle over the enemy lines in his log book shortly after he and James Child returned to Marieux, a facsimile of which is held by the RAF Museum at Hendon:

December 29th. Observer Lt Child. 2 hours 45 minutes. Height 6,500 feet. Reconnaissance to Cambrai and St. Quentin. Archie very good near Cambrai. Then met six Huns. Glen my escort, was shot down, followed by two of the Huns. I was then set upon by the remainder; Child my observer downed one Hun. We fought the remaining three for half an hour. Petrol began to get low and the engine sump was hit. So, relying on the stability near the ground of the B.E.2c against the Fokker came down in a steep spiral to 10 feet above the ground and came back from Cambrai skimming the trees as Huns shot like mad. Child turned the Lewis gun on to one lot of Huns by a farmhouse. Saw several small convoys and a staff officer on horseback. Fokkers left us a mile from the lines. Climbed to 800 feet and dived over the trenches. Engine failed and landed among French heavy batteries just south of Arras. About 100 holes in machine. Engine sump pierced an inch and a half from bottom.

First into the air of the Child brothers from Leytonstone was James, who served as an observer with No.8 Squadron in France before he returned to England and qualified for RAeC No.2377 on 31 January 1916. (RAF Museum)

James Child was not credited with the enemy aircraft he shot down well behind enemy lines on this occasion and Lt Sholto Douglas never received the Victoria Cross recommended by the CO of No.8 Squadron, Maj. A.C. Maclean. Wing HQ refused to sanction the award as the Victoria Cross was awarded for unselfish bravery and for saving the lives of others. Sholto Douglas had certainly saved the life of his observer and when he heard the Wing HQ had suggested he was also saving his own skin, typical of the man, Sholto Douglas considered it to be a fair enough comment on the whole affair.

The following week on Thursday 6 January 1916 *The Times* published a long and detailed account of the fight put up by Sholto Douglas and James Child, but in keeping with the times their identities were not revealed. The indomitable Lt William Sholto Douglas survived both the first war in the air and the Second World War, to become Marshal of the Royal Air Force, Lord Douglas of Kirtleside G.C.B., M.C., D.F.C.

James Child, having more than proved himself as an observer with No.8 Squadron, applied for pilot training and returned to England for instruction. He qualified for his RAeC 2377 at the Military Aviation School at Catterick, Yorkshire on 31 January 1916, less than five weeks after the epic battle with four Fokkers.

On completing his flight training, James returned to France and was posted briefly to No.4 Squadron at Baizieux from 14 until 29 April, when he reported to the Pilots' Pool at No.1 Aircraft Depot, St Omer. Whilst ferrying aircraft from St Omer to Home Establishment and back, he became unwell and was admitted to hospital in England with tonsillitis on Saturday 19 August, not returning to No.1 AD St Omer until 7 October but was not discharged fit for duty until 2 November, when he reported to No.19 Squadron at Fienvillers, under the command of Maj. Hubert Harvey-Kelly.

When Lt James Child arrived at No.19 Squadron they were equipped with the BE12 biplane, a single-seat version of the BE2c, the workhorse of the RFC and although fitted with a forward firing machine gun the BE12 had been a disappointment as a fighter. In December 1916, No.19 Squadron began to replace their BE12 machines with the French designed agile SPAD SVII biplanes fitted with the compact 150hp Hispano-Suiza engine.

Transition from the BE type that James Child had flown as a ferry pilot and with No.19 Squadron, to the much smaller, speedy SPAD with an excellent climb, apparently went well, in spite of No.19 Squadron's teething troubles with the new machines. James Child, flying SPAD B1537 was credited with his first enemy aircraft destroyed, an Albatros two-seater shot down on the afternoon of Monday 23 April 1917; it was observed to crash north-west of Douai. The CO of No.19 Squadron, Maj. Harvey-Kelly, destroyed an Albatros scout near Cambrai during the evening offensive patrol. Three days later during an afternoon offensive patrol in cloudy conditions near Arras, James Child came under attack from a flight of triplanes, not the Fokker variety, but Sopwith Triplanes of the RNAS! Badly shaken, James opened the throttle and put SPAD B1537 into a spinning nose dive. The rugged SPAD could dive like a brick; its small span biplane wings were not only well braced with wire and reinforced with ply strips sandwiched between the double wires bound with doped fabric, the bracing also had the extra strength of a secure attachment to compression struts between the centre section and interplane struts, giving the rugged little SPAD the appearance of a two-bay biplane.

Having escaped the attention of the Naval triplanes, James regained height to cross the frontlines and landed at Bellevue. It had been a narrow escape; his SPAD had bullet holes in both wings, the fuselage and tailplane.

Second Lieutenant J.D. Holmes also escaped in a dive from the gunfire of two Sopwith Triplanes, thanks again to the rugged construction of SPAD B1588. Such were the chaotic conditions that prevailed during the rapidly escalating air war in the spring of 1917, No.8N Squadron would claim two enemy machines forced down. Holmes made it safely back to Vert Galant on this occasion, but during an early morning offensive patrol on 18 May, engine failure in B1588 forced him to land behind enemy lines to be taken prisoner. The following day, anti-aircraft fire forced another No.19 Squadron SPAD pilot down into captivity.

During May 1917, No.19 Squadron had one pilot killed, two taken prisoner and a fourth wounded. During this period acting Flt Cdr James Child was mentioned in dispatches and promoted to captain. He would be officially credited with another enemy aeroplane destroyed, this action taking place on the morning of Thursday 7 June, when James claimed his last enemy machine flying a SPAD, this time B3502, when he destroyed a DFW two-seater near Menin.

Captain Child returned to Home Establishment on 16 June 1917 and after leave with his family in Leytonstone, he reported as a Flight Commander to No.84 Squadron at Lilbourne, near Rugby. Formed in January 1917, No.84 Squadron were in the process of equipping with SE5 machines before proceeding overseas for their first tour of duty. Although the SE5 was a product of the Royal Aircraft Factory, their Wolseley engines were copies of the Hispano-Suiza engine that Capt. Child had plenty of experience with flying SPAD machines with No.19 Squadron; faults were found with the engines of the first two SE5s that arrived at Lilbourne and they were returned to Wolseley for modification.

Major Sholto Douglas took over command of the Squadron on 8 August from Major H.R. Nichol. No doubt Sholto Douglas and his ex-observer – now Flight Commander – Jimmy Child had a lot to talk about since their days in No.8 Squadron. It was a busy time as the new squadron prepared to go to war; the CO and his three flight commanders, Capt. K.M. Leask (A Flight), Capt. E.R. Pennell (B Flight) and Capt. J.M. Child (C Flight), were the only members of the Squadron who had seen action in the air overseas.

Captain James Martin Child returned to France by air with No.84 Squadron on 24 September 1917, the ground personnel having embarked at Southampton for Le Havre three days before. No.84 Squadron Officers Record Book for the period has Captain Child's Christian names listed as James Maynard.

Based at Estree Blanche Aerodrome attached to the 9th Wing, Maj. Sholto Douglas and his experienced flight commanders were allowed to give their fledglings a further three weeks of intensive training in formation flying, getting familiar with their area of the front and practising one-to-one air fighting.

By the autumn of 1917 RFC High Command were at last aware that sending young, inexperienced pilots over the enemy lines was not helping the war effort, just providing the enemy airmen and anti-aircraft gunners with target practice.

Captain Child led six SE5as of C Flight on the first operational flight for No.84 Squadron in France by carrying out a line patrol. The squadron had their first encounter with the opposition on Monday 15 October, when they escorted DH4s of No.25 Squadron to bomb an ammunition dump at Harlebeke. 2nd-Lt Edmond Otto Krohn in B558 dropped out of the escorting Flight and on the way back to Estree Blanche he was attacked by Albatros scouts but managed – no doubt due to the 'one-to-one' training he had received from his flight commander – to put several bursts of fire into a DV that was observed by front line infantry to fall between Menin and Courtrai. Celebration of the first victory for the squadron was somewhat muted in the Mess that evening as they had an empty chair at the table. 2nd-Lt Teddy Vernon-Lord had gone missing during a free-for-all that developed in defending the bombers from the enemy V strutters awaiting their return journey. News eventually arrived that Vernon-Lord had been made POW having been shot down south of Courtrai by pilots of Jasta 27 under the command of Lt Herman Goring.

Major Sholto Douglas and his Flight Commanders had done their best to prepare the new pilots for their baptism of fire in three short weeks. Sholto Douglas recalled in later years:

All through October we fought up and down the Menin–Roulers Road to the east of Ypres. It was a hard school for a new and untried Squadron and at first owing to the inexperience of the pilots we suffered casualties. But bitter experience is a quick teacher.

Another SE5a failed to return from the morning offensive patrol carried out on 19 October – 2nd-Lt Stanley Park at the controls of B546 was forced down behind enemy lines and taken prisoner. The following day, while escorting DH4s from a bombing raid on Thielt, 2nd-Lt Wilfred Watts in B4876 failed to return, later confirmed to be POW. Two more machines were lost on 21 October, brief details in RFC communiqués indicate that No.84 Squadron was beginning to make its presence felt over 'Hun-land' by recording:

A patrol of 84 Squadron became involved in a fight with a large number of EA scouts lasting some 40 minutes and Capt. K. Leask, Capt. R.M. Child and Lt P.J. Maloney each claimed one EA driven down out of control.

Combat Reports reveal Capt. Child had been flying SE5a B562 during the morning offensive patrol when he sent an Albatros DIII scout down out of control at Gheluvelt. B562 would prove to be a lucky 'Bus' for the Flight Commander. The afternoon patrol were not so lucky in the dogfight with fifteen enemy aircraft above Roulers; No.84 Squadron lost three machines, two pilots POW and the unfortunate 2nd-Lt Bobbie Steele dying of wounds.

The next October casualty would be 2nd-Lt Arthur Rush, reported missing after a raid on Harlebeke Aerodrome on the 28th. He survived the ordeal as a POW – and it said a lot for the construction of the SE5a biplane that many a pilot had been able to walk or be carried away still alive after being shot down behind enemy lines at this period – but as fate would have it both No.84 Squadron pilots shot down on the last day of October 1917 were killed. Capt. Kenneth Leask, leading the afternoon offensive patrol, led his patrol in pursuit of four enemy scouts that may well have been acting as decoys for twelve more enemy machines that dropped out of the clouds to the rescue or to spring the trap. In the ensuing fight for survival, 2nd-Lt George Gray, who later died of his wounds, probably fell to the guns of the experienced 2nd-Lt Erwin Bohme, who already had 20 RFC machines to his credit. Bohme of Jasta 2 claimed SE5a B544 that fell near Zillebke Lake at 1715hrs German time. 2nd-Lt Edward Powell had been killed in action with 2nd-Lt Heinrich Bongartz of Jasta 36 above the Roulers–Menin Road at 1610hrs; Bongartz had shot down a SPAD and an RE8 during the morning to bring his victory score to twenty. Across the lines No.84 Squadron were facing stiff opposition from very experienced German 'war birds'.

A deterioration in the weather as November arrived brought some respite to the airmen both sides of the line No.84 Squadron had Flights on standby from the 1st, but unable to leave the ground until after midday on the 8th when conditions improved sufficiently to allow an offensive patrol to take to the air at 1300hrs. A large formation made up of two separate groups of enemy machines was engaged in combat above the battle of Passchendaele. Capt. James Child in B562 and Lt Frederick Brown, a Canadian who had joined the Squadron just a week earlier, sent an Albatros scout down out of control east of Poelcapelle, but once again there were empty chairs in the Mess that evening, as two aircraft had failed to return. Lt John Deans, a Canadian pilot, had been killed in the battle and 2nd-Lt Walter Kingsland had fallen wounded into captivity.

On 10 November, No.84 Squadron received orders to move to Izel-le-Hameau in preparation for a new offensive. The move began on the 12th and three days later, although ready for action, the weather again curtailed activities. Line patrols were, however, flown for familiarisation of landmarks and to shoo away enemy observation machines while preparations for the Battle of Cambrai were under way behind the British front line.

The attack by infantry and 386 tanks was launched without the customary artillery bombardment for the element of surprise at 0600hrs on 20 November 1917; low flying Camels, Pups and DH5s in spite of the bad weather carried out ground strafing with bomb and bullet in support. No.3 Squadron (Camels) sent out nine machines to raid enemy aerodromes, had three pilots killed, two made POW and three machines returned badly damaged. No.64 Squadron (DH5s), attacking mist and smoke shrouded trench and gun positions at Flesquières had two pilots killed, two wounded and two pilots shot down uninjured.

An improvement in the weather on the 22nd, found the SE5s of No.84 Squadron in the thick of things as usual, protecting the ground strafing machines, in consequence with most of the fighting taking place well under 2,000ft. Capt. Child was forced to return from an early offensive patrol with a stoppages in both guns; the over wing Lewis had jammed and the oil reservoir for the 'CC' Gear that synchronised the Vickers gun was empty. Refuelled and with both guns again in working order, Capt. Child took to the air again in B562 to lead C Flight on a second offensive patrol at 1055hrs. During a dogfight with Albatros scouts, north-east of Bourlon Wood, Capt. Child sent a DV down out of control at 1145hrs. Five minutes later he led C Flight in an ambush of a DFW observation machine and forced it down behind British lines to land near Flesquières, where the crew was taken prisoner. The following day No.84 Squadron suffered an unusual casualty when 2nd-Lt David Rollo was hit in the hand by a bullet; what made the wound unusual was he had been thumbing his nose at his opponents at the time!

No.84 Squadron had a busy day on 30 November; a German counter-attack south of Gouzeaucourt recaptured some of the ground they had lost in recent fighting. Four enemy machines were shot down during the fighting by No.84 Squadron, among them an Albatros DV that crashed at Malincourt after being attacked by Capt. Child. Three days later the Battle of Cambrai ended with a British withdrawal from the salient.

December brought with it a welcome leave for Capt. Child from the 6th to the 20th. The day before he left the squadron for the UK, he tested a 'Sidcot' one piece flying suit destined to replace the RFC issue leather flying coats. Both James and Maj. Sholto Douglas, after flying at 15,000ft, gave the 'Sidcot' the thumbs up and reported 'it was everything that could be expected of it'.

Whilst home on leave, Capt. James Child was awarded the Military Cross, no doubt celebrated in the Mess on his return to No.84 Squadron just in time for Christmas. Two offensive patrols were carried out on Christmas Day, but what few enemy machines were seen in the distance quickly made off out of sight.

Flez Aerodrome, February 1918. Captain James Child, C Flight, flanked by fellow flight commanders of No.84 Squadron. On his left, Capt. E.R. Pennell, B Flight; on the right is Capt. K.M. Leask, A Flight. (D.R. Neate)

On 29 December 1917, No.84 Squadron was ordered south to an aerodrome at Flez, where they came under the command of the 22 Wing of the 5th Brigade. The move presented no problem to the pilots and their machines, but the squadron vehicles travelling the snow- and ice- covered roads that were unsuitable for heavy lorries at the best of times had a memorable journey.

The first offensive patrols were carried out by No.84 Squadron from Flez Aerodrome on 2 January, with orders to fly high patrols from 8,000 to 12,000ft to deny air space to enemy aircraft along the 5th Brigade front line. During January No.84 Squadron claimed nine enemy observation and two fighter aircraft destroyed or out of control. Old habits die hard and Capt. Child, returning from a morning offensive patrol on the 20th with three members of his Flight, caught a working party of German infantry out in the open and strafed them from just 500ft before crossing the lines.

Because of bad weather, No.84 Squadron were taken off offensive patrols from 5–15 February. During this period Capt. James Child returned to Home Establishment in England and became a flying instructor with 1 Fighting School, Turnberry, where unfortunately he was accidentally killed attempting to rescue the pilot of a DH9 that had crashed after a mid-air collision on Friday 23 August 1918. Captain James Martin Child, MC, Croix de Guerre was brought home to Essex for burial in Chingford Mount Cemetery. Jack Escott Child, four years older than James and a married man living at Leigh on Sea, had followed his younger brother into the Royal Flying Corps in March 1917 and also became a scout (fighter) pilot, but unlike brother James who flew the SE5a compared with the Spitfire of the Second World War, Jack would fly the Sopwith Camel, equivalent to the Second World War Hawker Hurricane.

Following his flight training in the UK, 2nd-Lt Jack Child was posted from the Pilots' Pool to No.45 Squadron at St Marie Cappel under the command of Maj. Awdry Morris Vaucour MC on 6 September 1917. By this time No.45 Squadron had exchanged their venerable two-seat Sopwith 1½ Strutters for Camels. Within days of joining the squadron, Jack Child claimed his first enemy aircraft when the late morning patrol on 11 September engaged three Albatros scouts. During this engagement the newcomer to the squadron sent a DIII spinning down out of control east of Ypres.

During the Battle of Poelcapelle starting on 9 October, No.45 Squadron were busy ground strafing in support of the 'PBI' (Poor Bloody Infantry). The following day, Jack Child on a strafe in B2311 suffered engine failure and was forced to land, fortunately on the right side of the lines near Poperinghe.

As the Battle of Passchendaele began on 12 October, seven Camels of No.45 Squadron flying through rain and low clouds took on a large number of enemy scouts. During the bitter fighting one enemy scout went down out of control, but two newcomers to No.45 Squadron had been lost in the battle: twenty-three-year-old Capt. Horace Coomber in B2375 had been with the squadron for just twelve days and was buried at Dadizeele, nineteen-year-old 2nd-Lt Kenneth Willard who had been with No.45 Squadron only three days was buried at Harlebeke. By this time Jack Child had survived four weeks of offensive patrols over the enemy lines.

As the Battle of Passchendaele floundered in the mud, No.45 Squadron were out in force ground strafing – two low-flying Camels were brought down, B2327 by ground fire. Lt E.D. Clarke, although wounded, just managed to cross the front line before crashing into a slime-filled shell crater. The second Camel B5152, flown by Canadian 2nd-Lt E.A. Smith, fell behind enemy lines where the pilot was taken prisoner after being shot down by an Albatros scout, probably 2nd-Lt Joachim von Busse of Jasta 3.

Five Camels of B Flight led by Lt M.B. 'Bunty' Frew were carrying out a northern offensive patrol on the morning of 27 October and went to the aid of three Harry Tates under attack from Albatros scouts; Lt Frew, 2nd-Lt Raymond Brownell and Jack Child were credited with an Albatros DV that broke up in mid-air and crashed north-east of Comines. A second patrol from No.45 Squadron led by Capt. John Firth arrived at an opportune time 'Bunty' Frew who had now been separated from his Flight in the melee was surrounded by eight Huns looking for vengeance. Diving into the fray Capt. Firth sent an Albatros down in flames. As 'Bunty' Frew climbed to regain height he saw a smoking Camel spinning out of the dogfight above with a V strutter on its tail that he also promptly shot down in flames and watched it crash east of Moorslede. The spinning Camel B2382 from Capt. Firth's Flight had already crashed nearby, eighteen-year-old 2nd-Lt Cecil Phillips was later confirmed killed in action and like so many gallant young British airmen who fell behind enemy lines has no known grave.

Ferocious aerial battles were fought daily across the enemy lines and the more experienced pilots of No.45 Squadron, having soldiered on with obsolete Sopwith 1½-Strutter for so long, were making the most of the feisty little Camel that put them on equal terms with the German airmen.

Squadron records indicate that the next enemy machine credited to Jack Child was an armoured two-seat ground attack biplane, a 52ft-span Junkers J-1, that in spite of duralumin construction and 5mm armour plate protecting the crew, engine and benzine tank, fell to the guns of Jack Child's Camel B2443 near Westrosebeke at 1025hrs on Thursday 8 November. Jack's younger brother James, serving with No.84 Squadron 15 miles further down the line, drove down an Albatros DV out of control near Poelcapelle the same afternoon. In mid-November No.45 Squadron prepared to face another winter of fighting over the Western Front, but orders were received to transfer the squadron to the Italian front following an appeal from the Italians to their French and British allies for help. The Italian Army had suffered extremely serious losses of men and equipment after a well planned and executed surprise attack at Caporetto on 24 October by combined Austrian and German forces that resulted in 275,000 Italians troops captured, 10,000 killed, 20,000 wounded as the retreating demoralised troops also deserted in thousands. Had it not been for the river Piave 70 miles to the rear being in flood and forming a natural barrier to defend until help arrived, Italy would have had to sue for peace.

Thursday 15 November 1917 was memorable for the pilots of No.45 Squadron carrying out their last offensive patrols on the Western Front before leaving for Italy. Three Albatros scouts and a two-seater Rumpler were claimed without loss. That evening a 'farewell to St Marie Cappel' bash was held in the Mess the pilots of No.45 Squadron were hoping to fly their machines to Italy with their tails up. The following afternoon, however, when heads had cleared the aircraft were flown to No.2 AD at Candas where the Camels were dismantled for transportation by rail. However, their departure was set back by three weeks due to all available locomotives being required for the movement of troops and supplies for the Cambrai offensive about to be launched on 20 November. When the Germans launched a counter-attack at Cambrai on the 25th, Maj. Vaucour offered to unload No.45 Squadron machines from the railway wagons waiting in a siding at Fienvillers and take an active part. This offer was refused on the grounds that the squadron was already in Italy on paper! Part of the pilot's frustration was relieved by taking part in a short aerial gunnery course on the coast with HQ Command Flight at Berck-sur-mer.

The first of the two trains carrying the squadron to Italy puffed out of Fienvillers on Wednesday 12 December with A and B Flights on board. The second train followed with HQ and C Flight the following day, arriving at Padua on the 18th. A memorable Christmas Eve dinner was enjoyed by the officers at Storioni's Restaurant in Padua.

Delayed yet again, this time by mist and fog, the squadron's Camels were finally flown from the aerodrome at San Pelagio where they had been assembled a few days earlier, to a front line aerodrome at Istrana on Boxing Day, from where they became operational with VII Brigade RFC. No.34 and 42 Squadrons flying RE8s had arrived at Istrana earlier in the month and had already been in action. No.42 Squadron moved out on the 17th to make way for No.45 Squadron whose officers were billeted in a comfortable villa 2 miles from the aerodrome near the village of Fossalunga.

The RFC were already a thorn in the side of the Austro-Hungarian airmen, who sent a mixed force of bombers escorted by fighters to raid Istrana Aerodrome early on Boxing Day in retaliation for the earlier bombing of San Felice Aerodrome by RE8s of No.34 and 42 Squadrons. The pilots of No.45 Squadron billeted 2 miles away were spectators from the upstairs windows of the villa, as their machines were still at San Pelagio awaiting collection that afternoon.

Two Italian aircraft sharing Istrana Aerodrome with No.34 Squadron that was not operational that day were destroyed when a hanger went up in flames and most of No.34 Squadron's RE8s were damaged but none seriously. Italian pilots who managed to get their Hanriot scouts off the ground during the raid engaged the enemy and, with Italian anti-aircraft gunners, claimed seven of the raiders shot down.

The raid on Istrana was No.45 Squadron's pilots' introduction to the air war in northern Italy, they must have thought the arrival of the RFC had stirred up a hornets' nest, having never seen or heard of German airmen raiding British aerodromes in large numbers on the Western Front in daylight.

Offensive patrols by No.45 Squadron were first carried out from Istrana on 27 December but due to mist and snow little contact was made with the enemy until the 31st when the new arrival to the front made its presence felt. Lt Henry 'Mike' Moody leading A Flight in B6238 shot down an Albatros scout at 0945hrs, returned to Istrana to refuel and rearm and then shot down another enemy single-seater attacking an observation balloon behind French lines. By the time the pilots of No.45 Squadron returned to France in September 1918, they had claimed no less than 170 enemy aircraft destroyed and twenty-nine sent down out of control for the loss of three officers killed in action, three in accidents and seven wounded, during their nine-month tour of duty on the Italian front.

Sopwith Camel B2443 of No.45 Squadron marked 'K' in Italy. Lt Jack Child shot down enemy aircraft in both France and Italy flying this machine. (D. Whetton)

Lt Jack Child flying Camel B2443 on 22 February was one of a seven-strong escort for an RE8 carrying out a reconnaissance to the river Tagliamento. All went well until the Harry Tate almost reached the British lines. Disregarding or unaware of the escorting Camels above and behind, seven Albatros scouts attempted to put the prying RE8 out of action; hot on their heels came the Camels, quickly breaking up the enemy formation into a series of individual dogfights. An Albatros fired at by Jack Child, burst into flames and fell near Salgareda, and three more enemy machines were claimed by C Flight. Having escorted the RE8 back safely across the lines, Lt Raymond Brownell, the acting flight commander, returned to the fray, although by this time his Flight had won the day.

As in France, No.45 Squadron also carried the war to the enemy with low level raids on airfields and opportune targets, the 20lb Cooper bombs being very effective against machine gun emplacements. The enemy, however, was not the only dangers facing the British airmen in northern Italy; fog along the Venetian Plain in particular, where brilliant sunshine disappeared in minutes blotted out by ground mist and fog was a deadly menace to the airmen on both sides of the lines. British squadrons informed each other and anti-aircraft units by telephone when they were about to be fogged in; code letters in the form of large white canvas markers, possibly Ingram panels as used in France and the UK, would then be laid out to indicate to those airborne the nearest airfield free from fog.

Another menace No.45 Squadron encountered on the Italian front has been attributed by some historians to Italian temperament, undoubtedly they made bold and dashing fighter pilots and unfortunately, although the RFC/RAF machines carried large blue, white and red cockades, they were attacked in error by Italian pilots on more than one occasion. Members of C Flight were attacked by Italian fighters on Sunday 10 March, during the ensuing desperate free-for-all Lt Jack Child sent one Italian down out of control. No.45 Squadron fortunately had suffered no casualties this time, but the loss of their respected commanding officer, Maj. Awdry Vaucour later in the year, was also due to mis-identification when on 16 July Italian scouts opened fire at his lone Camel hitting the unsuspecting major fatally in the head.

St Patrick's day 1918, No.45 Squadron moved from Istrana to share with No.28 Squadron at Grossa Aerodrome near Asiago, some 30 miles to the west. From that date the Camel pilots air battles and bombing raids were carried out over mountainous terrain.

The four 20lb Cooper bombs carried by each of the six Camels of No.45 Squadron that left Grossa at 0930hrs on 4 May, were intended for the Hydro-Electric Power Station, north of Lake Garda at Trentino. Upon arrival at the target, Capt. Bush the flight commander realised the power station, lying deep in a valley among mountains, prevented the bombing taking place in single file at 500ft as planned, and released his Coopers from 2,000ft. Three other pilots in line astern – including Jack Child – released their bombs in turn that all fell short. Lt A. Lingard, due to engine trouble, had already dropped his bombs on army billets near Riva, probably inflicting the most damage during the raid as 20lb bombs were not heavy enough to cause much damage to industrial targets. The last pilot, having seen his comrades' bombs falling short of the power station, banked, flew south and dived into the valley following the river. Passing over the power station at just 100ft he toggled his bombs free, and two fell on the station as another hit a building close by. Lt Cedric Howell, the Australian pilot bringing up the rear, had used his initiative and at the end of the war Howell – known as 'Spike' in No.45 Squadron – would be their top scoring pilot in Italy with nineteen enemy aircraft to his credit.

On the return flight, two machines were forced to put down on an Italian aerodrome at Verona while Jack Child and Lt Jack Cottle, running low on oil, landed at Sovizzo to refuel. During May 1918, Camel pilots of Nos 28, 45 and 66 Squadrons claimed over sixty enemy aircraft shot down in addition to their low-level bombing and ground strafing attacks on enemy troops, without a fatal casualty inflicted by enemy fire.

Yet another hazard to flyers on the mountainous north Italian front is highlighted by the loss of B6282, a No.45 Squadron Camel returning low from a strafe on 24 May, after hitting an overhead power cable near Bassano. The shocked pilot Lt H.J. Watts crashed into the river Brenta. Having just escaped a fiery death, he now faced drowning in the fast flowing river. On seeing he was hampered by the weight of his waterlogged flying suit, two gallant Italian soldiers dived into the icy torrent to save him, but unfortunately Sergeant Guiseppe Maggi and Private Angelo Mori of No.62 Field Hospital were swept away to their deaths in the torrent. Lt Watts owed his live to an American Volunteer ambulance driver Bayard Wharton who also dived into the rescue and after a super-human effort pulled the semi-conscious airman to the river bank, where fellow American Red Cross Volunteers were able to drag them ashore.

Local leave was a welcome respite from the low-level bombing and strafing by the three Camel squadrons in Italy. Lt Jack Child was granted his leave from 4 June, returning to Grossa on the 19th. Venice that had been out of bounds, was now open at this period to British military personnel. During Jack's absence, the Austrians launched a massive offensive and succeeded in crossing the natural barrier of the river Piave by boat, raft and pontoon bridges; the three Camel squadrons used their 20lb bombs to good effect during daylight, considerably reducing the number of bridge heads gained by Austrian infantry.

By 20 June, Austrians now trapped on the wrong side of the again-flooded river came under siege from the Italian army and within 48 hours began retreating back across the Piave under cover of darkness. It was the beginning of the end of the Austro-Hungarian Empire, which sued for peace on 27 October, surrendering on 3 November 1918.

Sunday 7 July, Jack Child on offensive patrol in Camel D1975 was credited with another enemy aircraft; it would be the last officially credited to him. The LVG two-seat observation machine he shot up on that occasion was observed to crash at Val d'Assa.

As the war-weary Austrian army staggered towards defeat, the RAF were able to recall No.5 Squadron from Italy to France in September 1918 to reinforce the newly formed Independent Force. Lt Jack Child had already left the squadron by then, having been posted to Home Establishment on 4 August, where he reported for duty as a flying instructor to 188 NTS, based at Throwley in Kent, under the command of Maj. C.B. Cooke.

Jack Escott Child, who survived months of extremely hazardous low-level ground strafing attack and deadly air combat daily, was, like so many other war-weary men, weakened physically; he succumbed to influenza epidemic and passed away on Sunday 3 November 1918 at twenty-nine years of age. Jack was buried at Chingford Mount Cemetery, Essex, alongside his younger brother James who had been killed in an accident at Turnberry Aerodrome a few weeks earlier.

George Ebben Randall

Born on 19 January 1899 at 40 Morris Avenue, Little Ilford, Manor Park, Essex, George Ebben Randall was the son of Florence Maud and George Randall a railway porter. The baby's second name, Ebben, had been the maiden name of his mother who came from Scotland.

Britain had been at war for two and a half years when, at the age of eighteen, young George Randall was commissioned in the Royal Flying Corps as a second lieutenant on Wednesday 4 April 1917. The family home was by then at 73 Third Avenue, Manor Park.

With just six weeks' training, 2nd-Lt Randall reported for duty as an observer to No.3 Squadron based at Lavieville near Albert in France on Saturday 19 May 1917. No.3 was a corps squadron attached to the 15th Wing, V Brigade, engaged in artillery observation and contact patrols for which their Morane P-type two-seat monoplanes were ideally suited, if escorted when over the lines.

French-designed and built Morane aeroplanes had entirely equipped No.3 Squadron since December 1915 – the P-type monoplanes in service when 2nd-Lt George Randall arrived were fitted with 110hp Le Rhone rotary engines giving a top speed of 95 mph at 6,500ft.

Unlike the British BE2 biplanes in use with other corps squadrons, the Morane Parasol, so-called because the single wing attached by centre section struts was above the fuselage, was well braced with flying and landing wires. This configuration gave George, as an observer, an uninterrupted view of the battlefield below when engaged on artillery observation and photographic and reconnaissance patrols.

Thanks also to the close proximity of the pilot, George found he could converse by shouting at him and visa versa, unlike the BE machines where either the engine had to be shut off or hand signals relied upon.

Pilot Sgt Frank Courtney with a Morane-Saulnier L Type monoplane of No.3 Squadron RFC, at Auchel Aerodrome, August 1915. (Merle Olmsted)

As well as a drum-fed Lewis gun on a ring mounting for the observer, the pilot also at this period of the war had an air-cooled belt-fed synchronised Vickers gun that enabled him to fire forward through the propeller arc. In the hands of an experienced pilot the Parasol was a good 'Bus', as Capt. Cecil Lewis, who had flown Parasols with No.3 Squadron the previous year, recalled in his post-war book *Farewell to Wings*:

> In the Parasol I did my longest stint at the front – seven months on the Somme in 1916. In her I did my best work of the war, for which I was twice mentioned in dispatches and awarded the Military Cross. From her wings I saw sights that changed me in a few short months from a callow boy to a disillusioned young man. She was ropey, treacherous and dangerous to fly, permitted no liberties and needed attention every second she was in the air. But only once during 200 patrols did she ever let me down.

This was the type of machine that George Randall flew in as a fledgling observer over the enemy lines, it was all what Captain Lewis said it was and obsolete by the summer of 1917.

During the previous month of bitter fighting prior to 2nd-Lt George Randall joining No.3 Squadron in May, two pilots and two observers had been killed in action, another pilot and two observers had been wounded. Compared with losses sustained by other corps squadrons for the period that became known as 'Bloody April', No.3 Squadron with its Morane Parasols had fared much better than the aircrews of the BE2 and RE8 machines.

Small arms fire from the ground accounted for casualties among the low-flying Parasols of No.3 Squadron carrying out hazardous contact patrols with the British infantry on Thursday 3 May and Lt C.T. Cleaver, although wounded by ground fire, managed to return to Lavieville safely with his observer. Another Parasol returned to the aerodrome so badly damaged by ground fire it collapsed on landing, the fuselage breaking in two! However, the gallant crew had escaped with only minor injuries.

The Parasols of No.3 Squadron were engaged in artillery observation during the massive bombardment that immediately followed the detonation of 400 tons of high explosive mined under the German front line trenches on the Messines Ridge on Thursday 7 June.

Second Lieutenant R.A. Powell, carrying out counter-battery work, was wounded in the arm by ground fire. Although line patrols by RFC scout squadrons drove off many of the enemy machines attempting to prevent the corps machines from carrying out their duties, 2nd-Lt A. Denavon was wounded by an Albatros that surprised the Parasol crew carrying out a photographic reconnaissance above Bullecourt on 15 June.

Good fortune and line patrols protected No.3 Squadron from losses by enemy action during July 1917; however, both crew members of A6700 were wounded in a battle with enemy scouts on 9 August. 2nd-Lt George Randall had survived his first three months in a front line squadron on 19 August and had settled in as part of the team when rumours that the venerable Parasol machines were to be replaced by single-seat Sopwith scouts prompted George to apply for pilot training.

In early September the rumours came true and the experienced rotary engine pilots began to exchange their two-seater Moranes for single-seat Sopwith Camels and several new pilots arrived straight from flying schools in England, among them a fellow Essex

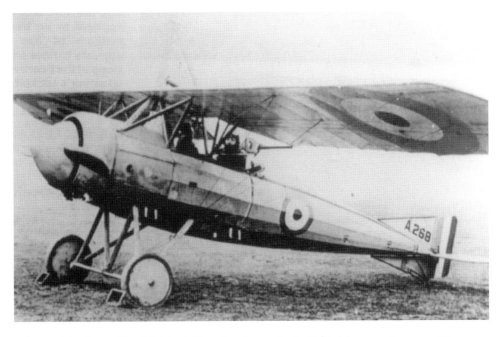

When 2nd-Lt George Randall joined No.3 Squadron at Lavieville in May 1917, they were fully equipped with the P type Morane-Saulnier. A268, shown here, had been shot down by Warrant Officer Edmond Nathanael of Jasta 5 on 6 March. Lt C.W. Short died of wounds; his observer, Lt S.M. Fraser, was wounded. (D.R. Neate)

man 2nd-Lt Herbert M. Beck from nearby Ilford. During the transition period, No.3 Squadron were to suffer the loss of two more monoplanes and crews to enemy fighters. Leaving Lavieville Aerodrome on 19 September at 1045hrs apparently on training flights, both machines were shot down over the lines by pilots of Jasta 5; the crew of one survived as POWs.

Two days later, on Friday 21 September, 2nd-Lt George Randall was posted as an observer to No.12 Squadron recently re-equipped with RE8 biplanes stationed at an aerodrome near Courcelles-le-Comte. Due to his application for pilot training being granted a few weeks later he once again packed his kit and left, this time for Home Establishment and leave on Saturday 10 November 1917.

Details of George Randall's flight training appear to have gone up in smoke along with the many 1914–18 training squadron records incinerated during the 1950s; however, we do know that pilot officer 2nd-Lt George E. Randall returned to France in June 1918, where he reported to No.20 Squadron at Boisdinghem equipped with the Bristol F2b Fighter. A few days later, on 2 July, he received his commission as lieutenant in the RAF.

No.20 Squadron had a reputation second to none in the RAF and by the end of the First World War had claimed no less than 630 enemy aircraft. Such was the fighting spirit of the pilots and observers of No.20 Squadron that 319 enemy aircraft had fallen to the guns of the great lumbering FE2b and later FE2d pusher machines before their replacement by the more orthodox Bristol Fighter had begun in August 1917. By the end of the First World War the squadron would also have one of the highest fatal casualty rates for a front line squadron, with 124 pilots and observers killed, and many more wounded.

In addition to daily fighting patrols, the men of No.20 Squadron carried out escort, reconnaissance and ground support roles. No.20 Squadron Bristol Fighters crossing the enemy lines on offensive patrols in 1918 usually carried one 112lb or up to twelve 20lb bombs for use on opportune targets. The 275hp Rolls Royce Falcon III engines that powered the Bristol Fighters flown by George Randall were the equal of the German machines in performance including what would be regarded as the best German fighter of the war, the Fokker DVII biplane.

It was with Glaswegian 2nd-Lt George Learmond, two years his senior, acting as observer gunner in Bristol F2b D8086, that Lt George Randall had his first successful encounter with a Hun during which he was credited with a Fokker DVII. The action took place during a series of dogfights over a large area behind enemy lines during an evening offensive patrol north of Wervicq on 24 July 1918.

In such good company George Randall would learn fast; he had to, as the already formidable 170hp Mercedes powered Fokker DVII met in combat daily over the lines were being replaced with the much improved 185hp BMW DVIIF, that were much sought after by front line Jasta pilots.

During the same patrol that George Randall had been awarded his first enemy aircraft, Lt John Colbert and observer Lt R. Turner in D7951 also shot down a Fokker DVII – it was Colbert's fourth victory. Lt L.W. Price and observer Lt A. Mills in C4672 also accounted for a third DVII that evening. However, that evening there were two empty chairs, both in the Sergeants' Mess, when C4604 failed to return from their patrol: Sgt H.G. Aldridge and observer Sgt M.S. Sampson had been shot down by Lt Hans-

Eberhardt Gandert of Jasta 51; fortunately it was learned later both men were confirmed to be alive as POWs.

No.20 Squadron claimed four DVIIs destroyed and another out of control on 25 July, but not without loss. C976 with Lt F.J. Shearer and Sgt D. Malpas were both killed while in combat with Lt Friedrich Ritter von Roth of Jasta 16, who claimed the Bristol Fighter over Gheluvelt at 0950hrs (0850 British time).

Monday 29 July was another good day for No.20 Squadron with four Fokkers driven down without loss. Six enemy fighters were claimed the following day after fifteen Bristol Fighters took off from Boisdinghem at 1930hrs and near Armentières engaged a mixed bag of Fokker DVIIs and Triplanes who quickly made off south-west. A second group of enemy machines were then encountered: about fifteen Fokker DVIIs with blue tails.

A former No.20 Squadron observer who had returned as a pilot, Sgt John Cowell DCM, MM and Bar credited with sixteen enemy aircraft, and his observer Cpl Charles Hill lost their lives in E2471 during a fierce combat with Lt von Roth of Jasta 16. Lt John Purcell in D7897 had attacked von Roth's Fokker sitting on the tail of Cowell's machine but was too late to save the unfortunate crew, as the DVII spun out of his line of fire; the crippled Bristol Fighter broke up and fell in flames carrying the two gallant NCOs to their deaths.

Lieutenant von Roth had only just escaped the fate of the Bristol Fighter crew he had sent down in flames; he would also survive another hard-fought three months to see the end of the war and be credited with twenty-eight victories. In the aftermath of Germany's defeat, overcome with despondency on top of the strain of living on his nerves as a front line fighter pilot, this gallant officer who had been wounded early in the war when serving with an artillery regiment and very badly injured in a flying accident during training to become a pilot, was unable to come to terms with the Fatherland having lost the war. He settled his affairs and with his service pistol committed suicide on New Year's Eve 1918.

There was no time to pay attention to the crew of the burning Bristol falling to their death without parachutes; suddenly without warning amid the chaotic mix up of swift turning, spinning, climbing, diving, machines of friend and foe, Lts Paul Iaccaci and Harold Edwards in D7915 found themselves head to head with a DVII. A short burst from the forward Vickers gun and Iaccaci quickly turned the two-seater to avoid collision, enabling Edwards to fire 100 rounds at the enemy machine that fell away and was seen by others to crash north-east of Bailleul. Observers with the strength to handle double yoked Lewis guns on the Scarff ring at this period of the war had the advantage of firing two ninety-seven-round drums before having to reload. Split up from the rest of the patrol, USAS pilot Lt George H. Zellers and observer nineteen-year-old Sgt John D. Cormack in C904 were last seen in a desperate fight with four DVIIs before falling in flames.

On the last day of the month, Bristol Fighter C859 failed to return from an evening offensive patrol. Lt W.H. Shell and Sgt J.D. Summers, suffering from engine trouble, fell behind the patrol unnoticed and were picked off by Lt Harald Auffarth of Jasta 29 for his sixteenth victory; both men were later confirmed to be alive as POWs.

A lull in the air fighting for the airmen of No.20 Squadron during early August was due to the ground support being given to the Allied 'push' that began on the 8th. On Sunday 11 August, led by Capt. Horace Lale and observer 2nd-Lt John Hills, sixteen Bristol Fighters, with full bomb racks, took off from Boisdinghem Aerodrome and once in formation headed towards the enemy lines to be joined by their escorts for the raid: no less than forty SE5a scouts from Nos 29, 75 and 85 Squadrons.

Crossing the lines at 8,000ft north of Thies the armada of British war planes droned towards their objective through a barrage of anti-aircraft fire. Their target: Courtrai railway station and sidings, packed with German troops. In response to a Very light from Capt. Lale in E2467 the Bristol Fighters dived in turn, releasing their 112lb bombs from a low level.

Direct hits were observed on the station building and locomotives; one bomb fell cutting the railway line and also five carriages and station buildings were seen to be damaged. SE5as of No.29 Squadron quickly followed, swooping in with four 25lb bombs apiece, and twenty more hits were observed on the station, sidings and a lorry.

The observers of the Bristol Fighters sprayed the congested target of troops and transport with their Lewis guns to deadly effect. The average height of the attacking Bristol and SE5a machines had been 400 to 900ft. On the return flight, under cover of their SE5 escort, two enemy observation balloons and a Fokker DVII were shot down by No.20 Squadron. RAF communiqués for the day state, 'All our machines returned from this enterprise'.

No.20 Squadron claimed a Fokker DVII on 13 August and another the following day. Lt George Randall with Sgt A. Newland as observer in D8086 carried out an evening patrol during which they engaged a formation of enemy scouts above Dadizeele. Two Fokker DVIIs and three Pfalz DIIIs were claimed by No.20 Squadron crews, including a Pfalz DIII sent down out of control by Lt Randall and Sgt Newland. One Bristol Fighter C987 was seen to go down during the fight; the pilot, nineteen-year-old Lt D.E.Smith, was later reported killed in action and 2nd-Lt J. Hills the observer had been taken prisoner.

A Fokker DVII and an observation balloon were claimed by No.20 Squadron on the 15th; Lt W.H. Markham attacked the Balloon at about 1,000ft with his front gun, setting it ablaze before he was badly wounded in the leg by ground fire. He managed to fly his observer 2nd-Lt E.S. Harvey back to Boisdinghem.

Seven enemy machines were claimed by the evening patrol on Wednesday 21 August without loss. The following evening George Randall and Lt G. Learmond in E2158 shot down another Fokker DVII that crashed at Dadizeele. Unfortunately No.20 Squadron lost Capt. D. Latimer and Lt T.C. Noel in D7993, when they failed to return from a morning offensive patrol. Capt. Latimer survived as a POW, twenty-year-old Thomas Noel died of his wounds.

On Monday 26 August, No.20 Squadron was transferred to the 22 Wing, V Brigade, moving to Vignacourt Aerodrome to replace No.48 Squadron, but were soon back in action.

A fierce battle took place above Havincourt Wood on 3 September when the evening patrol fought with a 'circus' of Pfalz and Fokker scouts. George Randall and Lt Learmond sent a DVII down out of control and four more enemy aircraft were claimed by No.20 Squadron for the loss of one machine B1344; the crew, nineteen-year-old Lt W.F. Washington and twenty-year-old 2nd-Lt K. Penrose were later reported killed. William Washington from Chingford had been another Essex man serving with No.20 Squadron, observer Keith Penrose was a South African. Another No.20 Squadron casualty during the battle above Havincourt Wood on 3 September, was the observer of E2181, 2nd-Lt Francis Ralph DFC, who had just shot down an attacking Pfalz before he was fatally wounded by another Pfalz. Frank Ralph, who had already been wounded during a dogfight the previous May, was twenty-five years of age and rated a first-class observer with thirteen confirmed enemy aircraft. Capt. H.P Lale DFC, the pilot, was unhurt and would survive the war credited with twenty-three enemy aircraft.

Although the German army was in retreat in the autumn of 1918, the Imperial Air Service with an increasing number of BMW powered Fokker DVIIs were fighting with a grim determination that made 'Bloody April 1917' pale by comparison. With what latter day historians term as 'Black September 1918', George Randall may have arrived at No.3 Squadron in the aftermath of 'Bloody April' but he was with No.20 Squadron in the thick of the ferocious fighting taking place that September.

With Lt Learmond manning the Lewis gun of E2249 during a scrap where No.20 Squadron claimed three DVIIs without loss, George Randall sent a Fokker down out of control near Cambrai on the afternoon of Thursday 5 September. With the exception of an Albatros DV sent down out of control the previous July when flying with Capt. Horace Lale, all nine enemy aircraft credited to observer 2nd-Lt George Learmond would be claimed whilst flying with George Randall. Capt. Horace Lale DFC would become one of No.20 Squadron's leading exponents of the Bristol Fighter, with twenty-three enemy aircraft to his credit by the end of the war.

Seven Fokker DVIIs were claimed by No.20 Squadron without taking casualties on Friday 6 September. Two were sent down in flames by Capt. H. Lale and 2nd-Lt H. Edwards during a dogfight over St Quentin. Horace Lale hit the first with his forward firing Vickers gun as it passed in front of E2181, Harold Edwards, the Canadian observer, returning the fire of an attacking Fokker saw it fall in flames. Four more fell to brothers August and Paul Iaccaci, two American pilots serving with No.20 Squadron, and their observers.

Lt August T. Iaccaci DFC, later captain, would survive the war credited with seventeen enemy aircraft. His brother Lt Paul T. Iaccaci DFC also survived the war credited with seventeen enemy machines. The seventh machine claimed during the day fell out of control having been hit by the guns of Lt R.B. Campbell and 2nd-Lt D.M. Calderwood.

It must be stressed that in the aftermath of the war, German losses did not tally with No.20 Squadron claims during the ever growing and intensifying dogfights that took place in 1918. Due to the offensive spirit of No.20 Squadron and indeed all British Commonwealth airmen, the fighting took place over the enemy lines. This made it easier for German airmen to obtain verification of their claims when successful, but as in the Second World War, more enemy aircraft were claimed in good faith than actually destroyed by both sides.

Day bombers of the RAF crossing the enemy lines flew in formation to enable their observer/gunners to cover each others' machines for mutual protection. Flying in formation also provided a stable firing platform for the observer/gunner, unlike the observer in a Bristol Fighter mixing it in fast and furious dogfights between large formations of fighters where it became every man for himself in a matter of seconds. In such situations it would have been fatal to watch the ultimate doom of a crippled enemy machine falling out of control.

Weather conditions closing in provided airmen on both sides of the lines with some respite, but not before Capt. H. Lale and Lt H. Edwards, carrying out an evening offensive patrol on Saturday 7 September in E2154, crashed another DVII, after which few enemy aircraft were encountered by No.20 Squadron crews, until the mid morning patrol led by Lt W. Thomson and 2nd-Lt H. Edwards on Sunday 15th engaged in combat a group of Fokker DVIIs from Jastas 6, 12 and 24 when No.20 Squadron records show that four enemy aircraft were destroyed and four sent down out of control in the fighting. Capt. Thomas Middleton and Lt Alfred Mills also had a scrap with a Hannover CL II, a formidable two-seat fighter to be treated with great respect, and shot it down. They made a fearful team, both Capt. Middleton with twenty-seven enemy aircraft to his credit and Lt Mills with fifteen were awarded the DFC and survived the war. At the end of the month after shooting down two more enemy fighters, Capt. Middleton was hospitalised, the traumas of daily air fights over the enemy lines no doubt responsible.

Post-war Britain had little time for out-of-work heroes and, discharged from the RAF in February 1919, like so many ex-servicemen in the 1920s ex-Lt Alfred Mills fell on hard times and was prosecuted for theft, given a three-month prison sentence and deprived of his DFC.

However, returning to No.20 Squadron on 15 September 1918, Bristol Fighter F5816 returned from the scrap with a wounded observer Sgt A.J. Winch, during which E2512 had gone down behind enemy lines with a wounded pilot Lt F. Finch, who along with his observer 2nd-Lt C. Russell was taken prisoner. Later the same day D7939 failed to return from the evening offensive patrol; 2nd-Lt A.R.D Campbell and Sgt T.A Stack were later reported alive as prisoners of war.

Keeping pace with the tide of war now running in the Allies favour, No.20 Squadron began the move to an aerodrome 23 miles to the east at Suzanne on 16 September. The move did not prevent the squadron from carrying out their daily offensive patrols over the enemy lines. Three enemy machines were crashed and four sent down out of control. Although C4718 was badly shot about, its crew managed to return to Vignacourt Aerodrome physically unharmed.

Another Bristol Fighter C951 was severely damaged in combat with enemy fighters during an evening offensive patrol on 18 September; the pilot, 2nd-Lt Andrew Strachan, managed to land his observer back at Suzanne Aerodrome. The twenty-two-year-old pilot ran out of luck on Friday 20th, gale force winds had kept aerial activity to a minimum the day before but the war birds were out in force as the weather improved.

A flight of SE5as from No.84 Squadron combined with the morning patrol of No.20 Squadron Bristol Fighters to tackle several Jastas numbering about twenty Fokkers in combat over St Quentin. The ever prevailing west wind had greatly increased since take-off and blew the dogfight that raged for half an hour ever deeper into enemy territory, during which No.84 Squadron pilots claimed two Fokkers shot down, while No.20 Squadron claimed seven DVIIs destroyed and three more last seen falling out of control.

In spite of the disadvantage of fighting so far over the enemy lines, just one Bristol Fighter failed to return: the unfortunate twenty-two-year-old 2nd-Lt Strachan and observer 2nd-Lt Calderwood falling to the guns of Lt Otto Schmidt, the CO of Jasta 5, who claimed a Bristol Fighter falling in flames over Fressnoy-le-Grand at 0940hrs. A second Bristol Fighter was claimed shot down in flames during the fight, but E2518 was the only machine that failed to return from the morning offensive patrol. What Jastas the dozen enemy aircraft claimed shot down during the battle belonged to is something of a mystery; Jasta 5, the main protagonists that morning, suffered no losses, as did the SE5as of No.84 Squadron.

Rain and strong winds on Monday 23 September accounted for the official RAF communiqué for the day stating that 'Enemy aircraft activity slight'. It was not so for the evening offensive patrol of No.20 Squadron who were engaged in a life or death struggle with a large formation of Fokker DVIIs to the east of St Quentin from 1815hrs. Four DVIIs destroyed and two out of control were claimed by the Bristol crews. Lt E.A. Britton and his observer Sgt R.S. Dodds in E2467 accounted for a DVII and sent another spinning down out of control; during the action Sgt Dodds had been wounded. Sergeant Kurt Ungewitter of Jasta 24 claimed a Bristol Fighter falling in flames at Levergies, the machine being E2562 of No.20 Squadron, the unfortunate crew twenty-year-old Lt James Nicholson and 2nd-Lt Brodie Wilson. Enemy aircraft activity had been reported as slight!

An RAF communiqué the following day reports 'Enemy aircraft activity was considerable'. Although No.20 Squadron was moved 5 miles south to an airfield near Proyart during the day, offensive patrols were maintained to keep up the pressure on the enemy. The evening offensive patrol claiming two enemy aircraft destroyed and two out of control in another fierce encounter south-east of St Quentin. Of the four aircraft driven down, Lt George Randall and observer Lt J. Hackett in E2470 were responsible for one destroyed and another shot down of control.

Although accounting for eight enemy aircraft during half an hour of dog fighting between Cambrai and St Quentin on the evening of Wednesday 25 September, there was only one casualty for No.20 Squadron to report, observer Lt R. Gordon-Bennett wounded in an exchange of fire with an enemy machine.

The endless daily round of offensive patrols over the enemy lines continued. 2nd-Lt Leslie Smith and observer 2nd-Lt Edwin Harvey were shot down in E2155 on 26 September. The twenty-one-year-old pilot was killed in the fight, the nineteen-year-old observer died of his wounds three days later.

At the end of the day on Friday 27 September as the PBI fought their way forward for the final push on Hindenburg Line, the RAF had lost forty-eight aircraft in supporting actions. No.20 Squadron Bristol Fighters had claimed three enemy aircraft destroyed and one out of control, for the loss of E2566 with twenty-one-year-old 2nd-Lt Fredrick Turner and eighteen-year-old 2nd-Lt Charles Clark. Both men were later confirmed as killed in action.

By this time nineteen-year-old Lt George Randall had survived nearly three months of facing death or serious injury daily, added to which he was now an acting flight commander responsible for the safety of others as well as his own observer. The effect on his nervous system like so many young airmen, friend and foe alike, can only be imagined.

Second Lieutenant Nicholas Boulton straight from training had only been with No.20 Squadron a few weeks and had already accounted for six enemy aeroplanes during September. He and his observer 2nd-Lt Charles Case in E2561, however, were no match for the Fokker DVII that singled them out during a battle in which No.20 Squadron claimed three enemy aircraft destroyed and three out of control, fought high above the outskirts of St Quentin on Sunday morning, 29 September. History has credited 2nd-Lt Josef Mai of Jasta 5 with E2561, the thirtieth victory of the thirty-one-year old German pilot. There is room for doubt as the time and place do not tally and the Bristol Fighter shot down by 2nd-Lt Mai could well have been one of the two that were also reported missing by No.22 Squadron that morning.

A question mark also hangs over the burial of the two young airmen. It was the custom on both sides of the lines to bury the pilot and observer killed in action side by side, unless one died later in hospital of wounds. As both Boulton and Case are reported killed in action on 29 September, why is nineteen-year-old 2nd-Lt Boulton buried at Bellicourt and twenty-one-year-old 2nd-Lt Case at Magny-la-Fosse?

The last day of September 1918 provided really foul flying weather with low clouds and heavy rainstorms giving many of the airmen along the Western Front a little respite. RAF losses for the day were light compared with the rest of the month: two machines and the crew of a low-flying Bristol Fighter of No.48 Squadron wounded by ground fire.

October brought better flying weather that resulted in some of the fiercest air fighting of the war and more casualties, but the morale of No.20 Squadron was high and tactics employed by the experienced flight commanders kept the squadron losses to a minimum. During the month twelve enemy fighters were claimed for the loss of three crews killed in action and two men wounded. A bombing raid by No.20 Squadron Bristol Fighters on Aulnoye railway station on the afternoon of Wednesday 23 October brought Fokker DVIIs swarming down for the kill. During the battle that followed no less than five enemy aircraft were claimed as shot down. No.20 Squadron casualties were E2470 with the loss of twenty-three-year-old 2nd-Lt Howard Pennal and nineteen-year-old Sgt George Aitken who were last seen low over the target and later reported killed in action. Lt F. Goodearle died and Lt A McBride was injured when E2590 crashed on landing.

Once again the airmen and ground crews of No.20 Squadron were ordered to move. This took place on Friday 25 October when their Bristol Fighters flew to Iris Farm Aerodrome at Clary, still with 22 Wing in support of V Brigade.

The first day of November began with the loss of 2nd-Lt P. Segrave and 2nd-Lt H. Kidd in F6116, shot down by enemy fighters while carrying out a midday offensive patrol; both men were later reported killed in action. Low clouds and heavy rain along the Western Front restricted aerial activity on Saturday 2 November to the loss of two RAF machines and one enemy machine claimed by a Sopwith Dolphin pilot of No.79 Squadron.

RAF communiqué for 3 November again reports 'Enemy aircraft activity slight'. No.20 Squadron encountered some of the slight activity when their midday offensive patrol was attacked by enemy fighters. During the fight amongst the clouds, Lt George Randall with Lt George Learmond as observer in E2429 crashed a Fokker DVII south-west of Berliamont. Two more Fokkers were sent down out of control by the patrol without loss.

A Fokker DVII that took on the formidable team of Randall and Learmond in E2429 on the morning of Saturday 9 November met his match and was seen to crash south-east of Beaumont.

Sunday 10th was not a day of rest for No.20 Squadron. The morning offensive patrol went to the aid of a formation of DH9 bombers under attack from a dozen Fokker DVIIs. George Randall and George Learmond in E2429 fired at one of the attackers that fell out of control and was observed to crash west of Louerval, but not by Learmond who was exchanging fire with another Fokker leading three others diving on their tail. The leader burst into flames and the remainder were engaged by other members of the flight.

Two more DVIIs were accounted for during the free-for-all above Charleroi where the flaming Fokker fell. 2nd-Lts F.H. Solomon and A.D. Sinclair claimed one, the other fell to the guns of 2nd-Lts H.W. Heslop and J. Hackett. Three hours earlier at 0830hrs, Capt. G.H. Hooper and Lt M.A. McKenzie had also sent a DVII down out of control over Charleroi. Two Bristol Fighters and crews were missing when the Flight returned to Iris Farm: F6195 with 2nd-Lts A.W. McHardy and W.A. Rogers killed in the action over Charleroi and F4421 WHICH had also been shot down in the scrap; Lt E.A. Britton survived the crash as a POW, his observer Sgt Reg Dodds unfortunately died of wounds. Lt Britton had been captured for less than 24 hours when the war ended with the signing of an Armistice at 11a.m. the next morning, Monday 11 November 1918.

For airmen like George Randall fighting daily for his life over enemy lines during the closing months of the First World War, the sudden cessation of hostilities came as a shock. There had been rumours going around the Mess for weeks, but rumours were only rumours – the Fokkers were always waiting over the lines as the next day dawned – but this time it was true: no more kill or be killed, the war to end all wars was really over. There was a riotous celebration in the Mess that night. In the sober grey light of a November morning later in the week, nineteen-year-old Lt George Randall and twenty-one-year-old 2nd-Lt George Learmond realised not only had they survived, they now had the future to contend with. George Learmond, who served with the Highland Light Infantry before volunteering for the Royal Flying Corps, had during his service with No.20 Squadron been credited with nine enemy aircraft; all but one of these claims were made when flying as George Randall's observer. Discharged from the RAF in May 1919, George Learmond, eventually dismayed with life in 'Civvy Street', re-enlisted with the army again in 1927.

At the end of May 1919, No.20 Squadron was on the move to India; George Randall, having elected to remain with the RAF, sailed on 5 June 1919. He was soon back in action. The 'war to end all wars' may have ended in Europe but much of the world was still under arms and the third Anglo-Afghan War had started on 8 May, when Afghan forces crossed the north-west frontier of India stirring up revolt.

Records show that Flying Officer George Randall took part in the Waziristan campaign 1919–1920 in support of the Indian Army. Adjacent to the Afghanistan border, Waziristan was home to three Pathan tribes: the Wazirs, the industrious Dhaurs and the troublesome Mahsuds, who once again waged war with reckless gallantry in the mountainous terrain of their homeland.

It was anticipated by the powers that be that the aeroplane, having recently played a key role in the defeat of the Central Powers, would soon force the rebel tribesmen armed with only small arms into submission. The bombing of village mud huts by Bristol Fighters did not have the same impact as the raids on German aerodromes and railheads in France; for example, 16 tons of high explosive bombs dropped on the village of Kaniguram was out of all proportion to the little material damage caused. As soon as the aircraft had flown off, the villagers returned, quickly rebuilding and repairing their homes.

Royal Air Force co-operation with the Indian army, however, was more effective. Flying low with small bombs and machine gun fire, Bristol Fighters were able to disperse and drive attacking tribesmen to cover. On one occasion, having dropped 25lb bombs and expended their machine gun ammunition, Bristol Fighters continued flying low over the battle to prevent the enemy attack from reforming until the hard-pressed defenders had been reinforced.

Fighting on the north-west frontier of India had been fierce and bloody in the past, but in the wake of the First World War modern rifles and ammunition now equipped at least half of the warlike rebel tribesmen. Although a war-weary George Randall did not fight for his life daily against enemy aircraft as in France, flying in mountainous terrain occupied by some of the finest marksmen in the world still made every mission hazardous. Add the risk of engine failure and possible capture followed by a slow agonising death at the hands of the fierce tribesmen no doubt also played on his nervous system.

With the end of the RAF operations in Waziristan, Flying Officer George Randall returned to Britain and reported for duty to No.39 Squadron at Grantham, Lincolnshire in July 1921. By January the following year he is listed as flying officer under instruction at the Central Flying School, Upavon, but sadly on 11 February 1922 Flg-Off George Randall was admitted to hospital suffering from neurasthenia, in other words, severe nerve exhaustion and fatigue.

Discharged from hospital on 20 March as non-effective sick, twenty-three-year-old George Randall was listed in RAF records as supernumerary in May 1922 and has no service records after January 1923. The author has been unable to locate details of the civilian life of this brave young Essex man who, like so many, had fought for King and Country.

To conclude this tribute, herewith are the two citations for the Distinguished Flying Cross and Bar dedicated to George Randall that were printed in the *London Gazette* in post-war years:

Saturday 8 February 1919
RANDALL. George Ebben. Lt. RAF. 20Sqn. (France)
A brave and resourceful flight commander, who has within the last four months previous to November 11th, led 71 offensive patrols. On 10th November, engaging a superior number of enemy aircraft, he himself shot down two and the remainder were driven off by his flight. In addition to the forgoing he has four other enemy machines to his credit.

Monday 12 July 1920.
RANDALL George Ebben DFC, FO. RAF. (Waziristan).
Bar to the Distinguished Flying Cross.

The FE2b biplanes of No.22 Squadron flown by Lt John Aspinall and his observer were more formidable than they look in 1916; unfortunately they were outclassed by the new breed of German fighters the following year. This painting depicts how the observer, often straight out of the trenches, had to have a head for heights. (M. Omsted)

John Vincent Aspinall

Born in the Essex market town of Epping on 11 April 1892, John Vincent Aspinall, at twenty-two years of age, like so many of his generation in the summer of 1914 answered the call to arms, volunteering for the Army.

Having served with the Worcestershire Regiment for eighteen months, he then successfully applied for a transfer to the Royal Flying Corps. On completing his training he qualified for a pilot's brevet with RAeC No.3347 taken at Brooklands Aerodrome, Weybridge, Surrey on 10 August 1916.

Such was the demand for pilots 'Over There' that with just 20 hours' flying time recorded in his log book, Second Lieutenant John Aspinall boarded the train at Victoria Station, packed with troops returning from leave to France via Dover and then by cross channel steamer to Boulogne.

The following morning at Boulogne railway station, having sought the help of an overworked Railway Transport Officer, he caught the next train to Amiens where he was collected by a RFC driver who stowed his kit into the back of a Crossley tender for the last leg of his journey. Twenty minutes later 2nd-Lt J.V Aspinall reported for duty with No.22 Squadron RFC at Bertangles Aerodrome on the Somme.

Formed at Gosport, Hampshire, in September 1915, No.22 Squadron arrived at Vert Galant, France on the first day of April 1916, moving to Bertangles Aerodrome 5 miles north of Amiens on the 16th. The squadron was equipped with FE2b aircraft, large clumsy-looking (even in 1916) pusher machines that were fortunately far more formidable than they appeared, until outclassed by new German fighter aircraft in the spring of 1917.

The 'Fee' – as the FE2b had become known in the RFC – was a design of the Royal Aircraft Factory at Farnborough, FE standing for Fighting Experimental. New pilots, such as 2nd-Lt Aspinall posted to a Fee squadron in 1916, considered themselves more fortunate than their contemporaries flying the aeroplanes such as the BE2c machine that had the observer/gunner situated in the front cockpit behind the propeller and engine but in front of the pilot.

The BE observer, surrounded by centre section struts, had a very limited field of fire, unlike the observer in the nose of a Fee that, along with the single-seat DH2 pusher and French Nieuport Bebe arriving at the front at about the same time, were responsible for ending the superiority of the Fokker monoplane fitted with an interrupter gear allowing a machine gun to fire through the propeller.

It was the death of Lt Max Immelmann, idolised by the German public, in combat with a Fee of No.25 Squadron in June 1916 that not only heralded the end of the so-called 'Fokker scourge', it also enhanced the reputation of the Fee in the eyes of the men who flew them.

Second Lieutenant Aspinall – as did all new pilots to a front line squadron – had to prove not only to Maj. R.B. Martyn, the commanding officer, but also his fellow flying officers and, just as important, the critical ground crew who repaired the damage, that he was really capable of handling the large pusher machine. The FE2b machines John Aspinall flew in England had been fitted with a reliable 120hp Beardmore engine. The machines in No.22 Squadron had been fitted with a more powerful 160hp Beardmore engine and a modified undercart dispensing with the nose wheel on the earlier models; this alone added another 2–5mph, giving the Fee with the more powerful engine a maximum speed of over 80mph.

As a new pilot arriving from a training squadron in 'Blighty', Aspinall had to prove his ability in the air, which in truth was a far more nerve-racking experience for the observer ordered to fly with him for the first time. After being shown landmarks that would enable him to find his way back to Bertangles, the observer accompanied the new pilot the following day for an inspection of the front lines without crossing them, again carefully pointing out landmarks for future reference. At the end of day three, having practised dropping dummy bombs on a target near the aerodrome, 2nd-Lt Aspinall was ready to go to war.

Bertangles Aerodrome was located a quarter of a mile west of the village, situated 5 miles north of Amiens on the Somme. Sharing the aerodrome with No.22 Squadron were No.24 Squadron flying DH2 single-seat pusher scouts (fighters). The two squadrons were separated by a single line track of the Amiens–Doullens railway. No.24 Squadron had arrived at Bertangles in February 1916, with the distinction of being the first single-seat scout squadron of the Royal Flying Corps.

No.22 Squadron of the 3rd Wing RFC attached to the IVth Army Brigade were engaged in offensive patrols, bombing and photographic reconnaissance of the German lines opposite the IVth Army. Coinciding with the arrival of Essex airman in France, the German Imperial Air Service – in the wake of losing the earlier advantage of Fokker monoplane fighters fitted with a synchronised machine gun firing forward through the propeller – had reorganised and had begun to unleash single-seat biplanes that were armed with twin machine guns. The daily casualty lists of RFC personnel again began to lengthen.

The crew of this FE2b appears to have escaped serious injury, thanks to the impact with the trees having been absorbed by the mainplanes. The heavy rear-mounted engine was an ever present threat in any crash landing. (D. Barber)

In September, No.22 Squadron saw two Fees return badly shot up from offensive and photographic patrols on the 3rd. Four days later, damaged in combat with enemy fighters, a No.22 Squadron Fee overturned after making a forced landing, fortunately recrossing the lines first, the shaken crew escaped serious injury.

The next day, Friday 8 September, the fate dreaded by airmen on both sides of the lines befell the crew of a No.22 Squadron Fee that fell in flames. The unfortunate crew had encountered Lt Oswald Boelcke, the Fatherland's most skilful fighter pilot with twenty-one allied aeroplanes to his credit.

As a fighting squadron, No.22 provided their own escort for bombing and photographic reconnaissance, the flight commander's Fee carrying the camera, with the remainder of the flight acting as escort over the enemy lines. It was an escorting Fee that fell in flames defending the all important photographs required at all cost by Headquarters.

Low clouds and unfavourable weather for reconnaissance flights intervened for a few days from 10 September. A Fee fell behind enemy lines on Wednesday 20 September and the crew became POWs. Although a Fee observer had a good field of fire forward, to use the rear mounted Lewis gun firing back over the top wing, he had to stand on a locker with just his feet and legs from the knees down inside the nacelle. More than one Fee pilot just managed to save his observer from falling overboard during violent combat manoeuvres.

Without safety harness or parachute the Fee observer, sometimes a volunteer from the trenches without any previous flying experience, had to be a special breed of man. Such was Cpl Arthur Winterbottom of No.22 Squadron. He was on an offensive patrol with his pilot, 2nd-Lt H.J. Finer, in FE2b 4938 on the evening of Friday 22 September and had sent an enemy machine down out of control near Sailly-Saillisel, shortly before they came under attack from two hostile machines, one attacking from the rear. 2nd-Lt Finer stalled the Fee and the observer climbed on to the locker to use the rear gun; as he unclipped the Lewis he was killed by a burst from the twin machine guns of their adversary. The gun fell from his lifeless hands knocking the pilot unconscious with a blow to the head. 2nd-Lt H.J. Finer remembered nothing until he recovered consciousness after crashing behind French lines. Had the Fee hit the ground nose first the unconscious pilot would have been crushed to death by the weight of the heavy Beardmore engine behind him.

The last day of September witnessed a fortunate escape for the crew of FE2b 6931. Engaged in combat with enemy fighters over the lines, the observer Cpl F. Johnson, changing drums on the Lewis, threw the empty over the side just as the Fee banked sharply. In a split second the suction of the 9ft-diameter propeller plucked the discarded ammunition drum back into the whirling blades resulting in a fearsome bang and vibration; Canadian 2nd-Lt C.F. Duffus, usually an aggressive pilot, was forced to recross the British lines and land.

In October 1916, no doubt due to bad weather, No.22 Squadron suffered no losses due to enemy action, until Sunday 22 when 2nd-Lt Alexander Cropper was severely wounded in a fight with three enemy scouts. He remained conscious long enough to land 6963 and get his observer Capt. R.H. Rushby back to Bertangles before dying of his wounds.

The previous day, Saturday 21st, RFC communiqués noted that: 'The activities of hostile aircraft were somewhat above normal on the IVth Army front', when 2nd-Lt Aspinall and his observer 2nd-Lt W.M. Taylor, in Fee 7012, carrying out an afternoon offensive patrol, engaged and shot down a Fokker which fell near Beugnatre.

Unfavourable flying weather with little action reported along the front for the next few days saw a corresponding reduction in RFC casualties from 23 to 27 October. The following day just one British machine failed to return, a No.21 Squadron BE12. The pilot, 2nd-Lt Maurice Sharpe, killed in action over the enemy lines, has no known grave.

The same day, the German Air Service suffered the loss of Capt. Oswald Boelcke, their leading fighter pilot with forty aerial victories to his credit. Son of a Prussian schoolmaster, he had been idolised throughout the Fatherland. Boelcke was killed as the result of a collision with a comrade in combat with DH2s of No.24 Squadron. Among the many floral tributes and wreaths surrounding the body of Capt. Boelcke as it lay in state before the high altar in the great cathedral at Cambrai was a wreath dropped behind German lines with the message 'To the memory of Captain Boelcke, our brave and chivalrous opponent. From the English Royal Flying Corps'. There was also a wreath sent by British Officer POWs from the Interment Camp at Osnabruck, inscribed 'to a much admired and honoured enemy'. The age of chivalry was still alive in 1916 but only just.

3 November, the day of Boelcke's funeral, was a bad day for No.22 Squadron, carrying out an afternoon reconnaissance mission. A break in the weather also brought the Albatros scouts out in force. The 'Recce Fee' fell to the guns of Jasta 2 pilots. Boelcke may be dead but his legacy of hand-picked pilots for his elite Jasta fought on. Capt. Auberon T.H. Lucas, the 8th Baron Lucas, pilot of the 'Recce' machine 7026, died of his wounds; Lt Anderson his observer, suffering injuries in the crash, survived as a POW.

Two of the escorting Fees also fell behind enemy lines: 5250 with mortally wounded Capt. Alan J.M. Pemberton who managed to land his observer L/Cpl Cook without injury; the crew of 6374, the second escort machine 6374, shared mixed fortune – the large bulk of the Beardmore engine at their backs shielded them from a hail of bullets, but a very strong wind blowing from the west forced 2nd-Lt W. Knowlden to land with his observer 2nd-Lt B. Ordish into captivity.

A Fee from No.18 Squadron had been lost earlier in the day – it was the seventh victory of an up-and-coming protégé of Boelcke, an ex-cavalry officer by the name of Manfred von Richthofen. The same afternoon the young pilot, in his best uniform, was designated to carry the *Ordenkissen* displaying his late commanding officer Oswald Boelcke's medals in the funeral procession.

Having survived the first crucial weeks as a new pilot at the front, 2nd-Lt Aspinall was now a seasoned veteran ready for anything, except the intense cold experienced by the aircrews of pusher machines as the cruel winter began to bite. The CO of No.24 Squadron sharing Bertangles Aerodrome, Maj. Lanoe G. Hawker VC, a pre-war aviator had, after consultation with Harrods, designed thigh-length fur-lined flying boots, which were marketed by Harrods under the trade name of 'The Charfor Boot'. Later, when issued to the RFC, they rejoiced in the name of 'Fug Boots' and were much appreciated.

As the battle along the Somme front slowed, bogged down in mud sludged by snow blizzards, 22 Squadron made use of any break in the weather to carry out reconnaissance flights. On Friday 17 November, Fee 6950 escorting a photographic machine was forced to land near Pozieres with both pilot, 2nd-Lt M. Helliwell, and observer, Pte F. Cox, wounded after being badly shot about by enemy fighters.

An Albatros DI was sent down out of control over Bancourt by Fee 7706 flown by 2nd-Lt N.H. Tolhurst and his observer Cpl F. Johnson on Wednesday 22 November. Sgt Frank Johnson DCM survived his tour of duty as an observer with No.22 Squadron and returned to England to train as a pilot. At the end of the war he had been credited with sixteen enemy aircraft and was awarded a Bar to his DCM in September 1918, a unique award in the RAF for a non-commissioned pilot.

On Thursday 23 November 1916, a patrol of DH2 pushers of No.24 Squadron left Bertangles at 1300hrs accompanied by Maj. Hawker VC. It would be the last flight of their CO who fell behind German lines during a desperate battle with Jasta 2. The odds had been stacked too high against the gallant airman, although his victor 2nd-Lt von Richthofen later had the single Lewis gun retrieved and the serial number cut from the fabric of Hawker's machine hanging as a mementos on his bedroom wall in the family home. Maj. Lanoe George Hawker VC, DSO has no known grave.

Fog grounded No.22 Squadron from 28 November until 4 December, when the morning patrol once again trailed their coats over the enemy lines inviting the Albatros pilots to give battle. 2nd-Lt Carlton Clement, a Canadian pilot, and observer 2nd-Lt J.K. Cambell in Fee 7703 sent an enemy machine down out of control. Five minutes later another Albatros fell to the guns of Capt. Chester Duffus and observer 2nd-Lt G.O. McEntee in 4883. The German pilot gave as good as he had received in the fight and Capt. Duffus was forced to land, fortunately behind British lines near Bapaume.

Capt. Duffus and observer 2nd-Lt McEntee were in action again near Bapaume on 11 December, shooting down an enemy observation machine that fell in flames. Continuing spells of bad flying weather hindered the RFC and although a very successful reconnaissance flight was carried out by the squadron on the 20th, it was not until 27 December that 2nd-Lt Aspinall and his observer 2nd-Lt J. Miller forced down another enemy machine, but it could not be added to the squadron tally as the Albatros scout landed in a field west of Ruyaulcourt behind enemy lines and therefore could not be counted as out of control or destroyed.

January 1917 brought a change of command for No.22 Squadron; Maj. Leonard Learmount replaced the capable Maj. Martyn, and a change of aerodromes when they moved closer to the front on 26th. Chipilly Aerodrome had been recently taken over from the French Air Service; the hutted accommodation provided better conditions for the other ranks.

Although the ground crews did not suffer the rigours of winter flying, the exposed bitter windswept airfield brought additional hazards. Apart from the obvious dangers of slipping on frozen ground swinging the 9ft-diameter wooden propeller by hand to start the water cooled Beardmore, the radiator had to be drained overnight. To start the engine the next morning, water was boiled in drums heated over a petrol fire in a small trench as close to the machine as possible; clambering about on wooden steps with buckets of boiling water to refill the radiator some 9ft above the snow and ice also had its share of risks.

Due to the frozen ground, wooden tail skids were easily damaged and became an urgent problem for the lack of replacements in Fee squadrons along the Western Front for several weeks.

On Sunday 28 January 2nd-Lt Aspinall and 2nd-Lt J.M. Miller in Fee 7681 claimed an Albatros scout shot down over Villers-au-Flos; it was also seen by other members of the flight to crash between Barastre and Bus. No.22 Squadron FE2b pushers were in the parlance of the times, 'keeping their tails up'; their casualties had been less than other front line pusher squadrons at this period. 2nd-Lt Geoffrey Hopkins, who survived the war, recalled, 'Our strength lay in our good formation flying, by which we were able to bring concentrated fire on attacking HA, so the Hun continued to treat FE2b formations with respect.'

The RFC had adopted the word 'Hun' not only for the enemy airmen, but also RFC personnel undergoing flight training, from the early days of the war when the Kaiser boasted to the world that his army would be feared as were the 'Huns' of old. In recent years young historians have queried the use of the word 'Hun', perhaps not being familiar with the British sense of humour during wartime!

Aspinall and Miller were again escorting a 'photo bus' on 2 February when, fighting off the Hun scouts, Fee 7711 was badly damaged and Miller wounded. They just escaped capture by clearing the front lines before crash landing.

Two days later while leading B Flight on an offensive patrol over the lines, Capt. H.R Hawkins and observer Sgt Frank Johnson in Fee 7697 took on three Albatros scouts above Haplincourt, claiming one DII destroyed. Capt. C.M Clement and observer Lt M.K Parlee in Fee A5461 were also attacked by three Albatros DIIs. One Hun hit in the engine by a burst from the observer's Lewis gun was seen gliding down under control with an idle propeller. The second Albatros engaged by Hawkins and Parlee crashed at Rocquigny, probably a Jasta 2 machine.

No.22 Squadron Fees were now engaged in daily photographic reconnaissance as the High Command were aware the Germans were up to something, winter or not. There were almost two empty chairs in the Mess on the evening of Tuesday 6 February when the crew of Fee 4971 were badly shot about defending a 'photo bus' from enemy fighters. Although wounded, the pilot Lt W.N McDonald managed to re-cross the lines to crash land near Eaucourt L'abbaye, his observer uninjured, and returned to the squadron.

RFC communiqué No.74 states, 'From the 4th to the 10th [February] inclusive 2643 [aerial reconnaissance] photographs were taken', as the British High Command sought to uncover what was going on on the other side of the lines. No.22 Squadron's daily photo recces gave them the answer at the end of February 1917. The German Army were preparing to retire from the Noyon Salient, their plan Operation Alberich had actually begun on 4 February and when complete would shorten the German front line by 25 to 30 miles, releasing thirteen Divisions into reserve and much-needed respite, behind the secretly prepared, well-fortified Hindenburg Line.

Intermittent spells of bad flying weather restricting reconnaissance flights favoured the continued German withdrawal during early March. The German Air Service did its best to put out the prying eyes of the RFC. Two No.22 Squadron Fees on line patrol were written off on Sunday 4 March. A5441 was set on fire during a battle with enemy scouts. The crew, 2nd-Lt L.W Beal and AM F.G. Davin, fought the flames with extinguishers but crashed on landing, both escaping serious injuries. 2nd-Lt E.A Mearns and Lt H. Loveland were also fortunate to escape injury crash-landing with a dead engine after being shot up from behind, the large bulk of the Beardmore engine shielding the crew from the hail of bullets.

Second Lieutenant Leslie Beal from north London had another narrow escape the following week when carrying out an offensive patrol – Fee 7685 fell to the guns of 2nd-Lt Werner Voss of Jasta 2. During the fight AM Davin had been severely wounded in the thigh; the pilot, with a dead engine and all but the elevator controls out of action, closely escorted by another Fee also badly shot up, managed to cross the lines before crashing. When the rescue party arrived to salvage the remains of 7685, they found Beal in a state of shock with bullet holes through the sides of his 'Fug' boots and sleeves of his heavy leather flying coat.

Apart from 7685, the squadron almost had another Fee struck off strength on 11 March but 2nd-Lt J.F Day, wounded in a scrap with an enemy two-seater, returned A5454 to Chipilly Aerodrome with his more seriously wounded observer.

Air Mechanic C. Belton, flying as observer with 2nd-Lt E. Mearns in A5459, became the next casualty when wounded in action with Albatros 'Vee strutters' on 15 March. The sesquiplane Albatros DIII, nicknamed 'Vee strutter' by the RFC, were replacing the formidable constant chord winged Albatros DII in the front line Jastas, that already outclassed the FE and BE machines of the Royal Flying Corps.

Enemy aircraft and unreliable engines were not the only hazards faced by No.22 Squadron over the enemy lines. On 16 March another observer, 2nd-Lt T.G Fawcett, watched the rear for enemy fighters as 2nd-Lt Hopkins was engaged in keeping the Fee on a straight and level course as the semi automatic camera attached to the side of cockpit exposed eighteen overlapping plates. German anti-aircraft gunners, known as 'Archie' in the RFC, quickly found the range of the English flyers. A steel splinter from a shell bursting less that 20 yards away hit the observer a glancing blow on the hand, but fortunately Fawcett, because of the intense cold, had worn three pairs of gloves and the wound only put him out of action for a few days.

Given the advantage of the Albatros DIII, many German pilots were to become aces during the next few weeks, among them 2nd-Lt Heinrich Gontermann of Jasta 5, who claimed a 'Lattice Tail' – as the obsolete pusher aircraft flown by the Allies were now known – for his fourth victory on 17 March. By the end of April he would be credited with seventeen victories including six observation balloons; fighter pilots of his calibre with the Albatros V strutter were increasingly crossing the lines to attack allied balloons. Gontermann's fourth 'Lattice Tail' had fallen behind British lines. No.22 Squadron had to write off 4900 and both the crew, 2nd-Lt F.R. Hudson and AM W. Richman, had been wounded.

The daily demand for photographic reconnaissance brought about another casualty for No.22 Squadron on 24 March, when Capt. W.E Salter was forced to land 4986 with a wounded observer 2nd-Lt E.D Galley.

Experience gained during the air battles fought in March would stand 2nd-Lt Aspinall in good stead to contend with what would be remembered as the 'Bloody April' of the first war in the air. The first No.22 Squadron loss during this period took place on the morning of Monday 2 April. Five Fees had left Chipilly at 0630hrs on a photographic reconnaissance, but one of the two Fees carrying cameras developed engine trouble and was forced to return. The remaining 'Photo Bus' with a close escort of three Fees, including Aspinall, droned on towards their objective to find Jasta 5 waiting for them. The remaining camera 'bus' 6953, in spite of the timely arrival of a flight of No.24 Squadron scouts, fell in flames on Gouzeaucourt Wood. 2nd-Lt Patrick Russell and Lt Henry Loveland were later confirmed killed in action.

The crew of A5486, 2nd-Lt G. Hopkins and AM H. Friend, escaped serious injury when, as the last machine on an offensive patrol the following afternoon, they were fired upon at long range by a V strutter. Hit in the fuel tank, they just cleared the front lines, landing with a dead engine. As they were helped away to the comparative safety of a 'dugout', the wrecked Fee came under fire from German artillery. 'Bert' Friend, a Londoner, was just one of the many unsung non-commissioned heroes who flew as observers with the RFC. He was also one of the many casualties due to the no parachute policy for allied aircrew during the First World War. AM Herbert Friend and AM Charles Loveland were the observers of two Bristol Fighters of No.22 Squadron that collided during an offensive patrol over the enemy lines on Friday 21 September 1917. Their pilots 2nd-Lt Sidney Spurway and 2nd-Lt Archibald Gilbert were also killed.

Bad weather, including a snow storm, curtailed aerial fighting on 4 April. Unfortunately, improved weather the next day brought with it a serious blow to the hard-pressed Fee squadrons waiting to be re-equipped with the promising new Bristol Fighter that had recently arrived on the western front with No.48 Squadron. Two out of a six-strong offensive patrol of Bristol Fighters that crossed the lines on the morning of Thursday 5 April 1917 returned to Bellevue Aerodrome after a scrap with four V strutters of Jasta 2; the remainder had fallen behind enemy lines.

It was business as usual for 2nd-Lt Aspinall and his Flight on Good Friday, 6 April; they were credited with the destruction of a V strutter in fighting over St Quentin and another Hun driven down near Fontaine Uterte.

Close formation defensive flying by No.22 Squadron crews paid off again for Aspinall and his observer 2nd-Lt M.K.Parlee when their Flight shared another V strutter destroyed in action over Regny and two others driven down.

Luck had been on the side of No.22 Squadron pilots now carrying out daily bombing raids as part of the planned 'New Push' due to begin on 9 April at Arras. Although No.22 Squadron were south of Arras, the bombing raids were intended to disrupt enemy communications and keep them guessing as to where along the front the attack would take place.

The six 20lb Cooper bombs carried on these raids had to be dropped from below 6,000ft to obtain some accuracy with the small missiles that were more suited for low-level trench strafing. As with photographic reconnaissance at this altitude the Fees were vulnerable to both Archie and Huns diving out of the sun. Sopwith Pups of No.54 Squadron provided escort for the Fees on the bombing raids, but the pilots of these nimble lightweight single-seat scouts preferred to fight at a higher level where they could meet the faster, heavier Albatros V strutters with twice the fire power on more equal terms.

2nd-Lt Aspinall and 2nd-Lt Parlee claimed another Albatros DIII destroyed and No.54 Squadron pilots claimed two out of control when returning from a bombing raid on Friday 13 April. During 'Bloody April' No.22 Squadron suffered the loss of twelve aircrew killed, wounded or POW.

Good fortune in the form of a posting to Home Establishment ensured John Aspinall survived his tour of duty as a Fee pilot over the Western Front in the spring of 1917. During 'Bloody April' alone, the eight RFC squadrons in France equipped with FE2 pusher biplanes lost no less than fifty-eight machines due to enemy action. Only the unfortunate fifteen BE2 equipped squadrons fared worse than the pushers, with the loss of seventy-five aircraft.

Captain J.V. Aspinall returned to France in the spring of 1918 to serve with No.11 Squadron as a flight commander. No.11 Squadron had exchanged their obsolete FE2b pushers for Bristol Fighters during June the previous year. The Bristol F2b Fighter biplanes powered by Rolls Royce Falcon engines from 230 to 285hp were greatly improved versions of the earlier F2a that made a disastrous debut during 'Bloody April' 1917. As a Bristol Fighter pilot, Capt. Aspinall now had a belt-fed Vickers machine gun synchronised to fire 800 rounds per minute through the propeller arc in front of him. The observer still had the lighter Lewis gun as used on the Fee pusher, or if he were strong enough to handle them in the slipstream, twin-yoked Lewis guns known as 'Huntley and Palmers' after a well-known biscuit manufacturer, and thanks to the excellent Scarff Ring mounting surrounding the observer's cockpit a 360 degree field of fire.

Unlike the obsolete Fee pushers Aspinall had fought in in the previous year, the Bristol Fighter was not vulnerable if the formation became split up; it matched enemy fighters in performance and had a sting in the tail. Prior to Aspinall joining No.11 Squadron, a Canadian pilot, Capt. Andrew McKeever DSO, MC and Bar, had become the chief exponent of the Bristol Fighter, credited with thirty-one enemy aircraft, many of them falling to his forward firing Vickers gun in six action-filled months from June to November 1917. His record would not be surpassed by two-seater pilots for the remainder of the war.

Although an experienced air fighter credited with five enemy aircraft, on his return to France Capt. Aspinall found the war in the air had intensified with larger groups of aggressive enemy machines waiting for the daily offensive patrols. The Essex airman at the controls of C4882 led his Flight over the enemy lines for the last time on the evening of Wednesday 15 May 1918. Deep inside enemy territory the Flight, having sent a large two-seater down out of control east of Cambrai, he then took on a mixed bag of Pfalz DIII and Fokker Triplanes from Jastas 5 and 6 that managed to break the British formation into individual dogfights.

During the encounter the flight commander and his observer, 2nd-Lt Paul Delacour, a South African, were seen to shoot down one of the Fokker Triplanes and Lt Joseph Seabrook and 2nd-Lt C. Wrigglesworth in C867 claimed a Pfalz shot down out of control.

Two Bristol Fighters failed to return to Remaisnil Aerodrome that evening and had to be reported as missing in action. C845 with Lt Herbert Sellars and Lt C. Robson and C4882 with Capt. Aspinall and 2nd-Lt Delacour had been shot down in the fierce fighting. Lt Robson fortunately survived the crash to be taken prisoner; Aspinall, Delacour and Sellars died of their wounds and are among the British and Commonwealth airmen listed on the Arras Memorial in France that is dedicated to those killed in action with no known grave.

Horace Martin Capon Ledger

Martin, as he was known to family and friends, was the eldest son of Horace and Kathleen Ledger, tenants of Warren Farm, Faulkbourne, Witham, Essex. Martin had an elder sister named Gertrude and three younger brothers, Philip, Ernest and Douglas. Unlike his father, Martin did not choose to become a farmer, or banker like his paternal grandfather.

Horace Martin Capon Ledger, who flew numerous aerial reconnaissance missions as an observer with French seaplane pilots of the Port Said Squadron in the Eastern Mediterranean, until killed in action on 22 December 1915. (K. Feline)

At the outbreak of the First World War, Martin was surveying in Ceylon, where he had married Ellinor on 14 October 1909 in St Peter's church, Colombo. The couple were living in Ramboda until 1914, when Martin, then thirty years of age, volunteered for the Indian Army Reserve for the duration of the war, and Ellinor returned home to England. Due to events unfolding in the Middle East, Ellinor would never see her husband again in her lifetime.

England and France declared war on the Turkish Empire on 5 November 1914, after Turkey had entered the war against her old enemy, Russia, as an ally of Germany and the Austro-Hungarian Empire two days earlier. Russia was now isolated from her French and British Allies in the west during the winter months, when her northern ports were icebound and access to her southern ports in the Black Sea via the Turkish Dardanelles now denied to the Allies.

Alarm bells were also rung at the War Office when it was discovered that large formations of Turkish troops were forming around Damascus, Jaffa and Akaba to attack the Suez Canal, cutting Britain's lifelines to India, Australia, New Zealand and the Far East.

An experienced surveyor in peace time, Second Lieutenant H.M.C. Ledger, now serving with the 27th Punjabis of the Indian Expeditionary Force, arrived in Egypt where he would be attached to the British Army Cartographic Service, specialists in the Sinai region then under the control of the Turkish Army that posed a threat to Port Said and Suez at the head and tail of the vital Canal. Even at this early stage of the conflict, it had been realised aerial reconnaissance would play a vital role over such a vast area. The four Farman box kite pusher aircraft of the Royal Flying Corps based at Ismalia did not have the range to carry out complete surveillance of Badiet et-Tih, the 'Desert of the Lost', but help was at hand from the L'Aviation Maritime Francaise.

The British Naval Attaché in Paris requested the loan of French seaplanes and aviators based at Bizerte in Tunisia for the purpose of 'surveillance of the Dardanelles, where the German cruisers *Goeben* and *Breslau* have found refuge' or 'for the defence of the Suez Canal'. With full approval of the French Admiralty, the seaplane carrier *Foudre* docked at Port Said on Monday 30 November 1914 to unload the first detachment of French Naval personnel along with crates containing Nieuport VI, single engined seaplanes, the following morning. This detachment would be placed under the command of the British High Command in Egypt to become known as 'The Port-Said Squadron', the first French Naval Aviation Squadron formed during the First World War.

Within days the first contingent of seven aviators with thirty-eight ground crew, assisted by native labour, erected five Bessonneau hangers and assembled five Nieuport VI 80hp seaplanes ready for action. A seaplane with a French crew flying from Port Said first came under fire on Saturday 5 December while carrying out a patrol over enemy territory east of Suez.

Two Royal Navy cruisers HMS *Doris* and *Minerva* were placed at the disposal of the 'Port Said Squadron' as seaplane carriers. British Intelligence officers with knowledge of the Sinai area were attached to the squadron to fly with the French aviators as observers.

In the harbour at Port Said were two German freighters that had been seized at the start of the war. The 5,000-ton *Aenne Rickmers* and *Rabenfels* were now flying the 'Red Duster' of the Merchant Navy; these were pressed into service as seaplane carriers with no modifications or armament added, their purpose to increase the eyes of the British Forces in the Eastern Mediterranean.

Captain Lewne B. Weldon, Dublin Fusiliers, came aboard HMFA *Aenne Rickmers* as officer in charge of reconnaissance operations along the coast of the Sinai Peninsula, a command he was well suited for having previously served fourteen years with the Egyptian Survey Department. He also had responsibility for landing allied agents along the enemy-held coast. Records show the reconnaissance flights of the Nieuport seaplanes from *Aenne* and *Rabenfels* during January 1915 were responsible for locating the strength and positions of the advancing Turkish armies.

The Anglo-French airmen arrangement worked very well; it was not, however, just the aerial reconnaissance reports of enemy troop movement taking place up to 50 miles from the coast, there was an occasional bombing with converted French artillery shells dropped through a tube clearing the struts and bracing wires of the floats. These 20lb missiles caused great panic among Arab caravans transporting for the Turkish Army. Flechettes, wicked-looking steel darts, were also dropped on the enemy in batches of 100. They had been used in France, but were found to be far too inaccurate and of little use when dropped over well-dispersed targets.

The pre-war Nieuport seaplanes had not been designed with folding wings for stowing on board ship and, with their 47ft wingspan, only two machines could be carried on the already cluttered decks of the freighters, protected from the elements by canvas screens. They were lowered over the side for take-off and recovered after alighting and taxiing back alongside, complete with their two-man crew, by the ship's wooden cargo booms.

As seaplane carriers, the ex-German freighters were primitive even by early 1915 standards, but the excellent work they carried out with French Naval airmen and British Army observers enabled the Anglo-Indian forces to successfully defeat the Turkish attempt to take control of or block the Suez Canal in 1915.

A Nieuport VI seaplane and crew of the Port Said Squadron about to be hoisted back on board HMS *Anne* after a mission. (JMB/GSL Collection)

Considering the inhospitable terrain of the campaign and the extreme heat during the hours of daylight, the 'Port Said Squadron' suffered few fatal casualties. French pilot QM Hervé Grall and Capt. F. Stirling with the cruiser *Minerva*, operating in the Gulf of Akaba on Thursday 31 December 1914, were very fortunate to escape after their Nieuport seaplane developed engine trouble and crash-landed about 30 miles from the coast. Both men were injured. As the Frenchman was unable to walk, the British officer handed over his water bottle and set off alone for help. Nine hours later an exhausted Capt. Stirling was back on board the *Minerva* and an armed party set off to rescue the stranded pilot. Having marched to the crash site as indicated by Stirling, an extensive search was carried out but there was no trace of the Frenchman to be found.

During the previous day Grall, having partially recovered from his injuries, set out on the long walk to the coast and had actually hidden from the 200 strong rescue party along the way, thinking they were Turkish troops. During the early hours of Saturday 2 January, the vigilant crew of the *Minerva* manning searchlights sweeping the beach picked out the sorry-looking figure of QM Grall just in time as he was suffering from dehydration and completely exhausted. The gallant French aviator lived to fly another day with the the 'Port Said Squadron', and among his observers would be 2nd-Lt Ledger whose life he would save the following December.

The second seaplane crew, QM Jean-Marie LeGall and 2nd-Lt Basil Partridge, forced down in enemy territory on Wednesday 27 January, were not so fortunate; they evaded capture to reach the British lines in the early hours of the following morning. When challenged with 'Halt! who goes there?' they were unable to give the correct password and were both shot at and killed by Gurkha sentries.

Martin Ledger first flew as observer with a French aviator from the armed merchant cruiser RIMS *Hardinge* in the Red Sea, but it was with the ex-German freighters *Aenne Rickmers* and *Rabenfels* in the Mediterranean that he carried out the majority of his flights with the 'Port Said Squadron'. A French aviator who thought highly of Martin Ledger as an observer was Ensign de Vaisseau Louis Barthelemy-de saizieu.

Throughout 1915, the 'Port Said Squadron', operating from the ex-German freighter HMS *Hardinge* and the light cruiser HMS *Doris*, were a thorn in the side of the Turkish Empire.

The career of HMFA *Aenne Rickmers* as a seaplane carrier almost ended on the night of Thursday 11 March 1915 whilst operating in the Bay of Smyrna with a mixed crew of Greek officers, seamen, British officers, plus a handful of Royal Marines, French Naval Aviation personnel and British Intelligence officers.

Torpedoed under cover of darkness by the Turkish TBD *Demir Hisar*, the Greek crew members took to the lifeboats and refused to come back on board! Fortunately the seaplane carrier still had holds full of German timber as cargo and remained afloat, eventually limping into the Royal Naval Base at Mudros on the Greek Island of Lemmos and beached waiting for emergency repairs to be carried out.

HMFA *Rabenfels* steamed into Mudros harbour on 19 March to take over the two seaplanes from the damaged *Aenne* now under orders to proceed to Alexandria for extensive repairs to be carried out in dry dock, not returning to Port Said until 1 July. Due to the poor showing of the civilian seamen on board the torpedoed *Aenne*, the *Rabenfels* had been commissioned into the Royal Navy as HMS *Raven II* in June with an all-RN crew. In August, after repairs had been carried out, *Aenne* became HMS *Anne*. Both seaplane carriers were now armed with a deck gun firing 12lb shells.

Not all of the reconnaissance flights carried out by Martin were from seaplane carriers. One of the most memorable took place on Wednesday 21 April with QM Hervé Grall at the controls of the Nieuport VI taking off from Port Said for a coastal patrol at 1000hrs. All went well for half an hour until engine failure caused them to alight on the sea and be carried by wind and tide for 5 hours until finally they were washed ashore 40 miles behind enemy lines.

Back at Port Said a second Nieuport seaplane set out during the afternoon following their planned route in search of the missing aviators. The Suez Canal Co. tug, the *Hardi* also set out to search the coast. Martin and Grall were walking along the beach towards the British lines (did they know the password?), when they spotted the *Hardi* looking for their machine and realised the best chance of escape was to return to the beached seaplane whose clear doped linen fabric was certain to be seen by the crew of the *Hardi*. In the meantime, the searching seaplane had run low on fuel and returned to Port Said without a sighting.

Jogging back down the beach they surprised three armed Arabs inspecting the seaplane, and although both Martin and he were unarmed, Grall brandished his water bottle like a revolver! Two of the Arabs ran off and the third, in fear of a weapon he had never seen before, raised his hands and surrendered. The search for the missing aviators was called off when the *Hardi* returned with Grall and Martin safe and sound to Port Said just before midnight.

Towards the end of May 1915 Martin received bad news from home – his brother Douglas, seven years his junior, serving with the Essex Yeomanry in France had been killed in action on the Frenzenberg Ridge on the 13th.

Martin Ledger was on board *Raven II* when she sailed out of Port Said at dawn on Tuesday 29 June, bound for El Arish, 80 miles along the coast. Nieuport seaplane N17, with the aristocratic French pilot Baron Louis Barthelemy-de saizieu and Martin Ledger, was lowered over the side, taking to the air at 1630hrs. Their orders were to reconnoitre the town of El-Arish. Martin estimated that there were not more than 500 enemy troops in and around the town, and before they left two bombs were dropped on fortifications along the sea front. Returning to *Raven II* at 1820hrs they found two crew members suffering from sunstroke.

Accompanied by the French cruiser *D'Entrecastaeux*, the seaplane carrier proceeded north towards Gaza. The next morning N17, with de Saizieu and Martin on board, was hoisted over the side, taking off at 0940hrs to check the progress of the railhead under construction at Ramleh.

The 80hp – and later 100hp – rotary engines of the Nieuport VI gave a top speed of 65mph. It was due to the well-designed, streamlined, three-stepped floats that it was able to unstick with a crew of two and loaded with bombs or bundles of propaganda leaflets, and later, in 1916, the weighty efficient Crouzet wireless set. As reliable as the air-cooled Gnome rotary engines were for the period, the extreme temperatures caused many engine failures such as the one that forced the crew of N17 above Akir who fortunately had enough height to reach the sea and be hoisted back on board at 1045hrs. A rough sea prevented another attempt by de Saizieu and Martin in N19 to reconnoitre the railhead at Ramleh during the afternoon; after several attempts to take off they were hoisted back on board.

Captain Louis Barthelemy-de saizieu of
L'Aviation Maritime Française, the pilot
who fought hand to hand with the Arabs
that killed his observer Lt Martin Ledger.
(K. Feline)

Cruising along the coast, *Raven II* took part in cloak-and-dagger missions. It was not until the morning of 6 July that the sea was calm enough for de Saizieu and Martin in N19 to be hoisted over the side – at 0700hrs – for a reconnaissance flight, during which they were to drop leaflets over Beirut. Shortly after crossing the coastline, de Saizieu's experienced ear detected all was not well with the rotary and indicated to Martin his concern and intention of returning. They touched down alongside *Raven II* at 0745hrs.

The following morning de Saizieu and Martin made another attempt, taking off in N17 at 0800hrs. The overhauled Gnome rotary ran well and they flew over Beirut at 4,200ft dropping leaflets. During the flight Martin had seen little to report when they arrived back on board at 0940hrs.

Thursday 8 July, N17 with de Saizieu and Martin on board set out at 0700hrs to reconnoitre Gaza and the railhead at Ramleh. Flying at 2,700ft, Martin found the railway had been extended by 2 miles with about 5,000 troops and labourers engaged in the construction work. On the return flight, they were fired upon as they came into range from four large army encampments and Martin was back on board making his report at 1015hrs.

Martin and his pilot carried out another reconnaissance of the railhead at Ramleh the following morning. Taking off at 0825hrs in N17, they climbed to 4,000ft and dropped propaganda leaflets in their wake as they flew over Jaffa. Above Ramleh, Martin made notes of three new camps that had been erected since the day before. After recovering N17 and her crew at 1100hrs, *Raven II* set course for Port Said.

On Monday 16 August, Martin and de Saizieu were back on board *Raven II* steaming out of Port Said to rendezvous with her sister ship *Anne* and the French cruiser *Jeanne D'Arc* in the Gulf of Alexandretta on the 18th. A severe thunderstorm put an end to the planned bombing of an important railway bridge at Chicaldere by the combined force of the two carrier's four seaplanes.

Weather again hampered operations when on 19 August, Adana and Tarsus were the proposed targets of the seaplane carriers off the coast of Anatolia. Thick mist inland forced de Saizieu and Martin in N17 and the crew of N14 to return to *Raven II*. The intrepid aviator, Hervé Grall, who had escaped near death when rescued by HMS *Minerva* the previous January, had been lowered over the side of *Anne* with Maj. H. Fletcher and carried on in N11 regardless of the mist to drop bombs on both Adana and Tarsus railway stations. N20, the second of *Anne*'s seaplanes, was unable to take off with a bomb load and had to be hoisted back on board. Taking off again without bombs, N20 was able to carry out a photo reconnaissance of Adana railway station.

Another attempt by the seaplanes of *Raven II* to bomb the railway stations during the afternoon had to be abandoned as both N17 and N14 suffered broken float struts attempting take-off, and were hoisted back on board, where it was found the engine bearers of N14 were also strained putting the Nieuport out of action for the rest of the operation.

A planned raid by the remaining three seaplanes on 20 August had to be cancelled when N20 from *Anne* again refused to unstick with two bombs on board for the lack of wind! Dense low cloud over the hills between the coast and the targets forced the remaining two seaplanes to return to their carriers.

Heading back along the coast during the afternoon, the three seaplanes were again lowered over the side for another crack at Chicaldere Railway Bridge. N11 taking off at 1500hrs struck first, exchanging two bombs that missed for several bullet holes in the wing fabric. N20 had managed to get airborne on this occasion but returned to *Anne* 20 minutes later with engine trouble. N17 from *Raven II* again crewed by de Saizieu and Martin also bombed the railway bridge without visible results and within an hour of touching down alongside *Raven II* the three ships were steaming south, *Anne* heading for Beirut and *Raven II* Jaffa before returning to Port Said.

Martin next had a tour of duty on board HMS *Anne* where he was amused to find a large portrait of Aenne Rickmers still hanging in the ward room: the ex-German freighter had been named after the daughter of the original owner. Perhaps as the *Aenne* had already survived being torpedoed before commissioned into the RN, it was retained for good luck; the fact that Aenne was a young woman had nothing to do with it.

Again teamed with de Saizieu, Martin sailed out of Port Said with HMS *Anne* on Saturday 9 October for operations off the coast at Wadi Gaza.

The now venerable N17, with de Saizieu and Martin, was hoisted out from the *Anne* at 1400hrs on the 10th and set off on a rescue mission. N14, crewed by QM Trouillet and Lt R.J. Paul, that had taken off on a reconnaissance flight to Beersheba at 1000hrs had failed to return. Although the search failed to locate the missing N14, on route to Beersheba Martin made notes of the railway from Tel El Sharieh, many store dumps, an elaborate trench system and a cavalry unit.

Luck had run out for the crew of N14 forced to land with engine trouble near Beersheba. Stunned by the crash landing, neither Trouillet nor Paul were injured apart from their dignity when they were dragged from the machine by Arabs who stripped them of their clothing, boots and the few personal items they carried. The timely arrival of the cavalry, albeit Turkish, saved the day and no doubt their lives. Thanks to the officer in charge, most of their belongings were recovered before they were led off into captivity.

The following morning low clouds prevented the crew of N17 carrying out a reconnaissance of the railway at Tel El Sharieh and a further two attempts during the afternoon were thwarted by rough seas and a damaged propeller. Returning to Wadi Gaza, *Anne* maintained an all-night vigil looking for the red distress flares that were carried on board the missing N14.

Rough seas on the 12th again prevented the 100hp Gnome rotary powered N17 getting airborne. After dark the crew of *Anne* resumed their all-night vigil along the coast of Wadi Gaza, in a vain search for the red glow of a flare. Choppy conditions again prevented use of the seaplane during daylight and *Anne* was ordered to Ruad Island, arriving at dawn on 14 October.

Although occupied by French forces, the island was vulnerable to attack from the mainland. N17 carried out reconnaissance flights over the Tarus area, but de Saizieu and Martin found no indication of enemy troops massing. Sailing from Ruad the same evening, *Anne* rendezvoused with the French cruiser *Dupleix* south of Jaffa the following morning.

The French cruiser arrived carrying a propeller for N17 as requested from Port Said by HMS *Anne*; it was fortunate as N17 would damage the last spare propeller attempting to take off during the day. The reconnaissance flights planned for the area were abandoned on the 16th after the long-suffering float struts of N17 collapsed after a bolt sheared its head. *Anne* returned to Port Said under orders to collect replacement seaplanes at midnight.

Martin was back on board *Anne* within 72 hours and not only did he have a replacement aircraft, he would now fly as observer with Lt Marcel-Antoine Destrem sporting a beard at the controls of N20. Their first mission on the afternoon of Thursday 21 October began with a successful take-off; however, it took the Nieuport over 40 minutes to gain enough height to fly over land high enough to be reasonably safe from small arms fire. Heading towards their objective, the railway at Kheima, the Gnome rotary began to misfire and Destrem prudently returned to *Anne* for the night.

As dawn broke on the 22nd, *Anne* again approached the coast. This time it was the turn of QM Bourgeois and Maj. Fletcher, flying N19, to carry out a reconnaissance of Ramleh railway station. Destrem and Martin set out in N20 – Kheima Railway again the object of the exercise – suffering the same engine problems they had encountered on the 21st they returned to *Anne*.

On their third attempt to carry out this important reconnaissance, Destrem and Martin changed to the more reliable N19 on the 23rd and followed the railway line to within 6 miles of Beersheba before Destrem detected a fault with the oil pump and turned back towards the coast. Airborne for over 2 hours, N19 landed alongside the seaplane carrier that had steamed southwards down the coast to meet them. With both seaplanes unserviceable, *Anne* returned to Port Said on the evening of Saturday 24 October.

Martin does appear to have been in his element flying as an observer in the cramped front cockpit of the Nieuport VI. He was mentioned in the Orders of the Day, issued by Admiral Moreau commanding the 'Nieuport Squadron' at Port Said, on 28 October 1915:

> An excellent aeroplane observer, has furnished extremely valuable information in the course of his numerous flights carried out in enemy country and frequently under dangerous conditions.

Martin's reconnaissance flights also received congratulations from Lieutenant General Sir John Grenfell Maxwell, Commanding Officer during the Egyptian campaign.

HMS *Anne* sailed from Port Said again with Martin and two Nieuport seaplanes on Thursday 5 November. In spite of putting more spies ashore along the enemy-held coast and the now familiar cloak-and-dagger operations to be carried out en route, it was business as usual for the seaplane crews.

Grall and Fletcher made a thorough reconnaissance of the Beersheba area with N11 during the morning of 6th. N22, with de Saizieu, Martin and two bombs on board was hoisted out to bomb the railway and camps detected near Beersheba by the crew of N11 earlier in the day, but was forced to return after 40 minutes in the air due to engine trouble.

Fletcher flew as observer with de Saizieu in N22 for a successful reconnaissance the following morning, obtaining details of the railway line and bridges northwards from Ramleh to Tul Keram. The seaplane crew had pushed the range of their machine to the limit and were out of fuel when de Saizieu put N22 down on the sea just 3 miles from *Anne*. Due to a heavy swell, N22 suffered damage being hoisted back on board the carrier. This is no reflection on the crew who, under favourable conditions, were able to hoist the frail seaplanes over the side for take-off in just 1 minute despite the superstructure on deck. Recovering a Nieuport after landing took half a minute longer!

Monday 8 November was cloak-and-dagger time again with *Anne* steaming close inshore for an agent controlled by Capt. Weldon, the intelligence officer, to point out his lone house on the coast at Athlit during daylight. That night a completely blacked out *Anne* returned to put the spy ashore under the cover of darkness.

Steaming south, *Anne* arrived off the coast of Wadi Gaza on the 9th to bomb Beersheba but weather conditions prevented this until the 11th. In ideal flying conditions Grall and Martin took off in N11 but were forced to return within three quarters of an hour: two of the nine cylinders on their rotary engine had burnt out. A spare engine replaced the damaged one for an attempt to be made during the afternoon. On the second attempt another cylinder gave out; the following day with the defective cylinder replaced, a third attempt by N11 and crew was again thwarted when yet another cylinder burnt out.

The seaplane carrier returned to Port Said on Saturday 13 November but little is known of Martin's activities ashore. Having acclimatised to the heat during his years in Ceylon stood Martin in good stead for service in the Middle East, but the hustle and bustle of busy Port Said bore no resemblance to the village life of Faulkbourne in rural Essex where he had grown up.

December 1915 would be a fatal month for Martin. On the 4th he and QM Grall set out from Port Said on a routine patrol and were forced to land off shore through engine failure. As the stranded airmen were just 12 miles from Port Said along the coast, it was decided to swim ashore and return to base on foot as quickly as possible, as they were behind Turkish lines. Martin, not a strong swimmer, was soon in difficulty and owed what was left of his life to the stocky French aviator who came to his rescue helping him to reach dry land.

Martin was again aboard *Anne* – steaming out of Port Said on Monday 20 December – who with her escort set out on an easterly course with a mission to reconnoitre the railway line under construction at Beersheba in the Sinai Peninsular. At 0900hrs the following morning Martin and his pilot, Lt Louis de Saizieu, climbed into the cockpits of N17 and were lowered over the side for take-off.

The reconnaissance flight was to have been a routine affair for the experienced crew – the biggest danger was engine failure over the desert, but the streamlined floats fitted to the Nieuport enabled emergency landings to be made on sand. There was also of course small arms fire to contend with, but to the dashing Baron de Saizieu, a pre-war aviator, and his English observer busy with his maps and sketch book it was all in a day's work; they had been fired at on many occasions during the year.

Their orders that morning were to examine the new section of railway track from Ramleh to Beersheba and then carry out a detailed reconnaissance of the Beersheba area, a task that could be accomplished well within the 3 hours endurance of their machine.

Circling Beersheba as his observer busied himself with matters military, de Saizieu kept an eye on the engine revolution counter that had fluctuated between 1,125 to 1,950 rpm on the outward journey and was no doubt relieved when Martin, having completed his task, directed with his arm towards the coast. The sea became visible in the distance and then the waiting *Anne* and escort were also discernible, when suddenly the 100hp Gnome rotary without warning ceased its noisy rattle. The bracing wires hummed as the pilot put the machine in a dive, increasing the revs of the now freewheeling propeller as he adjusted the throttle and mixture control. To their relief the Gnome burst into life again; the noisy rattle must have been sweet music to their ears.

During the flight above Beersheba they had encountered small arms fire; several holes in the wings were testimony. Along with the smell of burnt castor oil from the rotary exhaust there was now also a very strong smell of petrol. De Saizieu checked the fuel level in the front tank, and finding nothing amiss, concluded the rear tank had been hit and began to pump fuel from the rear to the front tank as a precaution.

Three minutes later just 12 miles from the coast, the engine died again forcing de Saizieu to dive the float plane in another desperate attempt to restart the engine. Now less than 3,000ft above the barren landscape the situation was desperate. As he tried every trick he knew to restart the engine, de Saizieu called out to Martin advising him to destroy his notes and maps apart from anything that would be useful in reaching their emergency rendezvous on foot.

At 600ft the Frenchman was searching an inhospitable, shrub-covered terrain filled with small ravines, when he saw a level area within gliding distance and warned Martin to put his flying goggles back on for protection from the dust and sand raised during the landing.

Intent as he ensured the rear of the floats touched the ground first, de Saizieu was caught unawares as the engine burst into life with the jolting, but with his hands full keeping the machine on an even keel the Gnome sputtered and quickly died again as the float plane slithered and shuddered to a halt. During the descent Martin had seen a group of Bedouin tents that he estimated to be about half a mile from them.

As senior officer, the Frenchman told Martin he would set fire to the machine to prevent it falling into enemy hands and as his job as pilot was over he insisted that Martin set out without him to reach the rendezvous with his report of the reconnaissance. Martin, aware the Arabs had seen their descent, refused to leave his comrade who had only a Browning automatic pistol with which to defend himself, whilst Martin had a rifle.

With the urgent need to destroy the grounded seaplane before the Arabs arrived, de Saizieu did not argue but told Martin not to fire unless he gave the order, as there was just a chance the Bedouins were in the pay of the British. The excited Arabs arrived, advancing in a semicircle. The Frenchman attempted to set fire to the machine after opening the petrol cock but this proved more difficult than he had expected.

By this time the airmen were completely surrounded by tribesmen brandishing rifles and swords. Their leader indicated to the airmen to lay down their weapons and move away from the aircraft; when they refused, the Arabs raised their rifles and de Saizieu shouted to Martin to open fire as he made yet another attempt at burning their machine.

Shots were exchanged, however, the tribesmen appear to have been reluctant to put bullet holes in the airmen's clothing. Still struggling to set the aircraft on fire, the Frenchman was jumped from behind by two Arabs intent on getting his life jacket off his back in one piece; reaching for his pistol he found the holster already empty.

Nearby Martin was now putting up a fight with the butt end of his rifle, having laid two of his opponents out. On seeing his pilot, struggling with a pair of the robbers, make one more attempt to set their aircraft ablaze, Martin broke free from the mob around him and ran to the assistance of de Saizieu, only to be shot dead as he reached his comrade's side. A bullet also wounded a Bedouin and as de Saizieu stopped struggling, awaiting the same fate, a Turkish cavalryman galloped up and calmed the situation.

Now their prisoner awaiting a Turkish escort, the Bedouins threatened to kill de Saizieu to avenge the deaths of their fellow tribesmen, but when they found out he was French and not British they became less aggressive. De Saizieu almost succeeded in bribing the Bedouin leader with an offer of £2,000 in ransom money for his safe conduct back to the Suez Canal; unfortunately the Turkish escort arrived first to take him into captivity.

Baron Louis de Saizieu finally returned home from imprisonment in Turkey in February 1919. Writing to the Ledger family, the French aviator had nothing but praise and admiration for Martin, but unfortunately was unable to confirm if or where the body of their son had been buried.

Second Lieutenant Horace Martin Capon Ledger, awarded the Croix de Guerre and Legion D'Honneur, is honoured on the Jerusalem Memorial that commemorates more than 3,000 men of the Egyptian Expeditionary Force 1914–1918 with no known grave.

Closer to home, in the village of Faulkbourne, there is a stained glass window in St Germanus church in memory of Martin, and below the window you will find a brass plaque dedicated to her husband from Ellinor Ledger.

The son and great-grandson of Baron Louis Barthelemy-de Saizieu were guests of honour when they visited the Village of Faulkbourne Millennium Exhibition in June 2000, when the church, Faulkbourne Hall, Warren Farm House gardens and the exhibition were open to the public. Reverend John Hall conducted a Remembrance Service at the church with members of both the Ledger and de Saizieu families present. Baron de Saizieu spoke about the death of Martin and the capture of Louis, saying 'that on behalf of his father, he was honoured to pay homage to Martin'. Great-grandson Charles Henri proudly displayed medals awarded to Louis. Local historian Christine Adam told the author, 'It was a very moving ceremony and flowers were also laid under Martin's window in the Church'.

The Woodhouse Brothers

Arthur Lionel Woodhouse JP, who came from Chester, was born in 1886 and became a successful wine merchant before he and his wife Frances moved down south to Broomfield in Essex. It was at Broomfield on 10 December 1896 that their first child, a future pilot in the Royal Flying Corps, Lionel Mostyn Woodhouse was born.

Their second child, Mosley Gordon Woodhouse, destined to serve as a pilot with the Royal Naval Air Service, arrived on 26 October 1898. As the family business that owned vineyards in Marsala in Sicily continued to flourish, so did the Woodhouse family, with the arrival of John Herbert, born 1900 and Peter Leigh, born 1906.

Three daughters, Barbara, Pauline and Nancy, completed the Woodhouse family who by then had moved to 'Tofts', a larger house at Little Baddow, a small village to the east of Chelmsford. The house is still known today as Tofts in the village.

Lionel, known as Lio in the family, was first to leave home, for him being the eldest son, it would be Eton via a boarding school in Broadstairs. Two years his junior, Mosley – whose family name was Mole – entered Radley College in Berkshire in 1913.

The third son, John, was just twelve years of age when he entered the Royal Naval College for two years, followed by his entrance to Dartmouth College in 1914. On 4 August that year, all three brothers were still at school; Lionel was a cadet in the Eton Officer Training Corps. He would be commissioned as a Second Lieutenant in the Essex Yeomanry on 1 July 1915, six months after his eighteenth birthday.

It is not known when Lionel actually applied for a transfer to the Royal Flying Corps, but by early 1916 it had become obvious to cavalry and mounted infantry men that the Western Front had stagnated into trench warfare and many volunteered for the so-called 'cavalry of the air'. Lionel's request for a transfer was granted on 18 June 1916 and even by the sparse flight training available at that period, Lionel progressed very rapidly to be appointed Flying Officer in less than two months.

On Wednesday 16 August, Lionel reported for duty to No. 52 Squadron based at Hounslow – where it had been formed three months earlier – and now in the process of working up as a corps reconnaissance unit for the BEF in France.

During October, No. 52 Squadron began to exchange their BE2c and BE12 machines for the latest product of the Royal Aircraft Factory at Farnborough, the RE8 or 'Harry Tate', named after a popular comedian of the period.

Captain Lionel Mostyn
Woodhouse MC, DFC, No.52
& 59 Squadrons RFC/RAF.
Killed on 29 September 1918.
(D.W. Empson)

At first the new machines did not prove to be as popular as the comedian, unfortunately the pilots of No.52 Squadron found them difficult to handle compared with the more stable and forgiving BE machines they had trained on. With misgivings, the Harry Tates of No.52 Squadron were flown to France on Friday 17 November 1916 and after an overnight stay at St Omer near the coast, flew on to an aerodrome at Bertangles as the last battle of the Somme was taking place.

As No.52 Squadron familiarised with life under active service conditions overseas, they received orders to prepare to make yet another move, this time to Chipilly Aerodrome east of Amiens. Due to severe weather conditions, the move did not take place until Friday 15 December.

The new year was just one week old when No.52 Squadron suffered their first fatal casualty due to enemy action; it was also the loss of the first Harry Tate behind enemy lines. Such are the fortunes of war that the commanding officer of No. 52 Squadron, Maj. Leonard Parker as pilot and 2 Lt F.A. Mann as observer, shared the dubious honour. They had left Chipilly in RE8 A74 at 1140hrs on Sunday 7 January to carry out a photographic patrol and were shot down by enemy fighters within the hour. Thirty years old, Maj. Parker died of his wounds, but his observer, although injured, survived as a POW.

When Maj. A.A. Walser MC took over the command of No. 52 Squadron, he found the pilots were prejudiced against the type of machine they were flying. The teething problems with the Harry Tate included the fear of spinning into the ground after a low-level stall, resulting in the machine bursting into flames. This fault would be partially cured by fitting a larger fin, unfortunately for some of the young pilots not as competent as Lionel Woodhouse, that simple remedy was not yet to hand.

Another move for No. 52 Squadron, on 25 January in wintery conditions, to an airfield at Meaulte, did not add to morale. Fortunately the squadron's first victory over an enemy machine, a two-seat observation 'bus' forced to land at Moriancourt by Lt Douglas Carbery and 2nd-Lt H. Mackay in Harry Tate A81, was the talk of the squadron mess that evening.

Two days later, on Sunday 27 January, Lionel Woodhouse and his observer Lt Hugh Nickalls were in Harry Tate A81 at 3,500ft above Moislains, directing the fire of the 141 Siege Battery, when they were forced to break off and engage an enemy aircraft; the Hun quickly made off without firing a shot. Later in the day, No. 52 Squadron was informed that front line troops had seen the action and observed the enemy aeroplane come down at Maurepas behind the enemy lines.

Another enemy machine was driven down out of control by the crew of Harry Tate A87, Lt Henry Mulock and his observer Cpl Boult, who had been engaged in a photographic patrol at midday on 29 January.

During February and March a gradual exchange of No. 52 Squadron RE8 and No. 34 Squadron BE2e machines took place. High Command reasoned the more experienced pilots of No. 34 Squadron would prove the worth of the Harry Tate that had already been ordered in large numbers to replace the obsolete BE2 machines at the front.

Twenty-five squadrons would be equipped with Harry Tates; it proved a reliable work horse that soldiered on and later saw service with the RAF in Russia and the Middle East after the armistice.

Although reservations about the Harry Tate persisted in No. 52 Squadron, it was not until 15 February that a second Harry Tate was lost in action. German records indicate that 2nd-Lt Georg Schlenker of Jasta 3, who had brought down Maj. Parker's machine, was again responsible. Harry Tate A87 fell behind enemy lines at Rancourt; Lt Henry Mulock and observer Pte T. Booth were reported missing but it was later learned they had had been killed.

On the Western Front in March 1917 there was a marked increase in German fighter activity. Lionel was now flying the BE2e biplanes exchanged with No. 34 Squadron and must have felt vulnerable. The Harry Tate with all its problems at least had the observer in the rear cockpit which was fitted with a Scarff ring mounting, giving the observer a good field of fire, as more than one enemy airman found out.

Due to this retrograde step, when under attack flying a BE, Lionel took such evasive action as the stable biplane would allow and was well aware his observer seated in the front cockpit, surrounded by the centre section struts and bracing wires, had to physically manhandle the Lewis gun from one spigot mounting to another in an attempt to fire at the manoeuvrable attacking Albatros scouts.

During the month of March 1917, the Royal Flying Corps lost as many aircraft in action as been lost for the whole twelve months of 1915. Among No. 52 Squadron casualties were a shot-up BE that crashed with a wounded pilot on 6 March; five days later a pilot was wounded by ground fire during an artillery shoot, and again, on the 19th, another pilot was wounded by the withering hail of small arms fire that greeted the BEs engaged in artillery spotting and contact patrols.

The ever waiting shark-like Albatros fighters shot down a lumbering BE2e carrying out a reconnaissance on the 23rd. Both crew members were wounded, the unfortunate observer dying later.

On 25 March another badly shot about BE2e returned to Meaulte Aerodrome; both the pilot and observer had been wounded. The last No. 52 Squadron casualty of the month was the BE2e forced down by enemy fighters and captured on the 28th.

As the month drew to a close, No. 52 Squadron – on 29th – moved yet again. This time it was to an airfield at Longavesnes, north-west of St Quentin, in preparation for the spring offensive planned by the British and French armies along 100 miles of the Western Front.

So far flying skill, nerve and Lady Luck had seen Lionel through his first three months on the Western Front. His younger brother Mosley, though, had been involved in a flying accident during March 1917.

Mosley had entered the Royal Naval Air Service as a probationary flying officer in November 1916 and, having completed his basic training, he reported to Redcar NAS in Yorkshire for flying instruction. It was at Redcar that he wrote-off Avro 504c 3304 in a landing accident, escaping with minor injuries.

Although under ever increasing pressure from Headquarters to carry out visual and photographic reconnaissance flights over enemy-held territory, No. 52 Squadron fared better than most squadrons when it came to loss by enemy action during April 1917. Attached to the XV Army Corps, No. 52 Squadron had a machine fail to return on the 11th when the crew of BE2e A2838 were killed in action over the enemy lines, and three days later BE2g 7241 fell in flames, carrying the unfortunate pilot and observer to their deaths behind the French front line.

Adding to the hazards facing Lionel and the airmen of No. 52 Squadron was the plan by High Command to send their BEs over the lines with a pair of 112lb bombs; to carry these the machine would have to be flown solo, leaving behind the observer and Lewis gun!

On 26 April, Lionel took part in the bombing of Bohain railway station, 25 miles behind enemy lines. Flying at 8,000ft, seven BEs of No. 52 Squadron were joined by six FE2bs of No. 22 Squadron also carrying bombs, which flew above the BEs protected by six high-flying Sopwith Pups from No. 54 Squadron. One BE dropped out with engine trouble to be followed by three Fees from the middle layer. As the remainder approached the target they encountered fierce anti-aircraft fire and could see enemy fighters closing in for the kill. Above the target the six BE pilots toggled their bombs free, well almost; one brave soul suffered a 'hang up' – in Second World War parlance – and landed very carefully back at Longavesnes Aerodrome with his bombs.

Flight Sub Lieutenant Mosley Gordon Woodhouse, 9N Squadron RNAS, was eighteen years of age when killed in action on 9 August 1917. (D.W. Empson)

BE2c 8623 came to grief four months after Mosley Woodhouse attempted to photograph Sleaford railway station from the air, whilst training at Cranwell on 11 May 1917. (S.Taylor)

Lionel's pair of 112-pounders hit the line north of the railway station. As the formation turned for the home run the two remaining Fees of No.22 Squadron, all that remained of the middle layer, were set upon by Albatros scouts of Jasta 5, who were no doubt unaware the lower BEs were unarmed and defenceless. The escorting Pups of No.54 Squadron were unable to prevent the loss of both Fees that fell behind enemy lines near Brancourt and their crews taken prisoner.

The third and last casualty for No.52 Squadron during 'Bloody April' was BE2e 7165, forced down just inside British lines by enemy fighters on the 28th. Although they came under artillery fire, the crew lived to fight another day.

Lionel's younger brother serving in the RNAS, PFO Mosley Woodhouse, having made satisfactory progress at Redcar, had arrived for advanced flight training at Cranwell, Lincolnshire, on 24 April 1917.

During the month of May, No.52 Squadron once again began to exchange their obsolescent BEs and this time the Harry Tates were more than welcome. The last No.52 Squadron BE lost in action fell to the guns of 2nd-Lt Werner Voss of Jasta 2 on Wednesday 9 May. Lt Rowland Coles and his observer, South African 2nd-Lt John Day, were engaged in an artillery shoot when the German ace shot BE2e 7209 to pieces as his twenty-sixth victory. The wreckage and bodies fell inside British lines.

At the end of May, young Mosley Woodhouse moved to Freiston, a substation to Cranwell, for weapons instruction, after being granted his seniority as Flight Sub-Lieutenant. On Sunday 10 June, with 40 hours solo in his log book, Mosley arrived at Dover NAS for overseas service. Fate was drawing the two Woodhouse boys together and, on 15 June, No.52 Squadron now fully re-equipped with Harry Tates flew north to Bray Dunes Aerodrome on the Franco-Belgian border.

A rear view of Maurice Farman Longhorn N5057, flown solo by Flt Sub-Lt Mosley on a cross-country flight from Killingholme to Redcar NAS on 14 March 1917. (JMB/GSL Collection)

On 25 June, young Mosley reported to No.12N Squadron at Dunkirk, awaiting posting to a front line Naval Scout squadron. During his short stay with 12N, Mosley logged another 2 hours' flying time on Sopwith Pups.

Flight Sub-Lieutenant Mosley Woodhouse, with just 6 hours in Pups, joined B flight of No.9N Squadron stationed at Guizancourt on Saturday 30 June. The squadron flew a mixture of Sopwith Pups and Triplanes. Mosley flew a Triplane for the first time on 7 July and recorded in his log book, '5365 quite liked it, made very fast but good landing'. Five days later he flew his first offensive patrol over the enemy lines. His log book entry reads, 'First flight in formation. Could not keep close enough. Saw nothing. Visibility fair'.

During June, brother Lionel in No.52 Squadron of the RFC destroyed thirteen enemy gun emplacements and caused a large number of explosions and fires whilst engaged in the daily round of 'Art Obs', artillery observation. For this he was awarded the Military Cross on 1 July 1917.

Young Mosley Woodhouse packed his kit and moved twice with No.9N Squadron during July. On the 7th the squadron aircraft were flown from Guizancourt to Izel le Hamel Aerodrome, followed by yet another move just three days later on the 10th to Frontier Aerodrome at Bray Dunes. Lionel, with No.52 Squadron, was at the nearby Middle Aerodrome; it was good news for their family at home in Little Baddow.

After collecting Sopwith Triplane N5356 from the depot at Dunkirk on the morning of Thursday 12 July, Mosley had a 55-minute flight in the afternoon, before taking off on an evening defensive patrol at 1920hrs. His flight commander, who also collected a Triplane from Dunkirk that morning, ran into a ditch and overturned attempting to take off. Mosley returned from an evening patrol with a badly vibrating engine.

When the two brothers met at Bray Dunes on a warm summer evening in the middle of July 1917, Lionel, a veteran pilot who had survived on the Western Front since November 1916, no doubt offered advice and caution to his eighteen-year-old brother, as they spent their brief time together remembering the happy days as children at Tofts.

At this period No.9N Squadron began to exchange their machines for two-gun Sopwith Camels. Mosley had been practising diving in Triplane N5356 on the morning of Friday 13 July, when a tyre burst on landing. The damage was quickly repaired and Mosley put the same machine through its paces during the afternoon and climbed to 10,000ft in 25 minutes.

Two Triplanes and two Camels of B Flight carried out an evening offensive patrol on 14 July; it would have been uneventful due to poor visibility but for Mosley's Triplane shedding another tyre on landing.

A six-Triplane ofensive patrol, led by Flt Cdr George Simpson, allowed Mosley his first sighting of distant enemy aircraft on Monday 16 July. Apart from a number of large smoke screens seen in No Man's Land there was nothing to report when the patrol returned after 2¼ hours.

Mosley carried out two patrols in a Triplane on 17 July. Once again, apart from 'seven Albatros stunting about well over the lines' there was nothing to report from the first. During the second patrol flying under thick cloud cover, Flt Cdr Simpson dived on enemy troops caught out in the open and dispersed them with a long burst from his Vickers gun.

An Avro 504B at Redcar. Young Mosley Woodhouse flew three of this type whilst under flying instruction at Redcar NAS. (JMB/GSL Collection)

Bad weather washed out a five-machine patrol after just 20 minutes on the 18th and the following was a rest day for young Mosley. A morning defensive patrol on 20 July was notable for the severe anti-aircraft fire encountered by the four Triplanes just south of Nieuport. During the afternoon patrol enemy aircraft were encountered. Flt Cdr Simpson fired several bursts at a red Albatros scout, and later a near miss by Archie fire shattered the propeller of Flt Sub-Lt (Sandy) MacDonald, who was forced to land on the beach near Nieuport. Hitting a patch of soft sand, the Triplane overturned without injury to the pilot.

Thick cloud down to 300ft the following morning washed out B Flight's attempted offensive patrol after just 5 minutes in the air. Mosley took part in an escort patrol over the lines with an RE8 on the 22nd, during which the flight encountered an enemy two-seater, but due to the Harry Tate's mission, they were unable to pursue the enemy machine. Flt Cdr Simpson fired a few rounds at long range 'just to put the wind up the blighter'.

Monday 23 July was a busy one for Mosley and his usual Triplane N5356 – airborne at 0700hrs, the patrol returned after 50 minutes due to bad visibility. No enemy aircraft were encountered during the 1300hrs offensive patrol. The last patrol at 1900hrs, consisting of four Triplanes and a Camel, also returned with nothing to report except poor visibility.

As No.9N Squadron prepared for yet another move, B Flight, on a 05.45 offensive patrol, encountered an enemy observation machine which the flight commander sent down out of control and claimed as his seventh victory. George Simpson had claimed the previous six enemy machines when serving with No.8N Squadron and been awarded the DSC.

During the afternoon five-Triplane offensive patrol, Mosley and Flt Sub-Lt Hazel Wallace observed two enemy machines flying below and dived to attack. Both sides withdrew unscathed, Wallace would survive the war with a total of fourteen victories, the last being an observation balloon.

On the same afternoon that his younger brother first came to grips with an enemy aeroplane, Lionel and his observer Capt. George Davies in Harry Tate A3549 were carrying out an artillery shoot at 6,000ft above a location given as MX5. The experienced Art Obs crew had seen an Albatros scout approaching from Middlekerke, Davies kept a wary eye on the Hun as it turned away towards the sea, Lionel continued to observe and correct the bombardment as needed. Hoping to catch the artillery machine off guard, the Albatros pilot turned suddenly and dived to the attack; Davies, anticipating this already, had the Albatros in his sights and opened fire with the Lewis gun at 250yds range. Realising he was not dealing with amateurs the German gave up the attempt and flew off in the direction of Ostend.

Captain Davies had been previously shot down with a wounded pilot Capt. R. Hall in A4225 whilst carrying out Art Obs on 15 July. Davies had not been Lionel's regular observer in the squadron, Lt Hugh Nickalls, an ex-school chum, had been until a high-spirited misdemeanour whilst off duty by the twenty-one-year-old airmen decided Maj. Walser to split the team up.

Friendly fire – in today's parlance – accounted for Harry Tate A4274, brought down by British anti-aircraft gunners in error on 28 July; the injured crew were rescued by front line troops. The following day Lionel's old school chum Hugh Nickalls was on an Art Obs mission with Lt Wilfred Roskelly in A4607 when they were attacked by enemy aircraft and shot down in flames.

Flight Sub Lieutenant Mosley Woodhouse flew Sopwith Triplane N5427 of 9 Naval Squadron during July 1917, prior to converting to Sopwith Camels. (E.F. Cheesman)

Sopwith Camel B3884, collected by Mosley Woodhouse from the Dunkirk Depot in exchange for a Sopwith Triplane on 4 August 1917; it was his first flight in a Camel, four days before he was killed in action. (JMB/GSL Collection)

As planned, Mosley's squadron moved to Leffrinckhoucke Aerodrome on Wednesday 25 July; it was a mere 10-minute hop along the coast by air for No.9N Squadron's eight Triplanes and seven Camels. The following day on an inner line patrol, engine failure forced Mosley to land his Triplane on the beach. He escaped injury, but N5356 had to be returned to the Dunkirk Depot for an overhaul.

A violent thunderstorm forced Mosley to land at Bray Dunes Aerodrome during the morning patrol on Sunday 29 July. At 1745hrs he returned to his own aerodrome and 45 minutes later he flew Triplane N4527 back to the Dunkirk Depot as B Flight were exchanging their last 'Tripes' for Camels. Mosley flew a Camel for the first time on Saturday evening, 4 August, having exchanged Triplane N5478 for Camel B3884. The 10-minute return flight to Leffrinckhoucke was through pouring rain.

He was allotted his own Camel B3870 the following morning and flew a patrol in it the same afternoon. Due to reasons not recorded, Mosley had not managed to get his Camel airborne until 1500hrs; the patrol had a 15-minute start on him and he was unable to catch up with them. He recorded in his log book, 'First patrol in Camel. Nothing to report, couldn't find formation'.

Canadian pilot Flt Sub-Lt Harold Mott, during the morning patrol on Wednesday 8 August, had been lucky to escape with just a broken nose after his Camel had been set on fire during a scrap with enemy fighters and forced to land just inside British lines. During the afternoon Mosley flew an offensive patrol in Camel B3870, but due to poor visibility he lost the formation in the clouds, returning after 75 minutes in the air with nothing to report.

Seven Camels of B Flight of No.9N Squadron took to the air at 0550hrs on Thursday 9 August 1917, led by Flt Cdr Simpson. As prearranged, Flt Sub-Lt Francis Mellersh and Mosley flying B3870 carried out an inner offensive patrol, whilst the four remaining Camels, including the tough Canadian Harold Mott, still recovering from his recent ordeal, flew the outer offensive patrol. The plan was to lure enemy machines to attack the split flights, or hopefully trap unwary German airmen crossing the front line in a Camel sandwich.

The first customer, an Albatros two-seater, was tackled by Simpson at 0620hrs above St Pierre Cappelle; the C type dived back across the lines only to return 10 minutes later to be driven off again by the patrol.

The next customer, this time an Aviatik two-seater, also dived away when fired upon. Simpson, having seen a number of enemy scouts waiting to pounce over the lines, declined the invitation to follow. The experienced flight commander had also seen the glint of wings 3,000ft above his patrol: it was a pair of Albatros scouts waiting to dive out of the sun.

At 0640hrs the two high-flying Albatros made a move; they had seen a Harry Tate engaged on Art Obs east of Nieuport and dived shark-like for the kill. Simpson, well placed to intercept the Huns, pulled back on the stick and with B3898 at stalling point fired a burst at the nearest V strutter. The startled German immediately turned and, followed by his companion, took on the three Camels that remained of the original seven in what was described later as 'a very hot engagement', during which the Germans, where possible, kept above and up-sun of the Camels.

George Simpson, already credited with eight enemy aircraft, and Francis Mellersh who would add another four to the one he had sent down out of control at the end of July, found they had their hands full as the two Albatros scouts repeatedly sniped at 'Woody', as young Mosley Woodhouse was known in B Flight.

With just 3 hours' experience in flying the tricky Sopwith Camel, and singled out by two very determined Huns, Mosley was unable to stay under the protection of his flight commander's guns. Finally, badly shot up and in sheer desperation, he stopped jazzing about and put the Camel into a dive towards the British lines. This is just what the Albatros pilots had been waiting for and dived in pursuit. George Simpson had also anticipated the young airman's desperate dash across the lines and followed firing at the nearest Albatros that span out of the line of fire only to be engaged by Mellersh bringing up the rear.

With the scared and exhausted eighteen-year-old pilot now a steady target in his sights the remaining Albatros pilot, 2nd-Lt Julius Buckler, quickly set fire to the Camel with a well aimed burst from his twin machine guns. The Woodhouse family motto was *Virtus in Arduis* (Courage in Difficulties); young Mosley now faced every First World War flyer's nightmare: falling in flames without a parachute.

Simpson and Mellersh fought with the two Albatros pilots for a further 10 minutes during which the flight commander suffered frustrating gun stoppages as he glimpsed the stricken Camel's flaming descent. The crew of the RE8 that had been the intended victim watched the burning machine pull out of the dive and begin side slipping as the pilot desperately sought to keep the flames away from his body.

Lionel Woodhouse at the controls of the RE8 knew from the markings on the Camels that 9N pilots had defended his machine and had an uneasy feeling the unfortunate Camel pilot falling in flames may have been his younger brother. 100ft from the ground the burning machine broke up throwing Mosley to his death. Flt Cdr Simpson and Mellersh returned to No.9N Squadron at 0720hrs to report the loss of Woody.

Across the lines, a victorious 2nd-Lt Julius Buckler of Jasta 17 landed at Ghistelle Aerodrome near Ostend to report, for his twelfth victory, a Sopwith down in flames south-east of Nieuport, and then prepared to go home on leave to Germany. Buckler would be credited with thirty-five allied aircraft and survive the horrors of two world wars, to die peacefully in Berlin in 1960.

Captain George Simpson DSC is known to have survived the First World War, as did Francis Mellersh who had a distinguished career in the RAF during the Second World War. Sir Francis Mellersh KBE, AFC, MA was unfortunately killed in a helicopter crash in 1955.

Lionel, having been informed that his younger brother's body had been found, penned the following letter to Woodhouse senior:

52 Squadron

R.F.C

B.E.F

My dear dear Dad,

I am writing to you not Mum, so that you may break it the more gently to her. Poor little Mole is dead. Oh it is to awful, first Nick [school chum Lt Hugh Nickalls] and then my favourite brother.

I saw the whole thing and at the time had a horrible feeling that it was one of our machines and not a Hun and if that was the case it would be him. He died protecting me. They went over to attack these Huns as they came up to the lines and fought for about five minutes, after one machine broke away on fire. It was the most glorious fight for life ever put up. All who saw it say the same thing, what a wonderful pilot he must have been? He was seen to be hit by his flight commander before the fire started and then with his machine under control, brought it down from 7,000 to 100ft in a series of side slips, so keeping the flames off himself, when it broke up.

I cannot give you any hope and think perhaps it was better for him to have been killed at the finish. I have kept nothing from you and will leave it to you to say what you feel the best for Mum. He was a wonderful and loved brother. It's nearly killed me to write this, but we must all try to bear up.

Your broken hearted son,

Lio

Six days after Mosley had been killed, the commanding officer of No.9N Squadron, as was the custom, had the task of writing the following letter of condolence to Mrs Woodhouse:

No.9 Sqn R.N.A.S.

15.8.17

Dear Mrs Woodhouse,

I hope you will not think my letter an impertinence at a time when you have had such a terrible loss. I know I can say nothing to lighten your trouble, but I should like you to know, that if there is anything I can do for you I will.

Letters such as this are always difficult to write and I can honestly say that this one is the hardest I have had.

Your son was not under my command for very long, but during that time I had come to hold a very high opinion of him. He would have become a very fine officer and I never had anything but praise in my thoughts of him.

During the time of his stay with us, he had become universally popular with us all and I know all feel his loss as keenly as I do.

His brother in the RFC saw the wretched affair happen, it seems to make it all the more sad. It was in doing his duty to protect his brother's machine that he lost his life.

The one consolation is, that he had no suffering, he was shot in the head twice and so all that happened afterwards, was mercifully saved him. His body fell out of the machine and was picked up in our front line trenches. It was brought down from there and buried by the Chaplain of 36 Casualty Clearing Station at Zuydcoote.

In due course we shall erect a cross over his grave, which will mark it until you can place one of a more permanent character if you wish to do so.

You will not want me to write more I dare say, but if there is anything further you may wish to know, write and ask me. You have my very deepest sympathy and may I say that your son died as he had lived, a gentleman.

Yours sincerely,

H. Fawcett.
Sq. Commander.

The same day that Sqn Cdr Fawcett sent the letter of condolence to Mrs Woodhouse, Lionel, who had already served for nine months with No. 52 Squadron in France, said farewell to his comrades. Maj. Walser had quickly applied for Lionel to be posted back to Home Establishment.

Home on leave at Little Baddow, Lionel told his parents of the propeller cross with an engraved bronze plate he had erected to mark his brother's grave.

Promoted to the rank of captain on 16 September 1917, Lionel had to adjust to a period of instructing. During October he took command of the artillery department at No. 1 School of Aeronautics based at Reading. Lionel's first hand experience of army co-operation from the air must have proved invaluable.

As the months of war dragged on, the RFC and RNAS were amalgamated to form the Royal Air Force on 1 April 1918 and as Lionel recovered in mind and body, the urge to return to active service prompted him to apply for a posting back to the BEF.

He set foot in France again on Monday 12 August 1918, arriving at Vert Galant Aerodrome, north of Amiens, the following day. Up to this period, Capt. Lionel Woodhouse MC had flown over 300hrs on a variety of aircraft, the most unusual a Short Bomber, a land plane version of the Short 184 seaplane.

Lionel's previous overseas service with No. 52 Squadron flying the RE8 stood him in good stead when he took command of B Flight No. 59 Squadron, that was also equipped with Harry Tates. No. 59 Squadron had been on active service in France for eighteen months when Lionel arrived, and he wasted little time in settling in.

The following morning he took up Harry Tate B5887, with a sandbag instead of a passenger in the rear cockpit, for a 20-minute flight. After lunch, with Lt James as his observer, Lionel once again flew over the enemy lines in a Harry Tate. On their return 2 hours later, the crew of A4687 had seen little enemy troop movement, except at some disused brick fields, map reference G9V, where they planted the two 25lb bombs that No. 59 Squadron machines usually carried with them on patrol.

On the morning of Thursday 15 August, Lionel and Lt Thompson flew a similar patrol, taking off from Vert Galant at 1100hrs in A6674. During the 2 hour and 20 minute flight, they noted a heavy enemy bombardment taking place at three different locations along the front. Before they recrossed the lines, the Harry Tate crew dropped two 25lb bombs and fired 150 rounds with their machine guns at German infantry massed at Achiet-le-Petit.

Lionel demonstrated that he had lost none of his skill at artillery spotting when the following day, with Lt Thompson as his observer in B6674, they carried out a 3¼-hour shoot for the howitzers of 495 Siege Battery. During the next six weeks, with the tide of war flowing in favour of the allies, Lionel was in his element assisting with the daily destruction of the retreating once-mighty German army.

Teamed with Thompson in B6674 on the morning of Saturday 17 August, Lionel carried out another artillery shoot; this time he actually controlled and ranged four separate Siege Batteries, the 95th, 244th, 277th and the 299th. Lionel did this by signalling each battery in turn to fire two ranging shots and when satisfied of their accuracy, he signalled 'Fire for effect'. This method proved successful as the targeted trenches were either damaged or demolished during the 3¼-hour shoot. To round off the day's work, Lionel carried out a 15-minute airborne engine test on D4896 with Flt Sgt Goodwin as his passenger during the afternoon.

An early morning photographic mission above Miranmont in B6674 on Monday 19 August encountered very accurate anti-aircraft fire. After exposing the eighteen plates in their camera from 7,500ft, Lionel and Thompson made their farewell gesture to the sweating anti-aircraft gunners below, with compliments from No.59 Squadron, a pair of 25lb bombs.

Two contact patrols were carried out by Lionel and Thompson on Wednesday 21 August. The first entailed flying at the height of 500ft in the direction of Achiet-le-Grand, a large village south of Arras, in order to ascertain the progress of advancing British infantry and tanks. On their return, they also had their maps well marked with enemy positions, such as the machine gun nests at map reference G19d and the locations of three grounded kite balloons.

During the morning contact patrol they had again encountered heavy anti-aircraft fire and had seen a flight of Pfalz scouts overhead that fortunately chose to ignore the solitary RE8, no doubt fearing a trap. That afternoon B6674, refuelled and rearmed, carried out another low-level patrol confirming the extent of the territory gained during the fierce fighting taking place.

Contact patrols were a speciality of B Flight; Lionel, like his younger brother who had lived up to thee family motto of 'Courage in Difficulties', set his own flight a good example in carrying out daily hazardous, low level reconnaissance flights to keep the Top Brass at HQ informed.

On Thursday 22 August, just twelve days after his return to France, Lionel, completely fearless, carried out a 2-hour contact patrol at an average height of 200ft with his equally fearless observer Lt Thompson. The next day, flying 500ft above the battle, several columns of German troops were seen retiring eastwards. Lionel reported these columns as being 'Engaged from the air and the retirement accelerated, a total of 400 rounds were fired'.

On the same day, as the slow, low-flying Harry Tates carried out essential army co-operation patrols, small arms fire from the ground inflicted the following casualties on No.59 Squadron: 2nd-Lt Thomas Hobbs, although badly wounded, managed to land his observer Lt C.R. Wallis back inside British lines before unfortunately dying of his wounds 24 hours later; observer 2nd-Lt J.B. Hyslop was wounded by ground fire; two more Harry Tates returned to Vert Galant badly shot about, but their crews had escaped physical injury.

This RE8???74 christened 'Windup' could be B6674, flown by Lionel Woodhouse when serving with No.52 Squadron in France. (JMB/GSL Collection)

On Saturday 24 August, B6674 suffered extensive damage from small arms fire during a morning contact patrol from Miraumont to Loupart Wood; both Lionel and Thompson again escaped injury.

During the afternoon three Harry Tates each loaded with a pair of boxes packed with small arms ammunition took off destined for the forward elements of the British advance that had out-paced the supply columns. Lionel, flying B5487, had Capt. C.T. Cleaver MC – known in the squadron as 'Hoppy' – as his observer. Having dropped the badly needed ammunition in the Iries-Loupart Wood area, they returned to give a farewell party for Hoppy that evening. Capt. Cleaver, a very experienced observer, left No.59 Squadron the following day as he had been transferred to No.16 Squadron as flight commander, a rare appointment for an observer, but Hoppy Cleaver was unusual having survived as an observer at the Front since 1916.

Another ammunition drop for Lionel and his regular observer Thompson with two boxes slung underneath F6011 on Sunday 25 August. Taking off at 1430hrs and flying alone, they made the drop to an infantry company at map reference M6d as ordered.

The next day entailed a mixed bag of duties for Lionel, taking off at 1500hrs with Thompson as observer; he carried out a now-normal routine contact patrol between 300 and 800ft for 1½ hours. Within an hour of landing Lionel was airborne again, this time with Lt James to carry out an artillery shoot. On their way to the target area, they dropped another two boxes of ammunition to troops in the forward area. The shoot was made interesting by the presence of twenty Fokker DVIIs flying at 7,000ft above Bapaume Wood, but they did not deter Lionel, who carried out the shoot as ordered.

Low clouds and heavy showers on the morning of Tuesday 27 August did not prevent Lionel and Lt James from carrying out a successful shoot before landing for breakfast at 0800hrs. Two hours later a report of a German counter-attack in progress saw Lionel and Thompson airborne again to reconnoitre and update the situation.

Apart from a short flight to carry out an engine test on F6011, Wednesday 28th was a rest day for Lionel. The next morning it was business as usual. With Lt Walter Peel MC as observer, Lionel carried out another counter-attack patrol. Unable to find any sign of an attack in progress, they flew low over the enemy front line failing to attract any small arms fire. During the afternoon Lionel and Peel carried out another successful artillery shoot.

A contact patrol at 1145hrs on Friday 30th found company strengths of British infantry in areas 1.31b and 1.32a on Lionel's map, with platoons as far forward as 1.19b and 1.13a. The Germans were dug in on the south-east outskirts of Riencourt and well shelling the village of Bancouver. Fifty-five minutes into their patrol, four enemy scouts dived on the Harry Tate, firing in turn as they passed. Pulling out of the dive they climbed back to attack; this time Peel was ready for them and fired a drum of ammunition into the leading machine that burst into flames and fell out of control north-west of Beugny. The three remaining scouts, thought by Lionel and Peel to have been Pfalz machines, withdrew.

The last day of August was business as usual for No. 59 Squadron, with a morning counter-attack patrol for Lionel and Peel; there was little sign of enemy activity in their sector. During the afternoon they made a now-becoming-routine ammunition drop at map reference 1.14c.

Lady Luck again flew with Lionel and his observer on the first day of September, an early morning contact patrol revealing enemy troops still holding trenches at map reference 1.14b to 1.27b in force. At 0645hrs a red signal rocket from the German trenches was quickly followed by a heavy bombardment of Freicourt and Bancourt. A spate of anti-aircraft fire suddenly directed against the Harry Tate was also heavy and a near miss damaged the starboard mainplanes. As Lionel attempted to regain control, he realised most of the control cables were damaged and only the elevator responded normally. With Peel leaning out of the cockpit holding the Lewis gun at arms length to balance the crippled machine, Lionel very carefully flew them home. Seven hours later, with F6011 repaired, Lionel and Peel carried out another contact patrol, and another the following day.

A line patrol flown by Lionel and Peel just after midday on Tuesday 3 September covered the front from Henduile to Quéant; that included a section of the formidable Hindenburg Line. East of Gouzeacourt seven trains shunted into sidings were noted and all the roads in the vicinity were choked with horse and motor transport trying to go east. Another horse-drawn column over half a mile in length was seen passing Metz. The most significant observation made during the patrol was the fact that no enemy troops were seen in occupation of the Hindenburg Line they had overflown.

No. 59 Squadron again suffered casualties from ground fire on 3 September; Capt. G.L. Scott and his observer 2nd-Lt J.N. Schofield were both wounded during a contact patrol and another observer, 2nd-Lt A. Dewhirst, was wounded in a bombing raid.

An opportunity to assist in 'hurrying the retirement,' as Lionel put it, occurred during an afternoon contact patrol when Lionel and Peel spotted enemy troops retreating towards Haurincourt Wood. Diving to within 100ft they both machine gunned the exposed troops, firing 250 rounds and inflicting twenty or more casualties.

The following day, the aggressive Harry Tate crew did some more 'hurrying the retirement' when carrying out an artillery shoot. Enemy troops were observed taking up positions at map reference P.18b, P.18, Q.113a and Q.13c. As Lionel dived firing 450 rounds from the forward Vickers gun, Peel added a further 200 rounds from the Lewis at the unfortunate PBI. Several machine gunners returned their fire hitting the mainplanes.

The now inseparable Lionel and Peel flew a morning contact patrol on Friday 6 September, returning with little to report. During the evening, flying D4865, they carried out an artillery shoot and dropped four 25lb bombs on Trescault. Following that they attacked and had a scrap with the crew of a Halberstadt two-seater that proved indecisive.

Low-flying Halberstadt two-seaters were carrying out the same duties for the German Army, as the Harry Tates above the front lines. On Sunday 8 September Captain Douglas Carbery, a fellow flight commander in No.59 Squadron and an old friend from No.52 Squadron the previous year, with his observer Lt J.B. Clements also attacked a low-flying Halberstadt, shooting it down and within minutes sending another down out of control.

On Monday 9 September, Lionel and Peel carrying out a contact patrol in F6011 were involved in trench strafing. After they observed the enemy firing green rocket signals at 0740hrs, Lionel dived to within 100ft of the ground to enable Peel and himself to fire 250 rounds into the trenches. They were greeted with machine gun and anti-aircraft fire that Lionel suspected came from improvised field guns. Having made notes on the extent of the British infantry advance, Lionel flew back over the 37th New Zealand Division and Corps HQ, to drop message bags containing their reports.

Bad weather conditions interfered with the work of No.59 Squadron for the next few days; Lionel and Lt Thompson flew a contact patrol at 50ft because of the very low clouds at 0630hrs on the 12th. They were able to confirm the infantry had taken their first objective south of Trescault – they came under fierce machine gun fire over 'Dead Man's Corner' and were surprised by an enemy machine that dived out of the clouds firing at them, before disappearing to the east. Message bags were again dropped at NZ and 37th Division HQ on the way back.

Friday 13 September found Lionel and Peel flying a contact patrol at 200ft with orders to drop their messages at the NZ and 37th Division HQ. Unable to do this, Lionel landed at 0910hrs but was airborne again at 0935HRS for the same purpose. The next day Lionel and Peel carried out another 3-hour artillery shoot.

Lieutenant Thompson accompanied Lionel on a counter-attack patrol in F6011 on the 15th; although they searched for 3½ hours, they found no sign of an enemy counter-attack, but low over Chapel Wood Switch, they provoked several volleys of rifle fire.

A 4-hour artillery shoot with Thompson as his observer on the 16th had Lionel once again sighting for the 95th Siege Battery. Out of the eighty rounds fired at hostile batteries during the shoot, Lionel was able to confirm one 'OK' and five 'Y's.

On Wednesday 18 September, eleven Harry Tates of No.59 Squadron were flown from Vert Galant to an advanced landing ground at Beugnatre 3 miles north-east of Bapaume. Lionel's turn to take off came at 1010hrs with Lt Thompson as a passenger. On arrival he dropped off Thompson, and with Lt Peel as his observer embarked upon a contact patrol to pinpoint the forward troops of both sides. They encountered very little Archie but, dropping to within 200ft of the ground, they flew into a hail of rifle and machine gun fire.

At 1900hrs that evening Lionel was informed of a German counter-attack taking place in the area covered during his morning patrol. Thirty-five minutes later he was airborne with Peel to assess the situation. It was serious; they found German troops were occupying trenches around Chapel Wood Switch which just a few hours earlier had been in British hands. Lionel flew direct to the IV Corps HQ, where Peel dropped a message bag containing the vital information.

The following morning Lionel and Peel climbed aboard C2553, a presentation aircraft inscribed 'Punjab No.42'. Taking off at 0630hrs and overflying the same sector, they found the situation had changed during the night, but enemy machine gun nests were still active.

As with the previous evening's patrol, Lionel flew back to IV Corps HQ to drop maps to the 5th and 37th Divisions.

Lionel's favourite Harry Tate F6011 was available for a counter-attack patrol over the same area that evening, again with Peel as his observer. They flew along the line checking German-held positions; there was plenty to be seen, heavy shelling, various coloured flares and rockets and other pyrotechnics, which Lionel described as 'golden rain', but no sign of a counter-attack. Undeterred by the heavy Archie and small arms fire, they dropped four Cooper bombs on Villers-Plouich and fired 600 rounds into enemy trenches before sighting a German two-seater over K.35 at 1845hrs which they attacked, firing 100 rounds before it dived away in great haste.

With little doubt a day of rest on Friday 20th was appreciated by Lionel and Peel. However, during the following afternoon they carried out a 3-hour counter-attack patrol during which about fifty enemy troops were observed in Chapel Wood Switch and Lionel immediately sent a GF (General Fire) signal. Twenty-five minutes later, with no bombardment forthcoming, they repeated the GF signal as the troops presented a perfect target. Eventually frustrated that no battery responded to their signals, Lionel dived to within 200ft of the Switch firing 200 rounds and dropping four 25lb bombs on the infantrymen.

Still looking for trouble, the Harry Tate's crew once again flew along the front lines, plotting the extent of the German-held territory. Locating movement on the ground at Q16b and 17a and running low on fuel, Lionel dispensed with the GF call and dived to 500ft, firing off 450 rounds before re-crossing the lines.

Lieutenant Thompson flew with Lionel for an artillery shoot on the 22nd; they were to be the eyes of the 495th Siege Battery. With a cloud ceiling at 500ft, the howitzers only fired two shells before Lionel had to signal a 'washout' due to heavy rain making observation impossible.

With Peel as his observer, Lionel carried out a shoot for the 95th Siege Battery the next afternoon. Their target was enemy gun emplacements located at R16c. During the next 3 hours the Harry Tate crew counted ninety-four shells burst around the target, achieving an 'OK' with one gun pit demolished, another damaged and two large explosions as ammunition went up in smoke.

The parents of Capt. Lionel Mostyn Woodhouse visit the cemetery where their son and his observer, Lt Walter Sidney Peel MC, the crew of RE8 F6011, were buried side by side at Grevillers, France. (D.W. Empson)

Counter battery work continued on 24 September when Lionel ranged for the 106th Siege Battery against a hostile battery at map reference R15v; forty-one shells damaged three gun emplacements and started a fire. To round off their day's work, Lionel and Peel fired 600 rounds into enemy trenches before heading for home.

The old team of Lionel, Peel and F6011 were over the lines at 1610hrs on the 25th, for a change their mission was a photographic reconnaissance. Flying at 7,500ft, twenty-eight photographic plates were successfully exposed and they returned without incident after 1 hour and 20 minutes.

Lionel did not fly on the 26th, but it was business as usual for the old firm on the morning of Friday 27 September, taking off with Peel at 0840hrs to carry out another low-level contact patrol in F6011.

Ten minutes after Lionel had become airborne, the crew of another Harry Tate from No.59 Squadron saw an aircraft fall in flames near Boursies. Lady Luck, who had accompanied Lionel and his equally gallant observers through the hail of small arms fire during the low-level contact patrols of the last six weeks, had deserted him.

As Boursies was in British hands, the bodies of Captain Lionel Mostyn Woodhouse MC and Lieutenant Walter Sidney Peel MC were recovered to be buried side by side in the British Cemetery at Grevillers.

A dreaded War Office telegram arrived at the Woodhouse family home in Little Baddow; once again like so many parents of that period, Lionel senior and his wife Frances had to bear the loss of yet another loved son.

The posthumous award of a Distinguished Flying Cross, gazetted on 2 November 1918, may have been of some comfort to Lionel's grieving parents. The citation read:

The church at Little Baddow, Essex, has two wall-mounted bronze memorial plaques dedicated to the Woodhouse brothers. Other members of the Woodhouse family are buried in the church grounds. (K. Feline)

> This officer displayed great gallantry during a counterattack by the enemy. Flying at 100ft, he engaged the advancing troops, causing heavy casualties. His bold action contributed materially to the failure of this counterattack. Having rendered this service, he continued his patrol, in which he was subjected to heavy fire and his machine was badly shot about.

A third member of the family, eighteen-year-old John Herbert Woodhouse, was serving as a Midshipman in the Royal Navy when the Armistice was signed. His parents, having suffered the loss of two sons, applied for the release of John – who was now the eldest surviving son – from the Navy. He returned home to Tofts in December 1918.

William Raymond Fish

The accidental death of twenty-four-year-old Captain William Raymond Fish MC of Woodford Green, was another tragic loss to the county of Essex. William had already been wounded in action on 24 March 1916 while serving with the 7th Suffolk Regiment. Convalescing in hospital, he applied for a transfer to the RFC and was accepted for flight training on 28 August.

Returning to France the following year as a scout pilot, Lieutenant W.R. Fish reported to No.32 Squadron at Lealvilliers, north-west of Albert. At least one other Essex airman is known to have served with No.32 Squadron, Lt Charles Edward Murrey Pickthorne of Ilford, who had been credited with four enemy aircraft while flying the obsolete out-gunned DH2 pusher scout in the early months of 1917; he was wounded and awarded the MC before returning to Home Establishment about the same time as William Fish arrived at Lealvilliers on Monday 2 April 1917.

The following month No.32 Squadron began to replace their DH2 pusher scouts with the DH5. Having the rotary engine in front of him in the new tractor machine, William found he still had the excellent forward and upward view of the outdated pusher design, thanks to the pronounced back stagger of the upper wing of the DH5 that was also superior in performance and armed with a belt-fed synchronized Vickers machine gun that did not require reloading every forty-seven rounds as had the drum-fed Lewis gun fitted on the pusher.

William was not destined to become one of the famous air fighters of the first war in the air, but some sources, such as Harborough's *Air Aces of the 1914-1918 War*, published in 1959, credit Captain W.R. Fish with five enemy aircraft; No.32 Squadron records do indicate he was credited with at least four; several of these were, however, shared victories. No details were found in squadron records of the DH5 flown by William or where over the lines he was credited with sending an enemy machine down out of control on 25 July. During the same month No.32 Squadron had four pilots killed, one wounded and four forced to crash land with battle damage, while claiming twenty-two enemy aircraft as out of control or destroyed.

It was soon discovered in action that the DH5 could not compete in performance with contemporary machines such as the Sopwith Pup above 10,000ft; this and the fact the DH5 was sturdy enough to be fitted with bomb racks was the reason the pilots of the five DH5 squadrons serving in France were ordered to carry out ever increasing numbers of low-level ground strafing patrols where the High Command thought they could be best employed.

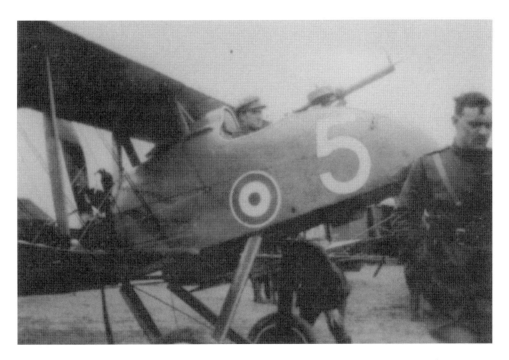

Although the FE8 single-seat pusher scout was obsolete by the spring of 1917, the pilots of No.41 Squadron fought on until July, when they were finally re-equipped with the Airco DH5. The stress of that period is evident on the faces in this unofficial photograph. (D. Barber)

Ground fire was responsible for six of the eight machines of No. 32 Squadron brought down during August. Lt William Fish escaped serious injury on the 10th when DH5 A9396 was hit by a passing shell near Kemmel, not an unusual incident for low-flying aircraft in the crowded airspace above the front lines in France during 1917/18. William managed to land the damaged machine behind British lines without injury. The same morning nineteen-year-old Lt Eric Seth-Ward, flying A9213, was not so lucky, hit by ground fire he fell to his death in Polygon Wood. During August 1917, six low-flying DH5s of No. 32 Squadron were brought down by ground fire; four pilots were killed, two wounded and two more – including William – were forced to crash-land the battle damaged aircraft. Five enemy machines were claimed during this period in spite of the demand for ground strafing patrols imposed on the squadron.

William had respite the following month from Droglandt Aerodrome where No. 32 Squadron had been based since 8 July. During fourteen days' leave, from 13 to 27 September, he had been awarded the Military Cross and promoted to the rank of temporary Captain. Casualties continued during September; two pilots had been killed, one wounded, two were POW and another injured crash landing after being shot up. Three enemy observation machines and an Albatros scout were claimed by the pilots of No. 32 Squadron during September.

On 16 October William had another narrow escape following an encounter with Albatros scouts south of Zonnebeke; with his machine badly shot up he was forced to land A9209 among shell craters just behind the front line.

Five days later, leading an offensive patrol in A9498, William, and 2nd-Lt C.J. Howson in A9311, drove an Albatros scout down out of control near Zonnebeke. 2nd-Lt B. Monkhouse managed to land the remains of badly damaged A9450 in one piece at Droglandt.

Another enemy machine fell to the guns of Capt. W. Fish in A9300 and 2nd-Lt Walter Tyrrell in B4916 over Passchendaele on 30 October; the Albatros DV was observed to crash by other members of the flight. Walter Tyrrell was destined to become the most successful pilot of No. 32 Squadron with seventeen enemy aircraft to his credit, twelve of them falling to the guns of his SE5a that equipped No. 32 Squadron from December 1917. Casualties for No. 32 Squadron were light for October; 2nd-Lt J.E. Johnston had been wounded on the 5th and four other pilots sustained injuries in crash landings, due to fierce anti-aircraft fire and no doubt nervous exhaustion.

Five enemy aircraft were claimed by No. 32 Squadron pilots during November. William, again flying A9300 with 2nd-Lt A.L. Cuffe in B4924 were responsible for an LVG two-seater that fell behind the enemy lines on the 13th.

The DH5 may have had its faults as a front line fighter, and by late 1917 was well out-gunned by enemy scouts; however, its rugged construction enabled many a young airman to fight another day, including 2nd-Lt William Jones who returned A9269 to Droglandt Aerodrome, having been hit by an anti-aircraft shell that passed through the wooden framed fuselage without exploding on 16 November.

In spite of the added dangers of low-flying patrols, No. 32 Squadron casualties for November – consisting of three pilots wounded – were light, but among the wounded was Capt. William Fish who, returning with his patrol after engaging a formation of enemy scouts across the lines on the 19th, was admitted to a Casualty Clearing Station

Captain William Raymond Fish MC, twice wounded in action, killed in a mid-air collision with a fellow member of 54 Squadron on 2 June 1918. (K. Feline)

with a bullet wound. Having previously been wounded while serving in the infantry no doubt stood him in good stead for the ordeal ahead in Le Tourqet and Prince Henry Hospitals. Discharged for light duties, he served with No.22 Wing HQ at Honnechy from the 25 December 1917, until passed fit enough for active service, reporting for duty with No.54 Squadron on 23 March 1918.

Based at Bertangles, No.54 Squadron was equipped with the formidable (in fearless hands) Sopwith Camel. William arrived as a replacement flight commander as No.54

Squadron had suffered heavy losses in ground strafing duties since February. Such was the desperate situation on the Western Front at this period following the German Army break-through, No.54 Squadron were forced to move to aerodromes at Conteville on 28 March, Clairmarais on 7 April and to Caffiers on the 29th.

The snub-nosed Camel looked a more conventional biplane than the DH5 and although armed with two Vickers guns and more aerobatic, it was a difficult machine to handle: more Camel pilots were killed or injured in accidents than by enemy action.

1 April 1918 found William settled in with No.54 Squadron who were not all that concerned about no longer belonging to the Royal Flying Corps, certainly not as much as the Royal Naval Air Service pilots that they had amalgamated with in the formation of the Royal Air Force. To most of the front line squadrons 1 April was just another day; No.54 Squadron had two pilots wounded and another injured when forced to land by small arms fire from ground strafing patrols.

William went home on leave on 6 April and was awarded a Bar to his Military Cross. During the month No.54 Squadron had eight pilots killed, six wounded, one POW and two injured in fierce fighting. Since the previous February, No.54 Squadron had written off forty aircraft in just three months. A move to Caffiers Aerodrome near Bailleul on the 29 April afforded a much needed respite for the pilots of No.54 Squadron. William was admitted to hospital suffering from scabies on 4 May, returning in time for the squadron move to St Omer on 1 June.

Just a few days later, a dreaded War Office telegram arrived at 'Sunnydene' in Woodford Green, the home of William's mother, stating that her son had been killed in action on 2 June 1918.

William, having survived being wounded in action with the Suffolk Regiment and again as a fighter pilot during ten months of perilous ground strafing action over the enemy lines, was fated to be killed in a flying accident when his Camel C1589 was in collision with another No.54 Squadron machine piloted by Lt C. Price-Hughes during the afternoon of Sunday 2 June. Lt Price-Hughes, although suffering shock, escaped serious injury when he crashed attempting to land Camel C1667l.

Twenty-four-year-old Captain William Fish MC was buried with Military Honours in Ebbingham Military Cemetery on 9 June 1918.

Another young Essex man who flew with No.54 Squadron during the war was Second Lieutenant Charles Henry Atkinson of Upton Park. He was shot down flying Camel D6494 in combat with Fokker DVIIs and last seen falling out of control above Estrees, on the evening of Thursday 4 July 1918. Like so many of his contemporaries, nineteen-year-old Charles Atkinson is today is just another of the many names on the Arras Memorial dedicated to the memory of the RFC, RNAS and RAF who were killed in France and Belgium during the First World War and have no known grave.

PART THREE
THE SEA BIRDS RNAS/RAF

Thank gawd we've got a Navy', was one of the more polite remarks made by military drill sergeants as they eyed up the latest batch of recruits on the parade ground at barracks all over Britain during the First World War. They did not realise at the time just how right they were.

The first Naval airmen were members of the Naval Wing of the Royal Flying Corps commissioned on 13 April 1912, from which the Royal Naval Air Service was formed as war clouds gathered over Europe on 1 July 1914.

A résumé of the rapid expansion and the many and varied duties undertaken by the RNAS during the First World War is beyond the limits of this book; however, the four Essex Naval airmen featured in this section, and of course the two younger brothers from the Petre and Woodhouse families who for the sake of family continuity you have already encountered, will give you an insight into the lives of Royal Naval Air Service airmen and also after they had merged with the Royal Flying Corps in the formation of the Royal Air Force on Monday 1 April 1918.

Edwin Harris Dunning

A visitor to St Lawrence's church at Bradfield Manningtree, Essex, will discover the grave of Commander Edwin Harris Dunning DSC. Within the thirteenth-century church, there is a large ornate commemorative wall plaque in the north transept that is dedicated to the memory of the Bradfield airman killed whilst flying during the First World War.

In recent years there has also been a montage of photographs on display, following a family service to mark the eightieth anniversary of the tragic accident that robbed the Royal Naval Air Service of one of their finest pilots.

Edwin Dunning, born on 17 July 1892, was the son of Sir Edwin Harris Dunning, Knight, of Jacques Hall, Bradfield. As a young teenager, Edwin Dunning served in the Royal Navy as a midshipman from January 1910 until March 1912, when it was suspected he was suffering from tuberculosis. He was declared fit again for active service at the start of the First World War and volunteered for the Royal Naval Air Service, entering on Sunday 4 October 1914.

Twenty days later, Flight Sub-Lieutenant Edwin Dunning qualified for Royal Aero Club Certificate No.949, flying a Short Biplane at the Eastchurch Naval Air Station on Saturday 24 October.

By January 1915, Edwin Dunning, having progressed to seaplanes, joined the recently commissioned seaplane carrier HMS *Ark Royal*. The keel of this 7,450-ton single screw vessel had been laid as a freighter; however, due to the threat of war the *Ark Royal* was redesigned for service with the Royal Naval Air Service.

On Friday 8 January 1915 Edwin Dunning, landing a Sopwith Folder on Southampton Water, encountered the problem that dogged the larger Sopwith seaplanes at this period: the struts attached to the floats of Sopwith 809 were prone to collapse due to poor suspension unless the sea was dead calm.

HMS *Ark Royal* set sail at midnight from Sheerness on Monday 1 February 1915, bound for the Dardanelles with six seaplanes (only one was suitable to use in choppy conditions) and four land planes.

An ambitious plan had been devised by their Lordships at Admiralty, with their French counterparts, to knock Turkey out of the war by forcing a passage through the 40-mile long Dardanelles Straight separating Europe from the sea of Marmora and Constantinople, leaving the capital open to bombardment. The success of this enterprise would have also ensured a secure all year round supply route to Russia, desperately in need of arms and ammunition for its enormous army. Had the Dardanelles and Gallipoli campaigns succeeded, the history of the First World War and indeed the twentieth century would certainly read a lot differently today.

Squadron Commander Edwin Harris Dunning DSC, who made the first successful aeroplane deck landing on an aircraft carrier. (The Dunning Collection)

HMS *Ark Royal* under the command of Squadron Commander Robert H. Clark-Hall, en route for the Aegean, put into Valetta harbour at Malta and, during the visit, *Ark Royal* lowered a Short Folder seaplane over the side. Short 136 actually made the first aeroplane flight ever seen by the excited Maltese spectators on Sunday 13 February 1915.

On Wednesday 17 February, *Ark Royal* anchored in a bay on the island of Tenedos off the Turkish mainland. With a force of no less than eighteen capitol ships and their protecting screen of cruisers, destroyers and torpedo boats, backed up supply ships and minesweeping vessels, much was expected from the little band of Naval aviators and their fragile seaplanes.

No time was lost in ordering a seaplane from the *Ark Royal* to fly a reconnaissance of the Turkish forts to ascertain if the defences to the entrance of the Dardanelles had been reinforced since the bombardment by an Anglo-French fleet in November the previous year.

Engine failure prevented the first two seaplanes from taking off; the third attempt was embarrassing as the under-powered machine refused to unstick in the early morning calm air and mirror-like Aegean Sea.

A 200hp Canton Unne radial engined Wight pusher seaplane eventually droned into the air 0730hrs, much to the relief of the two airmen on board at.

An hour and a quarter later, the crew of Wight 172 returned to Tenedos Bay and confirmed that the defences to the entrance of the Dardanelles had been reinforced.

During the first flight over enemy territory, the Wight dropped a calling card from the RNAS in the form of a 20lb Hale's bomb. In reply Turkish marksmen put seven bullets through the fabric-covered wings of the large seaplane.

The bombardment of the Turkish forts began on Friday 19 February. *Ark Royal* lowered four aircraft over the side during the day to carry out reconnaissance and observe the gunfire of the battleships. *Ark Royal* carried two wireless sets that were transferred from aircraft to aircraft; both sets could transmit but not receive signals.

The warships replied with Aldis lamp or searchlight. It was not as successful as their Lordships had hoped; the wireless sets were experimental and temperamental and the airman entrusted with their care, had received little or no training in the new skills of air to sea cooperation. Flt Lt Edwin Dunning, at the controls of Sopwith Folder 922, was among the airmen making up the rules of this new form of warfare as they went along.

A spell of bad weather prevented the *Ark Royal* seaplanes from taking an active part in the siege, during which time problems that beset the aircraft wireless sets were being attended to, but one airman recalled in later years, 'the wireless sets were at best home made affairs'.

When reconnaissance flights were resumed, the damage inflicted on the fortifications at the mouth of the Dardanelles had been enough to encourage a strike at forts deeper in the Straights.

By using the massive 15-inch guns of the dreadnought HMS *Queen Elizabeth*, with a range of almost 14 miles, it should be possible with *Ark Royal* seaplanes spotting, to lob 17cwt high explosive shells across the peninsular from the Aegean side, onto the heavy guns and fortifications known to be deployed all along the 15-mile narrows of the Dardanelles Straights.

Two Sopwith Folders were to spot for the *Queen Elizabeth* that took up position on Friday 5 March. The first Sopwith, No.808, fell into the sea 3 miles from the *Queen Elizabeth*; the two-man crew was rescued by a destroyer, although one had been seriously injured in the crash resulting from a shattered propeller.

The second Sopwith, No.922, crewed by Flt Lt William Sholto Douglas and Edwin Dunning, took over; unfortunately Sholto Douglas received a bullet wound in the leg and returned to *Ark Royal*.

Dunning took to the air again in Short seaplane No.136, a veteran machine that had taken part in the 1914 Christmas Day air-raid on the German Naval base at Cuxhaven. By the time 136 was ready to transmit, dusk had begun to fall; however, Dunning observed the fall of several more shells before the light faded, ending the shoot.

The next day and then the two following were stormy; rough seas prevented the seaplanes from taking off. During this period *Ark Royal* received orders to proceed to the Gulf of Saros in support of a bombardment planned as a diversionary tactic for the main assault on the Dardanelles Straights, planned for Wednesday 17 March.

Ark Royal returned to Tenedos on Friday 12 March and seaplanes immediately carried out reconnaissance flights and practised spotting mines from the air in cooperation with minesweepers.

Edwin Dunning had the floats of Sopwith Folder No.807 damaged attempting to take off on Tuesday 16th, because of its poor performance. Dunning had been flying it without an observer. Thursday 18 March 1915 was Dardanelles day: eighteen capitol ships of the allies steamed into the Straights to silence the guns in the enemy forts allowing the slower minesweepers to clear a passage through the narrows to the open Sea of Marmora.

Ark Royal received orders to send up seaplanes at hourly intervals. The first machine, a Wight Navy plane, did not get airborne until an hour after the bombardment had commenced; however, the second spotter machine over the Straights, a Sopwith Folder, reported the entrance forts had been badly damaged.

Moving further in, with guns blazing, the battleships *Irresistible* and *Ocean* struck mines and began to sink; *Inflexible*, already damaged by Turkish gunfire, also struck a mine but survived to take part in the Battle of Jutland in May 1916.

Further setbacks followed in quick succession: following a deafening explosion, the French battleship *Bouvet* sank after striking yet another mine and two more French battleships damaged by gunfire withdrew. It was a disaster for the Admiralty that had been so close to success. Minesweepers were sent in only to be greeted by a barrage of shells from field guns along the shore line. Operating in pairs towing a cable cutter between them, the minesweepers were sitting ducks and forced to retire.

It was a Catch 22 situation 1915-style; the minesweepers could not operate until the shore batteries had been dealt with and the mighty firepower of the warships could not deal with the shore batteries until the mines had been dealt with.

The twenty mines laid by the Turkish Navy on 8 March had not been discovered by the *Ark Royal* airmen due to the deadly weapons merging in with the rocks strewn across the bottom of the straights in that area. The ambitious plan of the Admiralty to breach the Dardanelles with the awesome firepower of dreadnoughts alone had failed. Enemy mines during the First World War sank four Royal Navy battleships, three cruisers, at least 250 merchant ships and 214 gallant little minesweeping vessels.

Phase two of the assault on the Turkish mainland at the Gallipoli peninsula began on 25 April 1915, involving 35,000 military and naval personnel, 17,000 ANZACS and a French division.

Edwin Dunning no doubt was both pleased and relieved when the *Ark Royal* began to receive new seaplanes. More seaworthy Short aircraft had been requested by Cdr Clark-Hall, but the first to arrive had been another Wight pusher.

More encouraging had been the arrival of Cdr Charles Samson and No.3N Squadron, with a mixed bag of aeroplanes to cover the Gallipoli campaign by flying from the island of Tenedos. The two large cranes of the *Ark Royal* performed well, unloading the crated machines for the aerodrome being prepared for the forthcoming offensive.

Although the land machines would be little or no improvement on the seaplanes, they would not be hampered by sea conditions that had prevented *Ark Royal* seaplanes from taking off.

The seaplane carrier had mobility giving its aircraft a greater range than land-based aeroplanes. The build-up to the Gallipoli landings was a busy time for the crew of *Ark Royal*, not only taking part in operations, but assembling and testing new aircraft.

Mid-April found *Ark Royal* seaplanes ranging the battleship guns from the Gulf of Saros on ammunition dumps close to the town of Gallipoli. On Thursday 15th, two Sopwith seaplanes bombed the Turkish battleship *Turgud Reis* but missed; however, another seaplane spotting for the battleship *Lord Nelson* destroyed an ammunition dump.

As troops landed on Gallipoli, *Ark Royal* had seaplanes over the ANZAC beachhead searching for enemy artillery – the well camouflaged enemy guns falling silent when the aircraft were overhead. The ANZACS requested this be done as often as possible during daylight hours.

Dunning took to the air in a hurry as 11-inch shells began to fall around the *Ark Royal* on Thursday 27 April. *Turgud Reis* had entered the straights again, and Dunning and his observer Flt Sub-Lt W. Park, on board the veteran Short No.136, directed the gunfire of HMS *Triumph*, forcing the Turkish battleship back out of range. The seaplane then flew lower, looking for gun emplacements ashore. A burst of anti-aircraft fire damaged the port wing and floats so Dunning returned to the *Ark Royal* where, alighting on a rough sea, the floats collapsed, but neither man was injured.

As the Gallipoli campaign stagnated into trench warfare, German submarines began operating in the Aegean. HMS *Triumph* was the first casualty, torpedoed on 25 May. Two days later the same U-boat sank another battleship, HMS *Majestic*.

At this early period of the war, warships were vulnerable to submarines unless moving at high speed. *Ark Royal*, which with a top speed of only 11 knots would have been a prime target, made for the island of Imbros and anchored in the bay safe from torpedoes to become a depot ship for all the RNAS aircraft land or seaplanes operating from the island.

It was still business as usual for the *Ark Royal* airmen; with new wireless sets and aircraft they carried the war to the enemy within range of Imbros and loaned seaplanes with handling crews to faster warships not so vulnerable to enemy submarines.

In November 1915, *Ark Royal* received orders to sail to Salonika where Allied forces had landed on 5 October. The Gallipoli campaign ended with the evacuation of the Allies on 8 January 1916. The terms of the Armistice, signed by Turkey on 31 October 1918, included the free passage of the Dardanelles for the Royal Navy.

British and French forces had occupied Salonika following the Bulgarian army invading Serbia on Monday 11 October 1915; Britain declared war on Bulgaria four days later.

Ark Royal aircraft operating from Thasos Island were active at the start of 1916, hunting for enemy submarines and keeping an eye on Greek military and naval forces awaiting orders to go to war, uncertain who the enemy was. Greece eventually joined the Allies on 5 July 1917.

German forces were sent to help the Bulgarians; the RNAS pilots over Salonika began to encounter enemy aircraft and were reinforced by the first contingent of Royal Flying Corps personnel and machines in July 1916.

Edwin Dunning received a posting to an aerodrome on the mainland of Greece when the *Ark Royal* returned to Mudros in March 1916. Flying from Stavros Aerodrome as part of No.2 Wing, Edwin Dunning flew a variety of aircraft on hazardous reconnaissance and bombing missions over the Bulgarian lines and the inhospitable Aegean Sea.

Details of his service at Salonika are sketchy. A confidential report from No.2 Wing for that period stated that Flight Lieutenant E.H. Dunning was reported to be 'a very efficient W/T officer'. Although orders were sent to No.2 Wing on 8 May for Dunning to return to England, he was flying a Nieuport 12 on reconnaissance of Port Lagos, with Sub-Lt C.B. Oxley as observer/gunner on Tuesday 20 June 1916. On the return journey Dunning and Oxley were attacked by two enemy seaplanes; during the fight Dunning received a leg wound, and having seen the enemy off, Oxley took over the controls of the Nieuport while Dunning applied a tourniquet to his leg.

The *London Gazette* on 14 March 1916 stated that Dunning had been mentioned in dispatches for Meritorious Service in Gallipoli and duly noted on 3 August the award of the DSC to Edwin Dunning for his presence of mind and gallant conduct, although wounded in the leg. By that time Edwin Dunning had returned to England and been promoted to Flight Commander.

On 14 September 1916 he took command of the Eastchurch Naval Air Station War Flight. During October and November he flew several times in search of hit-and-run daylight raiders along the Kent coast, flying Bristol D scout 8977.

A spell of duty with Air Department 'B' followed from 12 December 1916, until his posting to the Armstrong Whitworth works at Walker-on-Tyne six months later on 15 June 1917. Their Lordships at the Admiralty had decided, in the light of experience gained during the Gallilpoli campaign, to convert 22,000 tons of cruisers under construction at the Armstrong Whitworth yard into an aircraft carrier.

Experiments in launching aeroplanes from naval vessels had come a long way since the first successful flight from a moving ship had taken place on 2 May 1912, when Lt Charles Samson flew a Short Pusher Biplane from a ramp over the forward 12-inch guns of HMS *Hibernia*. The first successful wartime fly-off came on 6 August 1915 when Flt Lt W.L. Walsh flew a Sopwith Schneider float plane on jettisonable wheels from the deck of ex-Cunard liner, HMS *Campania*.

Right: Flight Lieutenant Dunning was wounded when he and his observer fought two enemy seaplanes in a Nieuport 12 of this type when serving with No.2 Wing RNAS. This unidentified RNAS observer demonstrates the French Lewis Gun mounting that was later superseded by the less cumbersome British Scarff ring. (D. Barber)

Below: One of the numerous attempts to launch from and land on the deck of an aircraft carrier had been this Sopwith 1½ Strutter fitted with skids in place of wheels that came to grief after taking off along rails attached to the deck of HMS *Vindex*. (C. Ross)

It would not be until the summer of 1917 that an aircraft carried out the first deck landing on a warship. Until that long awaited event, aeroplanes 'flying off' were ditched in the sea by nearby vessels or landed ashore if fuel allowed.

Whilst with Armstrong Whitworth, who were carrying out the conversion work on the cruiser HMS *Furious*, Edwin Dunning had been promoted to the rank of squadron commander.

The new aircraft carrier *Furious* had a forward 'flying-off' deck, 228ft in length and 50ft wide. The flying deck occupied the space intended for a massive 18-inch gun. A similar fearsome weapon had been mounted aft and it was said after a trial firing 'it had shaken her [*Furious*] considerably'. This gun would be removed in 1918 to make way for a 'flying on deck' and another hanger.

Complete with five Sopwith Pup biplanes that were capable of 'flying off' and four Short seaplanes, the *Furious* joined the fleet at Scapa Flow in July 1917. Although at this period *Furious* only had the one fight deck fitted forward of the carrier's superstructure and funnel designed for 'flying off', plans were made for an attempt to land a Sopwith Pup back on board.

Squadron Commander Dunning, with his nerve, experience and considerable skill as a naval aviator, carried out the first landing on board the first aircraft carrier on Thursday 2 August 1917. To perform this feat Dunning had practised deck landing ashore at Grain Naval Air Station the previous March.

Edwin Dunning, well aware of the terrible risk to life and limb, approached *Furious* steaming into the wind at 26 knots from the stem, flying to one side to clear superstructure – the plan was a simple one! – the Pup would edge in and hover above the 'flying-off' deck in the head wind where volunteers would take a firm hold on rope toggles attached to the Pup and manually pull it on to the deck.

Sopwith Pup N6452 flown by Dunning was almost the ideal little machine for such a venture, but unfortunately the 80hp Le Rhone nine-cylinder rotary engine could not be throttled back in a conventional manner, the speed had to be lowered for landing by cutting the ignition to several cylinders by the use of a 'blip switch', so-called by the blipping sound as the rotary engined aircraft came in to land.

As he drew alongside fighting the turbulence from the ship's superstructure, Dunning began to blip the rotary until the tiny biplane and aircraft carrier were side by side into the wind.

The tension among the landing volunteers increased as the Pup began to edge crabwise carefully over the forward deck, Dunning gradually lost height until willing hands grabbed the toggles and pulled the Pup safely down.

With sheer guts, skill and the unsung heroes of the deck party, Sqn Cdr Edwin Harris Dunning had carried out the first deck landing by an aeroplane in the history of the Royal Navy.

After more practice Dunning was convinced that he would be able to land a Pup unaided on the short deck and made another attempt at the controls of N6453 on Tuesday 7 August. Although the weather was squally, Dunning repeated this remarkable feat again with the aid of the deck crew. Dunning decided to make another attempt when a gust of wind slammed the tailplane against a hatch, damaging an elevator.

The first successful landing on board an aircraft carrier was performed by Sqn Cdr Dunning on board HMS *Furious*, Thursday 2 August 1917. (The Dunning Collection)

Although recovered after the fatal accident in which Sqn Cdr Dunning was drowned on Tuesday 7 August 1917, the wreckage of the badly damaged Sopwith Ships Pup N6452 was beyond repair and deleted. (The Dunning Collection)

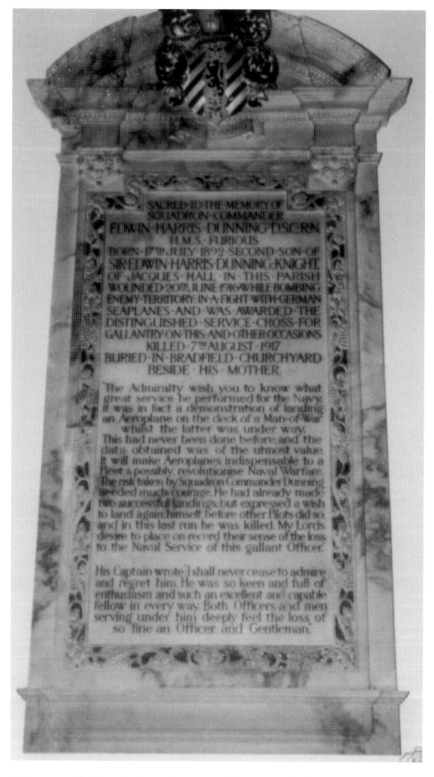

This ornate wall plaque in the north transept of St Lawrence's church was presented by the Admiralty in recognition of Sqn Cdr Edwin Harris Dunning DSC. (K. Feline)

Determined to make another attempt that day, Dunning took off again in Pup N6452, the same machine with which he had made the first successful landing on the *Furious* five days earlier.

Circling the *Furious* until the Le Rhône rotary had settled into a steady rattle, Dunning repeated the manoeuvre that had landed him back safely on board on two previous occasions. Unfortunately, due to gusting wind Dunning, again trying to land back on board unaided, touched down too far forward, the gallant deck crew rushed to his aid, several managed to grip the toggles until another severe gust of wind lifted the little Pup into the air, forcing them to let go.

The aircraft fell, veering to starboard, bouncing one wheel on the deck and, with Dunning desperately fighting for control, attempted to remain airborne. At that critical moment the Le Rhône engine choked and died. Powerless, the little biplane tumbled over the side into the sea in spite of valiant attempts made by the deck crew.

N6452 had been fitted with flotation bags but Edwin Dunning, knocked unconscious as the wrecked machine suffered a further pounding in the wake of the aircraft carrier, drowned still strapped in the cockpit of his machine before he could be rescued from the grey waters of the Scapa Flow.

The ornate wall plaque in the north transept of St Lawrence's church had been presented by their Lordships at the Admiralty in recognition of Squadron Commander Edwin Harris Dunning DSC. Part of the inscription reads as follows:

> The Admiralty wishes you to know what great service he performed for the Navy; it was in fact a demonstration of landing an aeroplane on the deck of a Man-of-War whilst the latter was under way. This had never been done before and the data obtained was of the utmost value. It will make aeroplanes indispensable to a Fleet and possibly, revolutionise Naval Warfare. The risk taken by Squadron Commander Dunning needed much courage. He had already made two successful landings; but expressed a wish to land again himself before other Pilots did so and in this last run he was killed. My Lords desire to place on record their sense of the loss to the Naval Service of this gallant Officer.

Also to be seen at St Lawrence's church are two stained-glass windows dedicated to the memory of Commander Dunning and a second memorial plaque on which the last lines in old English read as follows:

> He lovede chyvalrye
> Trouthe and honour fredom and curtesie
> He was a verray perfight gentil knight

George Henry Beard

Born in Dunmow, Essex, on 6 November 1886, George Henry Beard was the son of Richard Beard, master of the Church Schools in Dunmow.

Unable to obtain a commission in the Royal Naval Air Service after the outbreak of war, George enrolled at the Beatty Civilian Flying School at Hendon and qualified for his Royal Aero Club certificate No.1095 on Sunday 20 February 1915, flying a Wright biplane.

Once qualified, George immediately re-applied and entered the Royal Naval Air Service as Flight Sub-Lieutenant G.H. Beard the following week, reporting for duty to the Central Flying School. It was standard Royal Navy procedure at that period to reimburse airmen gaining their brevet at a civilian flying school, as George had done, the usual fee being £75.

On completion of his service training, George joined the rapidly expanding No.1 Wing RNAS at Dunkirk, where the Naval airmen flew on many and varied missions along the enemy-held Belgian coast, hunting U-boats, chasing Zeppelins and shooing off enemy seaplanes raiding both the French and English coasts.

On Sunday 26 September, a pilot returning to the aerodrome at Dunkirk reported a submarine on the surface moving west 4 miles north of Zeebrugge. George Beard took off in an Henri Farman armed with four 20lb bombs and set out in pursuit. After a lengthy search, he found the U-boat still on the surface heading at a snail's pace towards Ostend.

Without a bombsight and no doubt fingers crossed, George put the Farman in a shallow dive; levelling off at 700ft he toggled the bombs free. The small missiles exploded close to the U-boat, but not close enough to cause serious damage. As the submarine still made no attempt to submerge, George flew on to alert a Naval force bombarding Ostend docks. Without a wireless transmitter, George desperately began to semaphore with the aid of his handkerchief, it was not an easy task but at least he was in front of the slipstream created by the whirling propeller behind.

The well-tended grave of Sqn Cdr Edwin Harris Dunning in the grounds of St Lawrence church, Bradfield, is easily be identified by a bronze header. (K. Feline)

Ignoring the faster warships and flying as low as he dared, he circled the heavily armoured 12-inch gunned monitor, HMS *John Moore*. In spite of his valiant efforts, the crew of the monitor only managed to decipher the word 'submarine'; George's signals giving the position of the U-boat were unable to be read due to the smoke pouring out of the monitor's funnel obscuring the circling aeroplane at the critical time.

Not by any means were all the actions that George Beard took part in over the sea; one memorable occasion, flying Nieuport 10 aircraft as single-seaters carrying six 20lb bombs apiece, George in the company Flt Sub-Lt R.H. Mulock carried out a daylight bombing raid on the Zeppelin sheds at Evere near Brussels. Redford Henry (Red) Mulock, a Canadian pilot, became the first RNAS airman to claim five enemy aeroplanes forced down in the war.

George began the new year with a promotion to flight lieutenant on Saturday 1 January 1916 and would be commended for bombing raids carried out by day and night and for the successful spotting and correcting the fall of 12-inch shells fired by HMS *Marshal Soult* and other monitors against enemy artillery positions at Westend on 26 January.

Mentioned in dispatches for continuous Meritorious Service over the enemy lines on 15 February, George was also recommended for special recognition and reward with regards to spotting for the fleet in January, when he had worked in conjunction with Lt C.W. Nutting from the seaplane carrier HMS *Riviera*, a converted cross-channel ferry. Lt Nutting, aided by fellow officers on the *Riviera*, had devised a method for one aircraft to register the guns of five monitors firing systematic salvos.

1 Wing RNAS Nieuport 10 machines at Dunkirk setting out to bomb Zeppelin sheds near Brussels; Flt Sub-Lt George Beard was at the controls of the furthest machine. Note the burnt castor oil fumes emitted from the rotary engine of his Nieuport. (A. Longmore)

Promotion followed on 31 March 1916 when George became acting Flight Commander with the recently formed No.5 Wing based at Cloudekerque.

On 26 June the *London Gazette* reported that Flt Cdr G.H. Beard had been awarded the DSC, in recognition of his services as a pilot with the RNAS at Dunkirk.

The aircraft that George Beard flew with B Squadron No.5 Wing were Caudron GIV biplanes fitted with two 100hp Anzani radial engines. George and his observer Lt R. St John escaped serious injury in a crash that damaged Caudron 9116 beyond repair on Monday 3 July 1916.

Repeatedly attacked by the RNAS pilots of No.5 Wing were the enemy aerodromes at Ghistelles and St Denis Westrem in Belgium; George had taken part in a successful raid on Ghistelles Aerodrome on 3 September.

A few days later he was to be reported missing by the Admiralty when, on Thursday 7 September, he failed to return from an attack on another enemy aerodrome.

Flying solo in Caudron 9114, carrying a 250lb bomb load, George had set off from Cloudekerque once again to bomb St Denis Westrem Aerodrome, south-west of Ghent. Flown without an observer/gunner, the large Caudron would have been an easy prey for German fighter pilots who had found out by experience that 'Lattice tails' were vulnerable when attacked from the underside and rear, even with a gunner in the front cockpit.

On Sunday 24 September 1916, the Senior Naval Officer Dunkirk reported that the body of this gallant Essex airman had been recovered and been buried with honours at sea, this being why the Chatham Naval Memorial records that although the body of Flight Commander G.H. Beard DSC had been recovered from the sea, he, like so many of the British airmen killed in action during the First World War, has no known grave.

Christopher John Galpin

Born on 13 July 1892 at Witham in Essex, the son of the Reverend Galpin, a noted authority on medieval musical instruments, Christopher John Galpin became one of the elite band of British airmen who destroyed an enemy airship during the First World War.

Like so many men of the period, young Galpin volunteered to fight for King and Country, being accepted for the Royal Naval Air Service on Tuesday 30 March 1915. He eventually arrived as a flight sub lieutenant at the Chingford RNAS Station in Essex for flight training, where he qualified as a naval aviator in January 1916.

Such were the demands upon the RNAS by this stage of the war due to the ever growing number of merchant ships torpedoed by U-boats and the combined air-raids on Britain by Zeppelins and seaplanes, Christopher Galpin did not have to wait long for a posting. He was not, however, bound for foreign parts; his railway warrant only took him as far as Great Yarmouth on the Norfolk coast.

Great Yarmouth Naval Air Station had been opened on 15 April 1913 by their Lordships at the Admiralty who were aware of the threat posed to Britain by the bomb-carrying airships under construction in Imperial Germany.

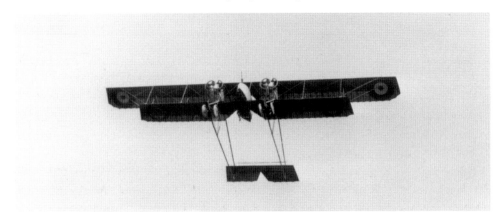

Above: An in-flight view of a Caudron GIV with two 100hp Anzani radial engines of the type flown solo by George Beard on his last bombing raid. (JMB/GSL Collection)

Right: Flight Sub Lieutenant Chistopher John Galpin, who qualified for RAeC Certificate No.2390 at Chingford RNAS Aerodrome Essex on 26 January 1916. Ft Lt Galpin was in charge of a Curtiss Flying Boat which destroyed Zeppelin L22 over the North Sea on Monday 14 May 1917. (RAF Museum)

Below: Flight Sub Lieutenant Christopher Galpin carried out numerous Home Defence patrols from Great Yarmouth Naval Air Station in a variety of aircraft. One of these, 8576, was a single-seat Avro 504C converted from the more famous Avro two-seat training machine for the RNAS. (JMB/GSL Collection)

After a short period of familiarisation, Galpin was soon flying the many and varied types of land and seaplanes at the air station. His first operational flight took place on Sunday 16 April 1916, when he carried out a patrol in Avro 504C 8576, a single-seat version of the famous training machine. At the end of his lonely patrol, Galpin returned to Yarmouth without a sighting of the reported enemy seaplane.

The following week, on St George's Day, Galpin escaped serious injury when he crashed Avro 504C 1474 on his return to Yarmouth at the end of another long patrol in search of an enemy seaplane.

During the night of 24–25 April Galpin was airborne in a Short 184 seaplane with Air Mechanic Pinn as observer on anti-Zeppelin patrol. The 225hp Sunbeam Mohawk powered seaplane, with a wingspan of 63ft 8ins and a top speed of 87mph at 2,000ft was not the ideal Zeppelin hunter.

Galpin and his observer were among the twenty-two assorted RNAS/RFC machines aloft during the combined hit-and-run raid on the east coast by German battle cruisers and Zeppelins.

High explosive shells fell on Lowestoft just after 0400hrs on Tuesday 25 April; four people were killed and twelve injured. The casualties would have been more if it had not been for the timely arrival of British light cruisers.

Once again Galpin had carried out a lengthy patrol in search of the elusive enemy without a sighting.

When short summer nights briefly curtailed the Zeppelin raids, the pace of life at Yarmouth Naval Air Station did not slacken. Galpin reverted to the single-seat Avro 504C 8576 and Sopwith Baby 8173, carrying out anti-seaplane patrols. He escaped injury when the latter machine, a small rotary engined seaplane, veered off the slipway on 6 July attempting to take off; the engine was salvaged but the airframe had to be scrapped.

Enemy seaplanes were making hit-and-run nuisance raids along the coast keeping the RNAS on its toes. Throughout July Galpin carried out routine anti-aircraft patrols in Sopwith Baby seaplanes Nos 8419 and 3776.

On the evening of Wednesday 2 August Galpin, flying 3776, encountered a Zeppelin and gave chase for 20 minutes with the airship gaining height until finally disappearing through the clouds out of sight. By now it was getting dark and, running low on fuel, Galpin had no option but to give up the chase.

In the fast-failing light, the pilot decided to put his machine down alongside a steamer at anchor 4 miles north of Cromer until daylight. Unfortunately, although alighting on a calm sea a strong tide immediately began to carry the machine away from the vessel Galpin had intended mooring to for the night.

The master of the Belgian steamship SS *Alberbircke* ordered two boats to be lowered and the Sopwith had been carried on the tide for 2 miles before the sweating seamen caught up with Galpin and towed him alongside where they finally hoisted the little seaplane aboard at 0415hrs.

Later in the day the *Alberbircke* disembarked Galpin and his machine none the worse for wear at Royal Naval Air Station Killingholme on the Lincolnshire coast. 3736 returned to Yarmouth on 5 August.

On 17 September 1916, Galpin carried out an uneventful anti-aircraft patrol in BE2c 8613, but life was seldom routine for long: no less than twelve Navy Zeppelins targeted London and the Midlands during the night of 23–24 September. Galpin, at the controls of Sopwith Baby seaplane 8149, was among the twenty-six Home Defence machines hunting them.

Having taken off from Yarmouth at 1825hrs, Galpin encountered a Zeppelin (probably the L21) 30 miles east of Lowestoft, bound for the Midlands at 7,000ft. He immediately gave chase, emptying a drum of ammunition at long range, but lost sight of the enemy whilst reloading – an all too common event for night flyers during the first war in the air.

The following night, again looking for trouble, Galpin patrolled in Sopwith Baby 8132, but it proved to be another cold and lonely airborne vigil. As we have seen from recent events, Galpin's routine patrols were seldom without incident; for example on 17 October a Short 184 type seaplane 8370 piloted by Galpin was reported as making a landing on the sea off Mundsley, a reason of engine failure or weather conditions is not recorded.

Two days later Galpin was once again airborne in BE2c 8498 on anti-aircraft patrol. His ability to fly any machine with wheels and floats at the station, from the diminutive 25ft-span Sopwith Baby with its tricky air-cooled nine-cylinder rotary engine to the large in-line water-cooled engine Short 184 was both a credit to the training received at Chingford and his own ability.

April 1917 saw the delivery of the first twin-engined Curtiss H12 patrol flying boat to Yarmouth. Compared with previous machines flown by Galpin and fellow pilots at the Norfolk Air Station, the majestic H12 was well armed with three Lewis machine guns and carried a 400lb bomb load. Not without good reason are the fifty Curtiss H12s ordered by the RNAS regarded as the most famous flying boats of the war.

Curtiss H12 8666 arrived at Yarmouth on Saturday 5 May 1917. With a wingspan of 93ft the graceful giant, originally fitted with 160hp American Curtiss engines, had been re-engined with two 250hp Rolls Royce Eagle VIII engines to give a top speed of 91mph at 5,000ft and a ceiling of 12,000ft. At long last the Yarmouth airmen had a machine suitable for long range patrols, enabling the hunting of enemy Zeppelins and U-boats in their own backyard.

With Galpin in command, 8666 roared out through the murk of pre-dawn mist and rain at Yarmouth on Monday 14 May to become airborne at 0330hrs. At the controls was Flt Sub-Lt Robert (Bob) Leckie who had collected the flying boat from Felixstowe nine days earlier, and to complete the crew, wireless telegraphic observer CPO V.F. Whatling and AM O.R. Laycock as the flight engineer. Their target was a Zeppelin that had unwittingly alerted Naval Intelligence monitors by transmitting coded wireless messages to base at Wittmudhaven en route for a routine patrol of the western area of the Dutch coast at Terschelling.

As commander of the winged boat, Galpin had the responsibility of navigation and plotted an estimated course to rendezvous with the unsuspecting Zeppelin. Forty-five minutes into the flight Galpin relieved Leckie at the controls (just three days earlier Galpin had flown a solo anti-submarine patrol in a tiny single-seat Sopwith Baby seaplane).

For Lieutenant Commander Ulrich Lehmann and the twenty men under his command on board German Naval Airship L22, a routine coastal reconnaissance well out of range of land-based British aeroplanes must have been a welcome break following a week of bad weather that confined the Zeppelins to their colossal sheds, depriving the Imperial Navy of its eyes over the North Sea. The L22, a four-engine Q type Zeppelin commissioned on 10 March 1916, had taken part in eight night raids on England during the year with Lt Cdr Martin Dietrich who, unlike the luckless Lehmann who had succeeded him, would live to see the end of the war.

On leaving Yarmouth Naval Air Station, Galpin ordered no wireless transmission to ensure the element of surprise as the Zeppelin crew was hopefully unaware of the long-range flying boat hunting them in their own backyard.

The Terschelling light ship came into view 5,000ft below at 0450hrs and there, 15 miles distant at a very low level, an unsuspecting enemy airship. Galpin opened the throttles and jettisoned three of the four anti-submarine bombs before Leckie took over the controls again.

Petty Officer Whatling was already manning the rear Lewis gun as Galpin slipped through the hatch to man the double yoked Lewis guns in the open bow cockpit. Unobserved, the flying boat closed the gap to within half a mile before the now alarmed Zeppelin crew raised her nose and began to climb rapidly.

With height and speed to spare, Leckie put the boat into a dive, overhauled the fleeing enemy and came up under the stern of the airship where at 50yds range Galpin, having cleared the Lewis guns, opened fire with the deadly mixture of incendiary and explosive bullets at the vast underbelly of the hydrogen-filled monster.

The port Lewis gun suffered a stoppage after a few rounds, but the starboard gun spat most of its lethal contents before it also jammed. As Galpin carried out the first Immediate Actions to rectify the stoppages, he thought he saw a glow inside the Zeppelin. Leckie put the boat into a tight banked turn to allow Whatling to bring the remaining serviceable weapon into action. The tormented monster was at an angle of 45 degrees when the stern erupted into flames and the stricken craft began to descend tail first. Whatling glimpsed the number L22 painted on the bow before the inferno engulfed the entire airship.

Galpin saw one crew member leap clear from the gun position at the tail and another from the rear gondola; neither man appeared to wear a parachute. Forty-five seconds later the skeleton of the L22, scorched bare of the rubberised fabric covering by the searing heat, crashed into the sea, leaving behind a thick brown column of smoke to the height of 1,500ft above an ever widening patch of oil and debris. It was still raining heavily when the flying boat returned to Yarmouth 4 hours and 20 minutes after the pre-dawn take-off, touching down at 0750hrs.

The German Navy would remain unaware of the menace of the flying boats operating in the German Bight for some weeks after the loss of the L22, despite another Zeppelin crew surviving an encounter with 8666 just ten days later.

Again with Galpin at the controls, 8666 became airborne at 0315hrs on the morning of Thursday 24 May, with fellow crew members Leckie, Whatling and Laycock. Their patrol area was once again the Dutch Islands in an attempt to cut off Naval Zeppelins returning from an unsuccessful attempt to bomb London, with craft now capable to operate at 20,000ft above the ceiling of defending night fighters and out of range of anti-aircraft guns.

'Old Eightysix-Sixtysix', the Curtiss H12 flying boat with which Flt Lt C.J. Galpin and crew destroyed German Navy Zeppelin L22. During its career this machine put the wind up two more Zeppelin crews, bombed two U-boats with visible results and rescued the crews of two RNAS land planes forced down in the North Sea. (JMB/GSL Collection)

With visibility deteriorating, Galpin, heading for Terschelling, was considering aborting the patrol when a Zeppelin suddenly broke cloud cover at 1600ft. The alert crew saw the approaching aircraft and fired two white flares, asking the aircraft to identify if friendly.

Flying at just 1,200ft because of the poor visibility, Galpin jettisoned the bomb load and roared up in pursuit of the Zeppelin as it began releasing water ballast, and climbed rapidly towards the safety of the clouds.

Galpin handed the controls over to Bob Leckie who tried to close the gap between the hunter and the hunted; Galpin managed to fire half a drum of flaming bullets at extreme range as the Zeppelin disappeared through the clouds.

In his report of the incident, Lt Cdr Erich Sommerfeldt stated that a dozen of Galpin's bullets had pierced gas cells of the L40 (the incendiaries no doubt burnt out long before they had struck home) and expressed the opinion that the enemy seaplane had been launched by surface vessel.

Fate was again on the side of the unsuspecting Lt Cdr Sommerfeldt and crew of L40 when they encountered 'Old Eightysix-Sixtysix' (as the H12 was now known back at Yarmouth NAS) on the morning of Tuesday 5 June 1917 during a routine westerly reconnaissance patrol off the island of Terschelling.

Galpin and crew glimpsed the L40 when still some 6 miles distant and made use of the mist and cloud to cover their stealthy approach. This time, in response to a white recognition flare from the L40, Leckie replied with a white Very light intended to put the enemy off their guard long enough to allow Galpin time to bring the Zeppelin within range of their .303 machine guns.

The crew of 'Old Eightysix-Sixtysix' on board HMS *Halcyon* on 8 September 1917. Flt Lt Robert
Leckie (third from left) had put the flying boat down to rescue the crew of a DH4 brought down
by anti-aircraft fire three days earlier. One account of the rescue attempt indicates that Flt Cdr C.J.
Galpin was in command; however, the remaining three crew members surrounding Bob Leckie in this
photograph are, from left to right, Flt Lt G.H. Trewin, Sqn Cdr V. Nicholl and Flt Lt A.H.H. Gilligan.
(JMB/GSL Collection)

The L40 had reached 10,500ft when all three guns opened fire from the 8666 below at
600yds range. Sommerfeldt wasted no time ordering the release of the water ballast and
full speed ahead. During the next 20 minutes, until the height climbing Zeppelin had
doubled the ceiling of the attacking H12, Galpin's crew emptied no less than ten drums
of the mixed explosive and incendiary ammunition at the rapidly diminishing target.

In spite of the fact that the L40 had patrolled for 5 hours without signs of British
warships being seen in the area, the Zeppelin commander again stated his opinion that
the aircraft had been put over the side of an adapted seaplane carrier and had posed no
real threat! The long range flying boats of the Royal Navy operating in the German Bight
were still undetected, but not for much longer.

The formidable team of Galpin and Leckie, this time with Leading AM Thompson and
AM Grant, had taken off to intercept a Zeppelin betrayed by its wireless transmissions
on 14 June.

Fate would be kind to the crew of Naval Zeppelin L46 flying blissfully along at 10,500ft
when they were overtaken by H12 8660 crewed by Galpin, Leckie and co.

Lieutenant Commander Heinrich Hollender heeded the warnings of '*Achtung Flieger*'
from his alarmed lookouts and immediately dumped a large amount of water ballast and
rapidly climbed to 15,000ft. Leckie at the controls again coaxed 8660 above 12,500ft and
at 0845hrs directly positioned beneath the enemy airship, Galpin opened fire and observed
the tracers were on target. Four drums of the deadly mixture of explosive, incendiary

and tracer were emptied with no visible result as Leckie endeavoured to push the H12 – already 500ft above its ceiling – even higher; obviously the phosphorous core of the incendiary bullets had burnt out before making impact. After half an hour of frustration, Leckie decided to call it a day. The Zeppelin had very wisely decided to keep well out of range; in fact, during the whole lengthy exchange of gunfire not one of the Zeppelin machine gunners hit the flying boat.

In his subsequent report of the incident, the Zeppelin commander identified his attacker as a single-engined seaplane with two occupants. Kvtlt Strasser assumed that this had been the same machine that had previously destroyed the unfortunate L43 and issued revised minimum altitude (13,000ft) for airships patrolling off the Dutch coast. At this height it was impossible to spot British submarines or new minefields, adding to the ever increasing hazards facing the U-boat crews.

Christopher Galpin had an encounter with a U-boat whilst on patrol in H12 8662 on 23 July, when he dropped bombs on rapidly submerging enemy craft without result.

In the early hours of Thursday 26 July 1917, wireless signals by three German Navy Zeppelins setting out to patrol the German Bight were once again intercepted by the RN Intelligence who wasted no time alerting the North Sea air stations.

'Old Eightysix-Sixtysix' became airborne from Yarmouth at 0725hrs with the experienced Zepp hunting team of Galpin, Leckie and co. One hour and forty-five minutes into their search they saw a Zeppelin and gave chase.

With the sun behind them the hunters came to within a mile of their quarry that suddenly released water ballast and began to climb at an angle of 20 degrees to 14,000ft and made off north-east towards Germany. The H12 managed to obtain 11,500ft and fired off four drums of Lewis gun ammunition without visible effect. Once again the flying boat had to abandon the chase of a height climbing Zeppelin – with an ascent rate of almost 3,000ft per minute – to get out of trouble. Galpin's adversary had again been the L46 commanded by Lt Cdr Hollender, who later confided to his observation officer that he was expecting to hear the report that the ship was on fire at any moment while the British bullets were seen and heard hitting their target.

Return fire from the Zeppelin had damaged the centre section of the upper plane and just missed the H12's built-in gravity fuel tank. If the two bombs dropped by the L46 during the engagement were aimed at Galpin's machine they fell wide of the mark and were probably jettisoned as ballast.

Continuing their patrol of the 'spider web', the crew was rewarded for their tenacity with the sighting of yet another Zeppelin about 10 miles away, flying at 8,000ft. The gap had been narrowed to 3 miles before the Zeppelin released water ballast and, turning east, climbed rapidly to 15,000ft and safety. Galpin, assuming that the L46 attacked earlier had sent out a wireless message warning sister ships of the flying boat menace, decided to call it a day and return to Yarmouth. Galpin's last quarry had been the L44, whose commander, Lt Cdr Franz Stabbert, had been warned by the L46 and called in turn for a fighter escort resulting in seaplane fighters from Borkum arriving on the scene too late to catch the long-gone 'Old Eightysix-Sixtysix'.

In an effort to overcome the advantage of the altitude reached by enemy Zeppelins operating over the North Sea, Yarmouth Air Station, on Wednesday 5 September, launched 'Old Eightysix-Sixtysix' teamed up with a single-engined DH4 two-seat bombing machine fitted with additional fuel tanks and capable of climbing to 17,500ft.

Attempting to attack the L44 scouting for German light cruisers covering mine sweeping operations, both British aircraft were damaged by accurate anti-aircraft fire; a shell splinter through the radiator of the DH4 did the most serious damage, forcing the land plane to ditch into the North Sea. 'Old Eightysix-Sixtysix' landed and taxied alongside and rescued the two airmen from a watery grave. Due to damage sustained to the hull of the flying boat by anti-aircraft fire, it proved impossible to get airborne again. It was three days later when the exhausted crew and their two passengers were rescued and 'Old Eightysix-Sixtysix' towed back to Yarmouth for repair. One account of this action published in recent years put Galpin, who had been recently promoted to Flight Commander, at the controls of the flying boat during the action. Records, however, indicate that he was not among the six survivors, but that the boat had been in the capable hands of Flt Lt Robert Leckie, who would continue taking 'Old Eightysix-Sixtysix' out on patrol. On 20 February 1918 he encountered two U-boats on the surface and badly damaged one with a pair of well-placed 230lb bombs.

Transferred to Felixstowe Naval Air Station, Galpin continued flying the large boats patrolling the 'spider web', and was in action on Saturday 3 November 1917 when, with Flt Sub-Lt G. Moody and the crew of H12 8694, they dropped bombs on a U-boat, again without visible results. Engine trouble prevented the flying boat completing the patrol and severe damage was sustained whilst under tow back to Felixstowe in rough seas.

Galpin and Moody were forced down again through engine failure onto the icy waters on Thursday 27 December; help was at hand when the destroyer HMS *Meteor* arrived in response to wireless signals from the floundering H12. A valiant attempt to tow the stranded flying boat to safety failed and the North Sea claimed the wreckage of 8676, but not the lives of her crew who were rescued to fight another day.

The new year brought changes and increased dangers for the flying boat crews who, on April 1 1918, were no longer Naval, but Royal Air Force personnel who were frequently encountering flights of enemy seaplane fighters.

A combined patrol of two Yarmouth and three Felixstowe flying boats along the Dutch coast on Tuesday 4 June 1918 ended with the biggest air battle fought above the North Sea during the First World War. It began with a broken fuel pipe forcing one of the Felixstowe boats down off the Dutch coast. Whilst the other four boats circled overhead, five enemy seaplanes arrived and began to strafe the crippled flying boat; they were quickly driven off and pursued by one of the other flying boats. Another fourteen enemy machines arrived on the scene and the remaining three flying boats, led by the redoubtable Capt. Robert Leckie, met them head on. In the ensuing battle one enemy machine attempted to strafe the downed flying boat and was brought down by return fire from the crippled boat crew and in turn another enemy seaplane alighted to rescue the pilot.

Two more enemy machines were downed in the fierce battle by the flying boats' gunners before another broken fuel pipe forced a second flying boat to descend. Repairs were quickly carried out and the fighting boat took off again, but the Germans had vanished as quickly as they had arrived. It would be several days before the fate of the boat that had chased after the five machines first encountered would be known at Felixstowe.

In a running battle with three enemy machines the flying boat was forced to land in Dutch waters and the crew interned for the remainder of the war. The three returning flying boat crews claimed six enemy machines forced down during the battle – perhaps the Germans were seeking revenge when two days later a patrol of four Brandenburg seaplanes attacked an H12, shot up the port engine and put it out of action. Yet again, the guardian angels looking after Christopher Galpin had their work cut out on Thursday 6 June 1918 as the damaged H12 4345 crashed into the North Sea leaving the crew, including Galpin and the Commanding Officer of Felixstowe Naval Air Station, Lt Col E.D. Robertson, clinging to the wreckage for 8 hours until they were finally rescued by the Royal Navy.

Three weeks after that ordeal Galpin again escaped serious injury when H12 8683 was completely wrecked in a crash on land, injuring all the crew slightly.

Major Christopher John Galpin survived the First World War. He was demobilised on 15 September 1919, after he had completed a twenty-seven-day Scandinavian tour by air that included Christiansund, Copenhagen and Stockholm at the controls of a Felixstowe F3 flying boat, returning to Felixstowe Naval Air Station on 6 August 1919.

Throughout and after the Second World War, Galpin worked for the Air Ministry until he finally retired with his wife to Brighton in Sussex.

William James Middleton and Stanley Jack Furze

William James Middleton had been resident at 54 Chingford Lane, Woodford Green, Essex, prior to the war, although he had been born at Farningham in Kent on 7 May 1897.

As a youngster William, like so many lads of his generation, was a keen member of the Boy Scout movement and became Assistant Scout Master of the local 2 Epping Forest Troop before volunteering for the Royal Naval Air Service to do his bit.

Having passed his medical he was ordered to report for training on Thursday 15 June 1916. His father, James Middleton, living at 10 Elm Grove, Woodford Green at that time, was recorded as his next of kin.

Prior to enlistment, William had been in reserved occupation, employed packing cordite in an ammunition factory, until enough women had been trained to take over and release able-bodied young men for the armed services.

In keeping with Royal Navy practice at that time, Aircraftman W.J. Middleton was on the books of HMS *President II* and HMS *Daedalus*; he actually received his training and served at the land-based Kingsnorth and Eastchurch Naval Air Stations.

It was at Eastchurch Naval Air Station that he qualified as Aircraftsman 1 Class Gunlayer, on 30 October 1917. Crossing the Channel via Folkestone, G/L Middleton arrived at Dunkirk NAS on 21 December, from where he reported for duty as an observer/gunlayer to No.5N Squadron, 5 Wing RNAS, based at Petite Synthe on Friday 1 February 1918.

No.5N Squadron had been based at Petite Synthe since April the previous year during which time the Naval airmen had exchanged their trusty but obsolete air-cooled rotary-engined Sopwith 1½ strutters for the more robust and better-armed Rolls-Royce-engined Airco DH4 bombers.

Just after the new observer had familiarised himself with the area, No. 5N Squadron were transferred with great urgency on 6 March to Villers-Bretonneux Aerodrome, 35 miles west of St Quentin in support of 22 Wing RFC, 5th Army Brigade.

On arrival the men of 5N found their new aerodrome had recently been bombed and still had a number of the craters to be filled in. The move on that Wednesday morning proved to be a minor disaster. No less than three DH4s crashed on landing at Villers-Bretonneux and another DH4, the crew having lost their way, crash-landed at Calais. However, to their credit, the remaining ten machines were in action the following morning, carrying out a bombing raid on Mont d'Origny Aerodrome.

When No. 5N Squadron paid a return visit to Mont d'Origny Aerodrome on 9 March, Gunlayer Middleton flew as observer/gunner with Flt Sub-Lt Geoffrey Ernest Siedle in DH4 N6005, taking off at 0910hrs.

Just after dropping their bombs on the target, the squadron came under attack from fifteen enemy machines. Regrouping in a defensive formation they fought their way back across the lines, but not without a suffering a casualty. Flt Sub-Lt B.R. Carter had been severely wounded in the neck; he was assisted by his observer H.F. Watson in making an emergency landing behind British lines.

Sergeant William J. Middleton flew more than 120 missions over the enemy lines as an observer with 5N/205 Squadron. This unknown DH4 observer is demonstrating the Scarff mounted Lewis gun for the family album without the ammunition drum. (D. Whetton)

Not one of the DH4s had escaped battle damage, but three German machines were claimed during the encounter. G/L Middleton and his pilot Geoffrey Siedle were credited with the first, an Albatros DV shot down out of control near Mont d'Origny Aerodrome at 1035hrs.

5N moved again on 11 March to Mons-en-Chaussée. As the one and only day-bombing squadron attached to the 5th Army at this period, the Naval airmen were attacking enemy aerodromes and ammunition dumps daily, in spite of the increasing number of German fighter aircraft along their sector of the front. Squadron 1, known to the allies as the 'Flying Circus', commanded by von Richthofen was now in direct opposition to 22 Wing RFC.

Although the Rolls Royce Eagle engines fitted to 5N DH4s were superior to the majority of British aero engines of the period, engine failure still occurred, as it did on Saturday 16 March when eleven DH4s set out at 0930hrs to bomb an ammunition dump and the aerodrome at Busigny, but only ten machines actually crossed the lines. Shortly after take-off, Flt Sub-Lt Siedle or G/L Middleton fired a Very signal flare indicating their machine A7587 had developed engine trouble and were forced to return to the aerodrome. Nine machines returned from the raid; Flt Cdr Omerod and Flt Sub-Lt Pattison had been killed when A7908 had been shot down in combat with Albatros scouts.

Twelve SE5as from No.84 Squadron had planned to use DH4 bombers as bait to lure the enemy scouts into a trap, but by the time they arrived on the scene 5N, thanks to their formidable firepower when flying in formation, had fought their own way back over the lines.

No.84 Squadron made amends the following day when the target for 5N was again the ammunition dump at Busigny, thanks to the SE5s that took on the twenty Albatros V-strutters and Fokker Triplanes; the unmolested bombers were able to obtain direct hits on the dump.

Gunlayer Bill Middleton, now a seasoned veteran with seven weeks' war flying experience, was about to take part in one of the largest dogfights of the war so far, that took place on 18 March. No.22 Wing in yet another attempt to draw enemy fighters into an ambush by No.84 Squadron SE5s, this time supported by Sopwith Camels of No.54 Squadron, ordered 5N to bomb Busigny for the third day in succession.

Nine DH4 bombers of No.5N Squadron took off from Mons-en-Chaussée at 0945hrs. in perfect flying weather; across the lines the German Air Service were waiting to draw the 'Tommies' into an ambush of their own. Outnumbered two to one by a mixed bag of Albatros and Fokker Triplanes, No.54 Squadron lost five Camels, two pilots killed, three POW, but claimed at least two enemy aircraft. The higher flying SE5as of No.84 Squadron lost two pilots killed in the action, but claimed eight enemy machines although surviving records indicate only six German fighters were lost along the entire front that day.

5N bombed Busigny Aerodrome before the enemy sprang their own trap, and fought their own way back to the lines; as usual two of the DH4s acting as escorts and carrying extra ammunition covered the rear of the formation bearing the brunt of the attackers. In spite of their valiant effort, A7663 with Flt Sub-Lt R.B. Ransford and G/L G. Smith had gone down fighting behind enemy lines, were reported missing and later confirmed as killed in action. A7587, very badly shot up by three Fokker Triplanes, managed to recross the lines to make a good landing at Estrees. Flt Sub-Lt C.E.Wodehouse, the pilot, had four bullet wounds, but his observer G/L L. James had a remarkable escape as bullets ripped his Sidcot suit in several places. G/L Middleton and his pilot, Flt Sub-Lt Siedle, in DH4 N6009, claimed an Albatros scout shot down, but due to the intensity of the fighting and number of enemy aircraft involved, they lacked confirmation.

For the record, Geoffrey Ernest Siedle, the No.5N/205 Squadron pilot Sgt Middleton regularly flew with at this period, was a year younger, born on 23 November 1898 in Swansea. Siedle had been one of the many Essex 'Chingflyers' when he qualified for his RAeC at Chingford Naval Air Station on 28 May 1917, followed by his posting to No.5N Squadron.

Rain and low cloud the following two days fortunately washed out another plan by HQ to have 5N lure the Huns into battle, in which sixty RFC fighters were to be involved.

The short respite for 5N came to an end on 21 March as the German Army in mist and fog launched an all-out major offensive on the Western Front, commencing with a terrific bombardment. At 0445hrs 9in shells began falling at regular intervals on the fog-shrouded aerodrome less than 8 miles behind the front line, forcing 5N to evacuate to Champien Aerodrome, then still 22 miles behind the lines. At 1330hrs the aircraft of 5N, taking advantage of a break in the fog to get away, bombed crowded canal bridges at Honnecourt before flying on to their new base. To the credit of the officers and men in spite of this major upheaval, 5N refuelled and rearmed to carry out a second raid on advancing enemy troops and their transport before dark.

As Champien Aerodrome also had four RFC squadrons sharing – having been driven from their own airfields – G/L Middleton slept two nights with the ORs in a hanger, while 5N officers shared one very over-crowded hut.

Fog again prevented any flying on the 22nd until the afternoon, when the canal bridges were again targeted, with a second bombing raid carried out in the evening.

Desperate times called for desperate measures: 5N were ordered to move to Bertangles, 5 miles north of Amiens on 23 March, but not before carrying out four more bombing raids from Champien, landing at Bertangles in the dusk after the last sortie. On arrival they found six RFC squadrons crammed into Bertangles and, as the last to arrive, again there were no living quarters available for the officers who had to sleep under canvas; the Ludendorff offensive had much to answer for.

The vital canal bridges at Bellincourt, already 15 miles behind the front lines, were again the target for No.5N Squadron on the morning of the 24th. Flying over the still shell-cratered Mons-en-Chaussée Aerodrome they had recently evacuated, they could see enemy machines taking off in pursuit. A second raid by the men of No.5N Squadron during the afternoon did extensive damage to Roisel railway station, starting several fires.

Exhausted as they were, the men of 5N worked round the clock on the aircraft out in the open to keep them airworthy. On 27 March, the situation along the front was so serious, 5N were ordered to engage in low-level bombing and strafing already being carried out by Scout and Corps squadrons. Unable to fly in defensive formation at low level, the DH4s were more vulnerable to German fighters and small arms fire from the ground; this no doubt accounted for the loss of D8379 the very same day. Flt Sub-Lt

E.C. Stocker and G/L C.M. Rendle, having no known graves, are listed on the Arras Memorial.

An enemy pontoon bridge across the river Somme was just one of the many targets bombed and strafed by aircraft of 5N on the 28th as yet another move, this time to Bois de Roche 10 miles west of Doullens, was carried out. The aircraft arrived long before their transport that had been delayed by the chaos on the roads and breakdowns, not arriving until 2300hrs in the pouring rain, in which the tent accommodation had to be erected before anyone could get some rest.

It is an ill wind that blows no good! A gale prevented the squadron from getting airborne the next day, giving the Naval airmen a chance to settle in their new quarters; but it was business as usual on 30 March; starting with an early morning raid on the Somme bridges. Gunlayer T. Jones was wounded strafing troops and transport at Villers Bretonneux; Flt Sub-Lt C.J. Heyward crashed attempting to land the shot-about DH4 N5992 with his wounded observer at Haute Visée Aerodrome occupied by No.101 Squadron.

The two morning raids carried out by 5N on the last day of March were to be their last action as Naval airmen. The Royal Naval Air Service and the Royal Flying Corps were amalgamated to form the Royal Air Force on Monday 1 April 1918.

Until he received a new uniform the only change affecting Bill Middleton was his remustering from his Naval rank as gunlayer to sergeant mechanic in No.205 Squadron (as all ex-RNAS squadron numbers were given a 200 prefix, No.5 Naval Squadron had now become No.205 Squadron).

The situation on the ground had eased sufficiently for No.205 Squadron to resume targeting aerodromes. A raid on Lamotte Aerodrome on 6 April brought the first casualties of No.205 Squadron when A7620 failed to return, with the loss of Lt G.M. Cartmell and AM A. Lane, later reported killed in action.

Mist, fog and rain assisted the enemy in launching another devastating assault that, within 3 hours, saw German storm troops in open country behind the British lines on 9 April. Once again British aerodromes near the front were hurriedly evacuated; sixteen fog-bound Sopwith Camels of No.208 Squadron had to be torched in the retreat. This time, however, Sgt Middleton did not have to re-pack his kit; No.205 Squadron were able to remain at Conteville until August.

The situation along the front became so serious, Field Marshal Douglas Haig sent out his now famous 'Backs to the Wall' order on 12 April 1918. Two raids were carried out by No.205 Squadron on Dampierre Aerodrome the same day; Fokker Triplanes were fought off by the combined firepower of the formation. N6001, that had developed engine failure, crashed on landing, but the crew were unharmed.

Captain C.R. Lupton and Air Mechanic A.G. Wood had a narrow escape on the 17th in N6000, when their rudder controls were shot away in combat and they were forced to land at Corbie, hitting telegraph wires; both men escaping serious injury. AM Albert Wood was destined to be killed in action less than one month later on 9 May.

A washed-out attempt to bomb Chaulnes railway station on 20 April had a tragic ending when 2nd-Lt R.C. Day had a foot blown off when his DH4 E4624 crashed, exploding a bomb and catching fire while attempting to land; his observer Sgt S.M. MacKay miraculously escaped serious injury.

German fighter opposition was on the increase: two Fokker Triplanes were claimed out of control on 22 April. An evening raid on the 23rd by five DH4s, again on Chaulnes railway station, saw them attacked by a large number of enemy machines. In the running battle five enemy scouts were claimed. Sgt Middleton and Lt Geoff Siedle in A8071 were credited with a Fokker Triplane out of control; all five of the DH4s suffered battle damage but no casualties.

DH4 A8071 proved to be a lucky 'Bus' for Lt Siedle and Sgt Middleton. Another raid on Chaulnes railway station by C Flight, led by the redoubtable New Zealand pilot Capt. Euan Dickson on the evening of Friday 3 May, cost the lives of Lt R.J.Scott and 2nd-Lt T.A. Humphries in D9243 shot down by Pfalz scouts. The combined firepower of the remaining eight DH4 gunners, including Sgt Middleton in A8071, piloted by Lt Siedle, were credited with two of the enemy machines, one falling in flames. Capt. Dickson and his observer AM C.V. Robinson shot down another Pfalz before leading the remainder of his flight home.

Returning from a raid on rolling stock and troop concentrations at Chaulnes on the morning of Thursday 9 May, where the anti-aircraft fire had been lighter than usual and a Jasta of enemy scouts encountered did not attack, it came as a shock when DH4 N6009 suddenly fell out of the formation as its wings folded, breaking up in the air over Amiens carrying nineteen-year-old Capt. Charles Lupton and AM Albert Wood to their deaths. They were another two gallant airmen who may have survived had parachutes been issued to allied airmen during the First World War.

The important railhead at Chaulnes continued to be targeted with ensuing battles on the homeward flights, until 11 May when the weather prevented raids being launched until the morning of the 15th. On the return journey a Pfalz scout was sent down out of control at Chaulnes by the crew of A7561, although during the encounter 2nd-Lt H.P. Bennett, the observer, had been wounded in the shoulder. The same evening 2nd-Lt Jones, an observer, was wounded in the arm.

On 17 May, observer 2nd-Lt J.A. Whalley sustained bullet wounds in both thighs in DH4 A7561. This machine had seen front line service with Nos 57 and 25 Squadrons RFC, prior to repair and being put to good use by No.5N/205 Squadron. DH4 D8401 failed to return from another raid on Chaulnes the next day; 2nd-Lt H.C. Conron and 2nd-Lt J. Finnigan were both later reported killed in action.

Luck almost ran out for the crew of DH4 A8071 when anti-aircraft fire badly damaged their machine, forcing Lt Siedle to put the machine down at Bertangles on the last day of May. Fortunately both Siedle and Middleton were unhurt, but it was the end of DH4 A8071, which had to be rebuilt and renumbered F6114, before being issued to No.57 Squadron in September.

Promoted to captain, Geoffrey Siedle left No.205 Squadron when he was posted to No.98 Squadron as a flight commander on 6 June. He was awarded the DFC on 2 July 1918 for his service with No.205 Squadron.

Lieutenant Stanley Jack Furze had been sent to No.205 Squadron at Bois de Roche on 4 June 1918 as a replacement pilot. Jack Furze was the son of an Essex farmer born on 3 September 1899 at Bromleys Farm, Harlow. Joining the army in November 1915, Jack had seen action on the Somme as a motorcyclist with the Army Service Corps before transferring to the Royal Flying Corps in August 1917.

He made his first flight with No.205 Squadron the next morning; the first of his many operational flights, both photographic reconnaissances took place on 26 and 27 June in DH4 A8030 with Lt J.B. Leach as observer. In spite of bad weather, they were able to take urgently needed photographs east of Amiens.

On 29 June with Sgt Murphy in D9238, in face of intense anti-aircraft fire, Jack took part in a successful bombing raid on Le Plateau ammunition dump. Again on 1 July, with Sgt Murphy in D9238, Jack flew two bombing raids on ammunition dumps at Bray and Chuignolles, during which the squadron was attacked by enemy aircraft and several DH4s were damaged.

No.205 Squadron targets for July included the railway stations at Bray and Rosières, a rest camp at Morcourt and ammunition dumps La Flaque, Omiécourt, Froissy and Trônes Wood, and the aerodrome at Cappy. Jack Furze flew on most of these missions with 2nd-Lt J.C. Walker as his Observer.

On 6 July the squadron bombed the enemy aerodrome at Cappy during which several DH4s were damaged by ground fire. The daily round of bombing and reconnaissance continued through July with No.205 Squadron sustaining just two casualties, Lt J.C. Wilson, pilot, on the 19th and 2nd-Lt P.S. Hartley, observer, on the 25th. Both men were wounded.

When weather conditions permitted, enemy dumps and railway stations were bombed in preparation for the opening of the battle of Amiens on 8 August 1918. The main task allotted to No.205 Squadron in connection with the opening of this 'Push' was the bombing of the Somme bridges.

During a raid on bridges at Brie and St Christ on the 10th, the formation were attacked by fourteen enemy scouts; No.205 Squadron gave as good as they got. Sgt Middleton, flying with Capt. J.M. Mason in D9255, sent a Pfalz scout down in flames; the formation sent another Pfalz and a Fokker down out of control. It had been a particularly fierce encounter, 205 were lucky to have had just one casualty – an observer, 2nd-Lt Herbert Hopton wounded by a Pfalz scout. The enemy pilot was probably wounded just after, as he was sent down out of control by the guns of observer 2nd-Lt Stanley Hamblin in A7587.

An unlucky Hun, climbing to attack 8421 from underneath, had a port wing shattered by a 112lb bomb as Lt Grossart and 2nd-Lt J.B. Leach released their load on Péronne railway station during a raid on 11 August.

Tuesday 13th saw more No.205 Squadron casualties: A7573 with Lt T. Fattorini and 2nd-Lt S.J. Parks failing to return from a photographic reconnaissance and later reported killed in action. A bombing formation was intercepted by a mixed bag of twenty Fokker and Pfalz biplanes. During the engagement, Sgt F.G. Manning, an observer in D8429, was killed and his pilot, Lt F.O. McDonald, wounded. Lt A.N. Hyde and 2nd-Lt W.W. Harrison had luck flying with them when DH4 D8387 was badly damaged by anti-aircraft fire on the 21st.

Doingt railway station, Trônes Wood, Roisel and Epehy were targets for No.205 Squadron until 25 August when the squadron moved from Bois de Roche to Bovelles Aerodrome. Maj. S.J. Goble who had been in command of the squadron since July 1917, contracted typhoid fever and command was taken over temporarily by Capt. J.M. Mason. Maj. A.J. Michell-Clarke arrived to take command of No.205 Squadron on the last day of August 1918.

September saw the German army falling back with deteriorating morale; however, the German Air Service fought on fiercely, as can be seen by the following casualties suffered by No.205 Squadron.

Observer 2nd-Lt J.C. Walker flew over the enemy lines with Jack Furze for the sixteenth and last time on 6 September. The next morning, with Lt D.J. Mellor in A7587, carrying out a reconnaissance, they were shot down. Walker was fortunate to escape serious injury as a prisoner for the remainder of the war; nineteen-year-old Douglas Mellor was killed.

Sergeant Bill Middleton was awarded the Distinguished Flying Medal, the citation for which appeared as follows in the *London Gazette*, 10 September 1918:

No F 16604 ACI (Gunlayer) William James Middleton (Woodford Green). He has taken part in 67 raids and has shown conspicuous gallantry and skill in bombing enemy lines of communication, dumps and aerodromes, on one occasion he obtained 6 direct hits despite intense anti-aircraft fire.

It was also the month that No.205 Squadron began to exchange the venerable but ageing DH4 for the DH9A. On 15 September, 2nd-Lt F.O. McDonald and 2nd-Lt J.B. Leach in DH9A F1009 engaged an enemy two-seater that fell in flames.

A relaxed Lt S.J. Furze at the controls of No.205 Squadron DH9A E1108, with fellow pilot Lt W.F. Taylor as a passenger, after the Armistice of 'the war to end all wars'. (D. Furze)

The next day as Jack Furze went home on leave No.205 Squadron ground crews were on the move to Proyart East; for the pilots and observers it was business as usual during the move.

At the end of the day, No.205 Squadron had two men killed, three wounded and another POW. Among the dead was nineteen-year-old Sgt Leonard Murphy who had flown as Jack's observer during June and July. Murphy's pilot, 2nd-Lt F.F. Anslow was taken prisoner when DH4 D9250 had been shot down by two enemy scouts near Bellenglise.

Badly shot about after bombing Busigny, DH4 B7764 was forced to land with pilot Lt G.C. Mathews wounded and observer Lt A.G. Robertson dying.

Returning from the same raid, 2nd-Lt H.F. Taylor, DH4 7964, landed at Proyart with his observer, 2nd-Lt H.S. Mullins, wounded. Also lucky to get back to the new aerodrome was DH4 D8429 with pilot Lt E.O. Danger wounded. It had not been a one-sided battle: two Fokker DVIIs and a Hannover had been shot down; the crew of DH9A F1016 claiming the two-seater and a Fokker DVII.

Busigny was again the target for No.205 Squadron, who were lucky to return with just one casualty on the 17th when observer to Lt H.F. Taylor in DH4 D8421, 2nd-Lt H.S. Millan, was wounded. Fighting their way back across the lines after bombing Villers Outreaux on 21 September, the formation saw DH4 A8089 – under attack by two Fokker DVIIs – break up in a steep dive carrying Lt A.N. Hyde and 2nd-Lt W.W. Harrison without parachutes to their deaths. During the running battle 2nd-Lt W. Tunstall, observer to Lt W.H. Clarke in DH9A F1015, was also wounded.

The battle of Cambrai began on 27 September with No.205 Squadron carrying out tactical reconnaissance patrols with single machines leaving at 90-minute intervals, while flights bombed troop concentrations at Brancourt and Beaurevoir, during which – on the 29th – the pilot of DH9A, Lt H.G. Kirkland, was wounded and observer 2nd-Lt C. O'Neill Daunt killed.

Returning from leave on 30 September, Jack Furze found that No.205 Squadron had a new commanding officer; Major Michelle-Clarke having been replaced by Major J.F. Gordon two days earlier.

During the next month Lt Furze flew twelve high- and low- level reconnaissance patrols in DH9A F1024. It was while flying as observer with Jack Furze, on 3 October, that fate caught up with twenty-one-year-old Sgt Middleton. While carrying out a low-level reconnaissance, Bill Middleton was severely wounded and died the following day.

Sergeant William James Middleton DFM from Woodford was buried with full military honours in what is known today as the Bronfay Farm Military Cemetery.

On 2 September 1919, James Middleton, on behalf of his son, received the posthumous award of the Medaille d'Honneur (Silver) from the French Government in recognition of his bombing of the bridge at Brie on 10 August 1918.

On the last day of October, Jack Furze, with 2nd-Lt A.D. Hollingsworth in DH9A F990, bombed Namur south-east of Brussels, and on the first day of November the railway station at Brussels was targeted. Not knowing at the time, Jack flew his last two bombing raids, again with Hollingsworth as observer, when Charleroi was bombed twice on 4 November.

Jack had one more hair-raising experience before the guns fell silent on 11 November when, the day before collecting a new DH9a from the Depot, it was run into by DH9 F6074 from No.107 Squadron crewed by Lt A. Holden and AM C. Chirgwin. Although DH9A E9731 was a complete write off, Jack and the No.107 Squadron lads escaped serious injuries.

Demobilised on 9 March 1919, Lt Stanley Jack Furze had flown over the enemy lines on fifty bombing raids and twenty-one photographic reconnaissance flights; thirty-four non-operational flights were also flown plus fourteen more offensive patrols that were aborted due to adverse weather or mechanical problems. Jack's total flying hours with No.205 Squadron amounted to 212; of these, 120 hours on DH4s and 92 on DH9As.

Although Jack Furze had been a member of the RFC/RAF, not the RNAS, he has been included in Part Three 'The Sea Birds' for the continuity of No.5N/205 Squadron, plus being Sgt Bill Middleton's pilot on his last flight over the lines.

Just before the outbreak of the Second World War, Jack Furze returned to the RAF as an Aircraftsman 2 Class, promoted to flight sergeant in 1940 and being demobilised in 1945 for the second time. On retirement from the Ministry of Agriculture & Fisheries, Jack lived at Clacton-on-Sea until he passed away in 1985 at eighty-five years of age.

The five Essex men of the RNAS/RAF remembered above, plus the younger of the Petre and Woodhouse brothers, gave an insight into the many and varied duties carried out by 'The Sea Birds'. The author would include Essex men who also served with RNAS amoured cars, kite balloons and airships. The same applies to 'The War Birds' of the RFC; this does not include, for example, Sergeant-Major Jillings MC, from Brentwood, Essex, the first British airman to be wounded by the enemy. However, as one can see by the following Roll Call of Essex airmen that the author was aware of at time of publication, it would be impossible to include them all.

If, as I take my leave, you find yourself wanting to know more about the First World War in the air, you can do no better than to look at:

Cross & Cockade International
The First World War Aviation Historical Society
http://www.crossandcockade.com

ESSEX AIRMEN 1910–1918 ROLL CALL

This roll is by no means complete, but may be of assistance to readers for future reference.

Ackroyd, 2nd-Lt Herbert Gibson, RFC RAeC 2621	Survived war 24 March 1916	Chelmsford
Adamson, Lt Gordon, RFC RAeC 495	Survived war 29 May 1913	Halsted
Allen, 2nd-Lt Francis R.L., No.213 Sqn RAF	Killed in action 14 October 1918	Manor Park
Anderson, PO Frederick C., Russian A/C Div. RNAS	Killed in action 16 April 1917	Forest Gate
Ansell, Lt Arnold E., Pilot No.48 Sqn RAF	Survived war	Laindon
Apling, Lt Stanley H., Pilot No.64 Sqn RAF	Survived war	Ilford
Archer, Major John O., RAF RAeC 2367	31 January 1916	Walton on the Naze
Armstrong, 2nd-Lt John L.P., No.25 Sqn RFC	Killed in action 22 June 1917	Felsted
Aspinall, Capt. John V., Pilot No.11 Sqn RAF	Killed in action 15 May 1918	Epping
Atkinson, 2nd-Lt Charles H., No.54 Sqn RAF	Killed in action 4 July 1918	Upton Park
Baker, AM Sidney A., No.27 Sqn RAF	Died of influenza 9 October 1918	Highams Park
Bardell, Flt Sub-Lt N., KB OBS RNAS	Survived war	Ilford
Barker, Lt Frank E., Ferry pilot	Killed whilst flying 13 January 1919	Walthamstow
Barlow, Lt Frederick C., No.49 W/T SQN RAF	Killed in action 21 August 1918	Ilford
Barlow, 2nd-Lt John L., No.40 Sqn RFC	Killed in action 23 September 1917	Wivenhoe

The photographer appears to be of more interest than this Morane Parasol that landed at Ingatestone, Essex, in the winter of 1916! Note the station master, paperboy and other locals rubbing shoulders with lads from the artillery. (R. Shelly)

Bateman, Lt John C., No.1 Sqn RAF RAeC 3727	Survived war 21 October 1916	Woodford
Beaumont, 2nd-Lt Charles L., 25 RAS RFC	Killed whilst flying 19 May 1917	Thaxted
Beard, Flt Cdr George H., DSC 5 Wing RNAS	Killed in action 7 September 1916	Dunmow
Beck, 2nd-Lt Herbert M., No.3 Sqn RFC	Killed in action 22 January 1918	Ilford
Bellerby, Sgt Herbert, No.27 Sqn RFC	Killed in action 23 September 1916	Chingford
Bence, Cpl Stewart J., No.211 Sqn RAF	Killed in action 14 August 1918	Leytonstone
Bennett, Cpl R., Observer RAF	POW details unknown	Ilford
Binney, Capt. Frank B., No.12 Sqn RFC	POW 26 September 1915	Tolleshunt D'Arcy
Boardman, 2nd-Lt Alex G., RAF	Killed in flying accident 29 April 1918	Woodford
Box, Lt George H., No.100 Sqn RAF	Killed in action 25 August 1918	Manor Park
Brand, Lt Francis R., No.29 Sqn RAF	Killed in action 27 June 1918	West Ham
Bray, 2nd-Lt Charles L., No.211 Sqn RAF	Killed in action 19 May 1918	Manor Park

Bridger, Sgt Ernest E.A., No.57 Sqn RAF	Killed in action 16 August 1918	Barking
Brinsmead, AM Alfred E., RAF	Killed by A/C propeller 13 July 1918	Forest Gate
Brown, Flt Cdt Charles D., RAF	Killed in flying accident 27 July 1918	Ilford
Browne, 2nd-Lt George E., No.42 Sqn RAF	Killed in action 23 September 1918	Southend-on-Sea
Brufton, 2nd-Lt Howard C., No.47 Sqn RFC	Killed in action 8 July 1917	Wanstead
Brunwin-Hales, Capt. Greville, No.13 Sqn RFC	Killed in action 24 March 1917	Colchester
Burton, 2nd-Lt Stanley G., No.99 Sqn RAF	Killed in action 30 July 1918	Westcliff-on-Sea
Carr, Major Hugh C., RAF RAeC 504	Survived war 2 June 1913	Walthamstow
Carpenter, Lt Eric E., RAF	Killed in flying accident 24 August 1918	Walthamstow
Cayford, 2nd-Lt George E., RFC	Killed in flying accident 16 July 1917	Wanstead
Chainey, 2nd-Lt F.H., Observer No.100 Sqn	POW 16 September 1918	Chingford
Chapman, Sgt Ronald C., Observer No.206 Sqn RAF		Manor Park
Cherry, Sgt E., Observer No.215 Sqn RAF		Stratford
Child, Lt Jack E., 188 Tr. Sqn RAF	Died of influenza 3 November 1918	Leytonstone
Child, Capt. James M., MC MID RAF	Killed whilst flying 23 August 1918	Leytonstone
Chrystall, Lt A.J., No.100 Sqn RAF Recording Officer		Buckhurst Hill
Clappen, Major Donald W., RAF	Served in Second World War Died 30 November 1978	Westcliff-on-Sea
Clarke, 2nd-Lt Herbert P., No.46 Sqn RAF	Killed in action 1 October 1918	Frinton-on-Sea
Claydon, Pte Harold A., No.18 Sqn RAF	Killed in action 25 July 1918	Grays
Clinch, Lt Stanley J., Pilot No.27 Sqn RFC/RAF	Served as Wg Cdr in Second World War	Seven Kings
Cooper, Lt Arthur G., Pilot No.28 Sqn RAF	Survived war	Essex
Cooper, 2nd-Lt George W., No.226 Sqn RAF	Killed in action 30 August 1918	Walthamstow
Collet, AM John, MiD Pulham AS RNAS	Killed in action 11 December 1917	Walthamstow
Connell, 2nd-Lt R.F., Observer No.99 Sqn RAF	Wounded in action 1 July 1918	Ilford
Cowan, 2nd-Lt Albert A., RAF	Killed in flying accident 16 July 1918	Stratford
Curtiss, 2nd-Lt Ralph L., No.48 Sqn RFC	Killed in action 21 September 1917	Rainham

Crosbie, Major Dudley S.K., RAF RAeC 735	Survived war 16 February 1914	Laindon
Crosswell, AM Thomas J., RFC	Killed in motorcycle accident 6 December 1917	Ilford
Daniel, Flt Cdt Harry T., RFC	Killed in flying accident 18 August 1917	Leigh-on-Sea
Daly Flt Sub-Lt Denis H., No.12 Sqn RNAS	Killed in action 17 July 1917	Leigh-on-Sea
Darrington, Lt Harold E., No.27 Sqn RFC	Killed in action 20 November 1917	Wanstead
Davidson, 2nd-Lt William, No.10 Sqn RFC	Killed in action 31 October 1917	Forest Gate
Davis, 2nd-Lt C.S., RAF	Killed whilst flying 7 May 1919	Ilford
Davis, 2nd-Lt Reginald, No.3 Sqn RFC	Killed in action 20 October 1916	Great Holland
Davis, Flt Cdt Charles W., RAF	Killed in flying accident 13 October 1918	Southend-on-Sea
Debenham, Capt. Horace G.W., No.46 & 208 Sqn RAF		Romford
Dendrino, 2nd-Lt Stephen, No.27 Sqn RFC	Killed in action	Great Waltham
Dennis, 2nd-Lt Charles C., No.11 Sqn RFC	Killed in action 25 September 1917	Ilford
Dennis, 2nd-Lt L.J., Observer No.97 Sqn RAF		Chingford
De Roeper, Major Bruno P.H., AFC 6N Sqn RNAS/RAF	Survived war	Forest Gate
Dismore, AM Frederick, RFC RAeC 580	Survived war 5 May 1913	East Ham
Docking, Lt Robert R., No.43 Sqn RFC	Killed in action 10 February 1917	Manor Park
Duddy, 2nd-Lt T.S., Observer No.115 Sqn RAF		Colchester
Duncan, 2nd-Lt H.E., Pilot No.100 Sqn RAF	Survived war	Upton Park
Dunning, Sqn Cdr Edwin H., DSC RNAS	Killed in action 7 August 1917	Bradfield
Dyke, 2nd-Lt E.P., No.98 Sqn RAF	Killed in action 30 October 1918	Southend-on-Sea
Edwards, Cpl Robert, No.48 Sqn RFC	Killed in action 30 April 1917	Canning Town
Ellery, Sgt Frederick A., No.107 Sqn RAF	Killed in action 14 September 1918	Walthamstow
Ellis, Sub-Lt L.G., RNAS/RAF	Former Ilford County High Pupil	Ilford
English, Sig. Henry A., RNAS	Killed in action 27 April 1916	East Ham
Eppstein, Flt Lt Maurice W.W., No.10 Sqn RNAS	Killed in action 12 May 1917	Lambourne
Evans, 2nd-Lt Hugh W., RFC	Killed in flying accident 30 August 1917	Seven Kings

Evans, Lt L.L.M., RAF RAeC	Survived war 6 July 1916	Brightlingsea
Everitt, PO Jesse, Dardanelles A/C Div. RNAS	Killed in action 6 June 1915	Southend-on-Sea
Felton, Sgt William R., RAF	Killed in flying accident 2 July 1918	Ilford
Firmin, Charles A., No.59 Sqn RAF	Wounded in action 19 October 1918	Ilford
Fish, Capt. William R., MC No.54 Sqn RAF	Killed in action 2 June 1918	Woodford
Fine, Lt Soloman, No.15 Sqn RAF	Killed whilst flying 18 May 1918	Southend-on-Sea
Fitzsimons, 2nd-Lt John B., RFC	Killed in flying accident 26 March 1917	Ilford
Flintoft, Lt Herbert T., No.56 Sqn RAF	POW 10 August 1918	Seven Kings
Fox, Lt R., DFC	Died of influenza 1 May 1919	Manor Park
Fox, 2nd-Lt Walter R., No.15 Sqn RAF	Killed in action 22 August 1918	Hornchurch
Fox-Rule, Capt. Gordon, DFC No.49 Sqn RAF	Survived war	Southminster
Fozzard, 2nd-Lt G., Observer RAF 1918	Survived war	Ilford
Freeman, Capt. S.T., RAF RAeC	Survived war 21 January 1913	Stratford
French, 2nd-Lt Thomas H., RFC	Killed in flying accident 13 January 1917	Ulting
Furze, Lt Stanley J., No.205 Sqn RAF	Survived war	Harlow
Galpin, Flt Cdr Christopher J., DSO RNAS/RAF	Survived war	Witham
Gardiner, 2nd-Lt D., No.80 Sqn RAF 1918	Survived war	Ilford
Gay, 2nd-Lt Frederick H., No.16 Sqn RFC	Died of wounds 25 March 1917	Romford
Gibson, Lt Ackroyd H., RAF RAeC 2645	Survived war	Chelmsford
Golding, 2nd-Lt W.A., No.23 Sqn RFC	Wounded in action 4 March 1917	Ilford
Greaves, 2nd-Lt W.H., Observer No.100 Sqn RAF		Leyton
Greif, Flt Sub-Lt Charles C., RNAS RAeC 2179	Survived war 17 December 1915	Grays
Greig, Lt Charles William, RAF	Killed in action 12 September 1918	Manor Park
Grenfell, Major Eustace O. MC DFC AFC No.1, 60 & 23 Sqns RAF		Southend-on-Sea
Gross, 2nd-Lt Robert J., RFC	Killed in flying accident 25 February 1918	Dovercourt
Groves, Lt J., Pilot RAF 1918	No further details	Ilford

Haley, 2nd-Lt Arthur, No.55 Sqn RAF	Killed in action 1 June 1918	Buckhurst Hill
Harris, Capt. Trevor W., RAF	Killed in flying accident 4 October 1918	Ilford
Harrison, Capt. William R.E., RAF RAeC 688	Survived war 21 November 1913	Colchester
Hart, 2nd-Lt Frederick W., RAF	Killed in flying accident 22 July 1918	West Ham
Harvey, AM Frederick A., KBS RFC & RAF	Survived war	Hainault
Herrett, 2nd-Lt G.R., Observer No.100 Sqn RAF	Survived war	Brentwood
Herring, Lt Albert H., No.25 Sqn RAF	Killed in action 20 May 1918	Ilford
Hill, Flt Sub-Lt Austin B., DSC 2 Wing RNAS	Invalided out September 1917	Chigwell
Hillebrandt, 2nd-Lt Frederick, RFC	Killed in flying accident 22 March 1916	Ilford
Hollick, Lt John, Pilot No.210 Sqn RAF	Killed in action 18 May 1918	Upminster
Horton, Capt. John H., RAF RAeC 2456	10 February 1916	Hockley
Hyde, Capt. Frank, No.13 Sqn RFC, No.260 Sqn RAF	Survived war	Walthamstow
Ingleby, Major Clement R., Pilot RAF	Survived war	Ilford
Isaacs, Flt Sub-Lt Walter A., A Sqn RNAS	Killed in action 3 November 1917	Leytonstone
Jakins, 2nd-Lt Walter V., RFC	Killed in flying accident 10 July 1917	Woodford
Jameson, Capt. Wilfred C., RAF	POW killed escaping 15 September 1918	Ilford
Jarvis, Sgt Charles E., RFC RAeC 524	Survived war 17 June 1913	Harwich
Jeffkins, 2nd-Lt Eric C., No.215 Sqn RAF	Wounded 17 September 1918	Ilford
Jillings, Sgt-Maj. David S., MC No.2 Sqn RFC	Wounded 22 August 1914	Brentwood
Jones, Sgt W.E., MM No.211 Sqn RAF	POW 28 September 1918	Ilford
Keddie, Capt. George, 198 (N) TS RAF	Survived war	Southend-on-Sea
Keen, Lt Stephen W., MC No.60 Sqn	Killed in action 21 August 1918	Manor Park
Kimpton, Sgt Ernest F., No.108 Sqn RAF	Died of wounds 2 September 1918	Walthamstow
King, Lt William H., No.7 Sqn RAF	Killed in action 11 April 1918	Colchester
King, AM Albert E., DSM No.2 Wing RNAS	Killed in action 12 June 1917	Forest Gate
Knox, 2nd-Lt Charles D.,	Killed in action	Westcliff-on-Sea

No.43 Sqn RFC	17 March 1917	
Know, 2nd-Lt F.W.,	Survived war	Ilford
Observer RAF		
Knight, Lt George B.,	Died of wounds	Ilford
No.53 Sqn RAF	7 April 1918	
Landon, Capt. Edward G.,		Brentwood
RAF RAeC 1908	17 October 1915	
Landon, Lt Col. J.H.A.,		Shenfield
DSO RAF RAeC 458	12 April 1913	
Lawson, Cpl Benjamin,	Killed in action	Chingford
No.42 Sqn RFC	3 August 1917	
Ledger, 2nd-Lt Horace MC	Killed in action	Witham
att. HMS *Anne*	22 December 1915	
Leete, 2nd-Lt Sidney J.,	Killed in action	Wickford
No.57 Sqn RFC	28 July 1917	
Link, 2nd-Lt Frederick L.,	Killed in action	Ilford
No.74 Sqn RAF	7 June 1918	
Lloyd, Lt David R.C.,	Killed in action	Kirby-le-Soken
No.60 Sqn RFC	16 June 1917	
Lloyd, AM William M.,	Killed in action	Leyton
No.4 Sqn RFC	21 July 1917	
Long, 2nd-Lt John T.,	Killed in action	Ilford
No.53 Sqn RFC	10 October 1917	
Loomes, Edgar Ferdinand,		Chelmsford
RAeC 2342	28 January 1916	
Loton, Lt A.G., Pilot RAF	Survived war	Ilford
Love, Flt Sub-Lt Harold E.,	Killed in action	Leytonstone
RNAS Egypt	28 March 1918	
Malcolm, Lt J.,	Former Ilford	Ilford
Pilot RAF	County High Pupil	
Marsh, Capt. Phillip E.G.,	Died of influenza	Wethersfield
MC RAF	30 December 1918	
Mathews, Lt A.H.,		Harold Wood
Pilot No.100 Sqn RAF		
Maver, Sgt Ernest G.,	Survived war	Ilford
Observer RAF		
McCreary, Lt Harry Charles,	Killed in action	Southend-on-Sea
No.20 Sqn RAF	2 July 1918	
McCutcheon, 2nd-Lt Bernard J.,	Killed in action	Westcliff-on-Sea
No.48 Sqn RAF	8 August 1918	
McMahon, AM Sidney,	Killed in action	East Ham
No.42 Sqn RFC	29 June 1917	
Meadway, Lt Brian W.,	Killed in flying accident	Chadwell Heath
RAF	4 June 1918	
Melville, 2nd-Lt David C.,	Killed in flying accident	Manor Park
RFC	21 January 1918	
Middleton, Sgt William J.,	Died of wounds	Woodford
DFM No.205 Sqn RAF	4 October 1918	
Miles, AM Lionel H.	Killed in enemy air raid	Walthamstow
RAF	24 September 1918	
Mitchell, 2nd-Lt Leslie E.	Killed in action	Leytonstone

No.62 Sqn RAF	29 September 1918	
Monk, Capt. Ernest W.,	Died of wounds	Leytonstone
No.8 Sqn RFC	29 March 1918	
Moreton, Lt Norman H.,	Killed in action	Westcliff-on-Sea
No.34 Sqn RAF	16 May 1918	
Morgan, 2nd-Lt Albert S.,	Killed in action	Leytonstone
No.3 Sqn RFC	22 April 1917	
Nash, 2nd-Lt Henry A.,	Killed in action	Romford
No.55 Sqn RAF	14 May 1918	
Neil, Lt D.,	Survived war	Essex?
Observer No.97 Sqn RAF		
New, Lt Hedley B.,	Killed in action	Brentwood
No.3 Sqn RFC	31 October 1917	
Newman, Capt. Arthur,	Survived war	Ilford
MC DFC No.57 Sqn RAF		
Nickels, Lt Christopher C., RAF	Killed in flying accident	Forest Gate
	9 June 1918	
Nicholas Capt. Charles H.N.,		Chelmsford
RAF RAeC 2277	14 January 1916	
Norton, Capt. John Hamilton,	Survived war	Hockley
MC No.13 Sqn RAF		
Oliphant, 2nd-Lt J.L.M.,	Wounded in action	Southend
Observer No.99 Sqn RAF	25 September 1918	
Orfeur, Sub-Lt Charles B.,	Killed in action	Colchester
2N Sqn RNAS	1 July 1917	
Orange, 2nd-Lt Harold S.,	Killed in action	Walthamstow
Observer No.55 Sqn RAF	25 September 1918	
Pacey, Sgt Joseph W.,	Killed in action	Orsett
No. 206 Sqn RAF	29 July 1918	
Palmer, Sgt Thomas N.,	Died POW	Walthamstow
No.30 Sqn RFC	13 March 1916	
Parker, 2nd-Lt G.L.R.,		Leigh
Observer No.216 Sqn RAF		
Parker 2nd-Lt Percy D.,	Killed in flying accident	Bradwell
RFC	4 January 1918	
Parker, Lt William L.O.,	Killed in action	Faulkbourne
No.13 Sqn RFC	31 October 1917	
Pearsall, PO Bertram H.,	Killed in action	Ilford
Dardanelles A/C Div.	11 October 1915	
Petre, Major Henry A.,	Survived war	Ingatestone
No.30 Sqn RFC, No.75 Sqn RAF		
Petre, Sqn Cdr John J.,	Killed in action	Ingatestone
DSC 6N Sqn RNAS	13 April 1917	
Pheby, Sgt Henry T.,	Killed in action	West Ham
No.215 Sqn RAF	4 August 1918	
Phillips, Flt Sub-Lt George H.,	Killed in action	Romford
No.6 Wing RNAS	7 January 1918	
Philpott, Capt. John R.,	Died POW	Southend-on-Sea
MC No.63 Sqn RFC	15 January 1918	
Pickthorne, Maj. Charles E.,	Survived war	Ilford
MC Nos 32 & 84 Sqn RAF		

Potter, Sgt Frank A., No.20 Sqn RFC	Died of wounds 10 September 1917	Leyton
Potter, 2nd-Lt S.B., No.214 Sqn RAF	Interned in Holland 30 June 1918	Ilford
Powell, Flt Sub-Lt Leslie A., 3N Sqn RNAS	Killed in action 7 March 1917	Hornchurch
Puncher, Lt H.R.A.V., No.216 Sqn RAF	Survived war	Pitsea
Raby, 2nd-Lt Laurence F., No.53 Sqn RAF	Killed in action 9 October 1918	Westcliff-on-Sea
Randall, Lt George E. No.20 Sqn RAF	Survived war	Manor Park
Read, Major Geoffrey J., RAF RAeC 2034	Survived war 7 November 1915	Brentwood
Richardson, 2nd-Lt J.B., Observer No.215 Sqn RAF	POW 15 September 1918	Woodford
Ridgewell, AM William E., RFC Egypt EF	Killed in action 30 December 1917	Collier Row
Roberts, 2nd-Lt Gavem B., No.19 Sqn RFC	Killed in action 26 September 1917	Loughton
Roberts, Sgt William H., No.20 Sqn RFC	Killed in action 11 September 1917	East Ham
Ross, Cpl Ernest A., Observer RAF & Army	Survived war Co-operation School	Becontree
Rowley, Lt Charles E., No.91 Sqn RFC	Killed in action 19 January 1918	Barking
Ryan, Flt Cdt Henry H., RAF	Killed in flying accident 28 August 1918	Leytonstone
Scotcher Capt. William G., MC No.50 Sqn RAF	Killed in action 15 September 1918	Ilford
Scott, Sgt Ernest, No.27 Sqn RAF	Killed in action 16 June 1918	East Ham
Scott, 2nd-Lt Harold G., No.52 Sqn RAF	Killed in action 30 July 1918	Southend-on-Sea
Simons, Flt Sgt Alfred S., No.44 Sqn RAF	Died 8 November 1918	Hackney
Smith, Lt Eric, St C. RFC	Killed in flying accident 2 July 1917	Forest Gate
Smith, 2nd-Lt Frederick L., No.108 Sqn RAF	Killed in action 9 November 1918	Leyton
Smith, Cdt John C.S., RFC RFC	Died of appendicitis 26 April 1918	West Ham
Smith, Lt Leonard H., No.74 Sqn RFC	Killed in action 2 November 1917	Westcliff-on-Sea
Smith, AM Percy L., No.111 Sqn RFC	Died of wounds 3 December 1917	Thundersley
Smith, 2nd-Lt Walter S., Observer No.48 Sqn RFC	Killed in action 9 January 1918	Loughton
Smith, Capt. W., Pilot No.97 Sqn RAF from Sqn Records		Ilford
Smither, 2nd-Lt Harold,	Killed in action	Westcliff-on-Sea

Pilot No.48 Sqn RFC	6 July 1917	
Spelling, Capt. Alfred I., RAF Admin officer	Survived war	Ilford
Stephens, 2nd-Lt Donald E., Pilot No.57 Sqn RAF	Killed in action 19 September 1918	Ilford
Stone, Lt Charles O., Pilot No.2 Sqn Australian Flying Corps	Survived war	Chingford
Storrar, Lt Sidney E., Observer RAF	Survived war, AVM in Second World War	Leigh-on-Sea
Swinfen, 2nd-Lt Percy C., RFC	Killed in flying accident 20 September 1917	Leyton
Taylor, Capt. Ashley D., Pilot No.99 Sqn RAF	Killed in action 24 August 1918	Wansted
Taylor, Capt. Thomas, St. C.G. No.35 Sqn RFC	Killed in action 17 March 1918	Ilford
Thornton, Lt Harold V., Observer No.34 Sqn RAF	Killed in action 11 May 1918	Leytonstone
Thorp, 2nd-Lt Charles E., Observer No.55 Sqn RAF	Killed in action 30 August 1918	Leytonstone
Thrower, 2nd-Lt Leonard A., 406 Seaplane Flt RAF	Killed in action 18 July 1918	Leigh-on-Sea
Tinsley, Lt William, No.88 Sqn RAF	Survived war	East Ham
Tolhurst, Lt Bernard J., No.11 Sqn RFC	Killed in action 22 April 1917	Southend-on-Sea
Tower, Capt. Hugh C., No.60 Sqn RFC	Killed in action 19 September 1916	South Weald
Troth, 2nd-Lt George N., No.101 Sqn RAF	Killed in action 21 September 1918	Ilford
Turnell, 2nd-Lt Robert D., MM No.52 Sqn RFC	Killed in action 27 March 1918	Chelmsford
Underwood, Lt Roy G., No.39 Sqn RAF	Killed in action 25 September 1918	Southend-on-Sea
Uniacke, 2nd-Lt Desmond P.F., No.48 Sqn RFC	Killed in action 21 September 1917	Upminster
Viney, Flt Lt Taunton E., DSO No.5 Wing RNAS	Killed in action 21 May 1916	Frinton-on-Sea
Walker-Hodges, Flt Sub-Lt Charles R., No.4 Sqn RNAS	Killed in action 18 August 1918	Thaxted
Ward, Major George B., MC No.10 Sqn RFC	Killed in action 21 September 1917	Foxearth
Ward, 2nd-Lt Percival H.B., No.22 Sqn RFC	Killed in action 19 May 1917	Waltham Abbey
Washington, 2nd-Lt William F., No.20 Sqn RAF	Killed in action 3 September 1918	Chingford
Wates, 2nd-Lt Leslie C., No.29 Sqn RFC	Killed in action 9 October 1917	Leytonstone
Welch, Capt. Hubert I. No.80 Sqn RAF	Killed in action 29 September 1918	Dunmow
Welford, Lt Leonard C., No.80 Sqn RAF	Killed in action 7 June 1918	Loughton

Whitmill, Lt George H.,	Killed in action	Westcliff-on-Sea
No.202 Sqn RAF	21 April 1918	
Wiffin, AC Ernest,	Killed in action	Romford
13 Kite Balloon Section RAF	23 October 1918	
Wignall, 2nd-Lt G.	POW	Ilford
No.80 Sqn RAF	14 August 1918	
Wiles, PO Edward,	Survived war	Ilford
RNAS & RAF		
Williamson, 2nd-Lt Gerald D.,	Killed in action	Hockley
No.7 Sqn RFC	1 January 1918	
Wilsdon, PO William H.,	Killed in action	Walthamstow
Dardanelles A/C Div.	30 April 1915	
Wilson, Lt Conrad Thomas,		Chigwell
RAF RAeC 3476	2 September 1916	
Winkley, Lt Stanley H.,	Killed in action	Hockley
No.84 Sqn RAF	1 April 1918	
Winn, Flt Sub-Lt John H.,	Killed in action	Chingford
1N Sqn RNAS	20 September 1917	
Wood, Lt Maurice H.,	Killed in action	Woodford
No.59 Sqn RFC	13 April 1917	
Woodhouse, Capt. Lionel M.,	Killed in action	Little Baddow
MC DFC RAF	27 September 1918	
Woodhouse, Flt Sub-Lt Mosley M.,	Killed in action	Little Baddow
9N Sqn RNAS	9 August 1917	
Woodman, 2nd-Lt Douglas,	Killed in action	Clacton
No.56 Sqn RFC	11 March 1918	
Woods, Lt E.,	Wounded in action	Ilford
No.55 Sqn RAF	25 August 1918	
Wooley, Sgt Hardy J.,	Killed in flying accident	Chadwell Heath
RAF	23 October 1918	
Wrapson, AM Arthur E.,	Killed in action	West Ham
RFC details unknown	30 November 1917	
Young, 2nd-Lt Frederick J.,	Killed in flying accident	Chelmsford
RAF	1 May 1918	
Young, AM Sidney T.,	Killed in action	Ilford
KBS RFC Egypt EF	30 December 1917	

ABBREVIATIONS

A/C	Aircraft
ALG	Advanced Landing Ground
AM	Air Mechanic
BEF	British Expeditionary Force
Capt.	Captain
Cdr	Commander
Cdt	Cadet
CFS	Central Flying School
Col.	Colonel
Cpl	Corporal
CPO	Chief Petty Officer
DFC	Distinguished Flying Cross
DFM	Distinguished Flying Medal
Div.	Division
DSC	Distinguished Service Cross
Flt Cdr	Flight Commander
Flt Lt	Flight Lieutenant
Flt	Flight
Flt Sgt	Flight Sergeant
Flt Sub-Lt	Flight Sub Lieutenant
G/L	Gunlayer
HMA	His Majesty's Airship
HMFA	His Majesty's Fleet Auxiliary
HMS	His Majesty's Ship
IFC	Indian Flying Corps
Jasta	Jagdstaffel
KBS	Kite Balloon Section
KIA	Killed in Action
L'AMF	L'Aviation Maritime-Française
Lt	Lieutenant
Lt Col.	Lieutenant Colonel
Maj.	Major
MC	Military Cross
MM	Military Medal
NAS	Naval Air Station

NTS	Night Training Squadron
PBI	Poor Bloody Infantry
POW	Prisoner of War
QM	Quarter Master
RAeC	Royal Aero Club Certificate
RFC	Royal Flying Corps
RIMS	Royal Indian Marine Ship
RMA	Royal Marine Artillery
RNAS	Royal Naval Air Service
Sqn Cdr	Squadron Commander
Sgt	Sergeant
SS	Steam Ship
Sqn	Squadron
TBD	Torpedo Boat Destroyer
TS	Training Squadron
USAS	United States Air Service

BIBLIOGRAPHY

Books

Adam, C. & K.: *1914–18 A Village Remembers*, Faulkbourne Press, 1999
Bowyer, C.: *The Flying Elephants, History of No.27 Sqn*, Macdonald, 1972
Bowyer, C.: *Royal Flying Corps Communiqués 1917–1918*, Grub Street, 1998
Brett-Dallas, R.: *The History of British Aviation 1908–1919*, Air Research, 1987
Colbrook, E.W.: *ABC of the Great War*, Odhams, 1919
Cole, C. & Cheeseman, E.F.: *The Air Defence of Britain 1914–18*, Putnam, 1984
Cole, C.: *Royal Flying Corps Communiqués 1915–1916*, Donovan, 1969
Cole, C.: *Royal Air Force Communiqués 1918*, Donovan, 1969
Cronin, D.: *Royal Navy Shipboard Aircraft Developments 1912–1931*, Air Britain, 1990
Douglas, Sholto: *Years of Combat*, Collins, 1963
Franks, N., Bailey, F., Guest, R.: *Above the Lines*, Grub Street, 1993
Halley, J.: *The Squadrons of the Royal Air Force*, Air Britain, 1980
Henshaw, T.: *The Sky Their Battlefield*, Grub Street, 1996
Hobson, C.: *Airmen Died in the First World War 1914–1918*, Hayward, 1995
Jones, H.A.: *The War in the Air*, Oxford Press, 1937.
Layman, R.D.: *Naval Aviation in the First World War*, Chatham, 1996
Lewis, C.A.: *Sagittarius Rising*, Peter Davies, 1944
McKinty, A.: *The Father of British Airships*, Kimber, 1972
Macmillan, N.: *Offensive Patrol*, Jarrolds, 1973
Poolman, K.: *Zeppelins over England*, Evans, 1960
Rimell, R.: *Zeppelin!*, Conway Press, 1984
Robertson, B.: *Air Aces of the 1914–1918 War*, Harleyford, 1962
Robertson, B. & Nowarra, H.: *Von Richthofen and the Flying Circus*, Harleyford, 1958
Robertson, B.: *British Military Aircraft Serials 1911–1971*, Ian Allen, 1971
Shores, C. & Franks, N.: *Above the Trenches*, Grub Street, 1990
Sturtivant, R. & Page, G.: *Royal Navy Aircraft Serials 1911–1919*, Air Britain, 1992
Sturtivant, R. & Page, G.: *The Camel File*, Air Britain, 1993
Wallace, G.: *Claude Grahame-White*, Putnam, 1960

Weldon, L.B.: *Hard Lying Herbert Jenkins*, 1925
Werner, J.: *Knight of Germany*, John Hamilton, 1938
Woodman, H.: *Early Aircraft Armament, Arms & Armour*, 1989

Journals

Aeromodeller, Aeroplane, Cross & Cockade USA, Cross & Cockade International, Essex Countryside, Flight, Flying, Over the Front, Popular Flying, Windsock International.

INDEX
PEOPLE, PLANES AND PLACES

If you are interested in purchasing other books published by Tempus,
or in case you have difficulty finding any Tempus books in your local bookshop,
you can also place orders directly through our website

www.tempus-publishing.com